TRICHOTOMY OF SELF

WHO YOU ARE IS THE PATTERNS YOU REPEAT DAILY, THE STORIES THAT GUIDE, AND THE PURPOSES YOU SERVE

MARK LOUDERMILK

PHOENIX & SAGE PUBLISHING

First Edition

ISBN: 979-8-9935188-1-7

Published by Phoenix & Sage Publishing

This book is designed to provide accurate and authoritative information on the topics covered. It is sold with the understanding that neither the author nor the publisher is engaged in rendering legal, accounting, or other professional services. If expert assistance is required, the services of a competent professional should be sought.

The stories, experiences, and examples shared in this book are based on the author's real-life experiences and observations. Some names and identifying details have been changed to protect the privacy of individuals.

Success in business, as in life, is the result of preparation, hard work, learning from failure, loyalty, and persistence. This book provides guidance, but results will vary based on numerous factors specific to your situation.

To everyone who has ever whispered in the darkness: "There has to be more than this."

There is.

And to my mother, who asked the question that changed everything: "Son, are you happy?"

"Every man has two lives.The second begins when he realizes he only has one."—Confucius

"We are what we repeatedly do.Excellence, then, is not an act, but a habit."—Aristotle

"The cave you fear to enter holds the treasure you seek."—Joseph Campbell

PREFACE

Who This Book Is For

This book is for the person who has read all the self-help books and still feels helpless.

It's for the successful professional who has everything but feels nothing.

It's for the parent who is present in body but absent in spirit.

It's for the dreamer whose dreams have been buried under "someday."

It's for anyone who has ever felt like they're living someone else's life.

But most importantly, this book is for the person who is ready to stop reading about change and start creating it.

Who This Book Is Not For

This book is not for people looking for shortcuts. There aren't any.

It's not for those who want to feel better without doing better.

It's not for anyone unwilling to look in the mirror and see who's really there.

It's not for those who believe their patterns are permanent, their stories are truth, and their purposes are fixed.

And it's definitely not for anyone who thinks reading equals transformation.

My Promise to You

I won't waste your time with platitudes you've heard before.

I won't pretend change is easy when we both know it's not.

I won't give you motivation that expires by tomorrow morning.

What I will do is show you exactly how human identity works—through patterns, stories, and purposes—and give you the tools to consciously reshape all three.

But you have to do the work.

My Story (The Short Version)

I was raised in gangs during the 1980s and 1990s Los Angeles. People I grew up with are either dead or serving life sentences. I spent my teenage years incarcerated. By every measure, I should have become another statistic that was my pathway in life.

Instead, I became a respiratory therapist, then a registered nurse working emergency medicine, then computer science major and then someone who refused to accept that past determines future.

But education didn't transform me—examining my patterns, stories, and purposes did.

This book contains what I learned in that examination, validated by decades of studying human behavior, ancient philosophy, modern psychology, and the lived experiences of transformation.

I'm not a guru. I'm not special. I'm just someone who discovered that you can change who you are by changing what you repeatedly do, what you deeply believe, and what you ultimately serve.

If I could transform from a gang member to someone teaching others how to transform, then you can become whoever you're willing to practice becoming.

How to Use This Book

The Three Reads Method

First Read: Recognition: Read straight through. Don't journal yet. Just recognize yourself in these pages. See your patterns, stories, and purposes reflected back. Let the framework sink in.

Second Read: Examination: Now read with a pen. Do every exercise. Answer every prompt. Write in the margins. Argue with me. Agree with me. But engage with me.

Third Read: Implementation: This is where transformation happens. Choose one chapter that spoke to you most. Live it for 30 days. Apply its principles daily. Then move to the next chapter.

The Non-Negotiable Tools

1. **A Journal** - Not digital. Paper. There's something about the physical act of writing that digital can't replace.

2. **A Morning** - You need 20 minutes each morning. If you don't have 20 minutes, you don't have a life.

3. **A Commitment** - Six months minimum. Anything less is tourism, not transformation.

The Chapter Structure

Each chapter follows the same pattern (because patterns matter):

- **Opening Story**: Real transformation in action

- **The Problem**: What's keeping you stuck

- **The Framework**: How the Trichotomy applies

- **The Practice**: Specific actions to take

- **The Journal Prompts**: Where the real work happens

Skip the journal prompts and you might as well skip the chapter.

A Warning and a Promise

Before you turn another page, I need to be brutally honest with you.

This book will not change your life.

You will.

Or you won't.

The difference between those two outcomes has nothing to do with the words I've written and everything to do with what you do with them.

The Journaling Imperative

Socrates said, "The unexamined life is not worth living." Twenty-four hundred years later, that truth hasn't changed—only our willingness to face it has.

This book demands more than your eyes. It demands your pen.

Not because I say so, but because transformation happens in the writing, not the reading. Every profound thinker from Marcus Aurelius to modern psychologists understands this: **You don't know what you think until you write it down. You don't know who you are until you've had an honest conversation with yourself on paper.**

Yet most people will read these words, nod in agreement, and never pick up a pen. They'll consume these ideas like entertainment, file them away as "interesting," and wake up tomorrow exactly the same person who went to sleep tonight.

They'll say journaling "isn't for them." They'll claim they "think better in their head." They'll insist they're "too busy" to write for ten minutes a day.

What they're really saying is: "I'm not willing to face myself. I'm not willing to do the work. I'm not willing to give up who I am for who I could become."

The Six-Month Challenge

So here's my dare to you:

Try this for six months. Not six weeks. Not until it gets hard. Not until you "don't feel like it." Six months.

Write every day. Examine your patterns, your stories, your purposes. Face the uncomfortable truths. Document the small changes. Track the resistance. Notice the evolution.

After six months—and only after six months—you've earned the right to say this doesn't work.

But if you're not willing to show up for yourself for six months, then let's be clear about what you're really saying: Your life isn't worth six months of effort. Your transformation isn't worth ten minutes a day. Your future self isn't worth meeting.

The Book That Doesn't Exist

If you're looking for the book that you read once and wake up transformed—the magic pill in paperback form—I wish you luck finding it. In thirty years of searching, I've never encountered such a thing.

Transformation isn't a download. It's a practice. Change isn't an event. It's a process. Growth isn't consumption. It's application.

The reason most people don't change isn't lack of information—we're drowning in information. It's lack of implementation. They read about change instead of creating it. They think about transformation instead of practicing it. They hope for different results while maintaining identical patterns.

Your Choice, Right Now

You're holding a book about the Trichotomy of Self—the patterns you repeat, the stories you tell, and the purposes you serve. These three elements are creating your life whether you're conscious of them or not.

You can read about them and remain unconscious.

Or you can write about them and become conscious.

You can treat this book as entertainment and stay exactly who you are.

Or you can treat it as a workshop and become who you're capable of being.

The Stoics journaled daily. Socrates examined everything. Modern psychology has proven what ancient wisdom knew: **Writing is thinking made visible. Journaling is transformation made tangible.**

Yet you'll probably skip it. You'll probably read these words, feel momentarily inspired, and then turn the page without making the commitment. You'll probably choose the comfortable prison of who you've been over the uncertain freedom of who you could become.

Prove me wrong.

Get a notebook. Any notebook. The dollar store sells them for $1.99. Your transformation is worth at least that much, isn't it?

Write this on the first page:

"Today, [date], I begin the six-month challenge. I will examine my patterns, my stories, and my purposes daily. I will not judge the process until I've completed it. I will show up for myself because my life is worth the effort. I understand that reading without writing is entertainment, not transformation. I choose transformation."

Sign it. Date it. Mean it.

Or close this book now and save us both the time.

Because if you're not willing to journal, you're not willing to change. And if you're not willing to change, these words are just marks on paper, and your life will be the same story, different day, until the day you die having never truly lived.

The unexamined life is not worth living.

The examined life begins with a pen.

Your move.

Note to the reader: Every chapter in this book ends with journaling prompts. Skip them at your own peril. Do them, and discover who you really are beneath the patterns, stories, and purposes you've inherited. The choice—as with everything in your life—is yours.

Final Prefatory Note

One Last Thing

There's a moment in every transformation where you'll want to quit.

Not because it's too hard, but because it's working.

Your old identity will fight for survival. Your comfortable patterns will scream for restoration. Your limiting stories will insist they're truth. Your small purposes will beg you to come back.

This is the moment that matters most.

This is when you'll discover whether you're serious about change or just curious about it.

When that moment comes—and it will—remember:

You bought this book for a reason. Something in your life isn't working. Something in you knows there's more. Something brought you to this page, this moment, this choice.

Honor that something.

It's the part of you that's ready to live instead of exist. It's the part that's tired of same shit, different day. It's the part that knows you're capable of more than you're currently being.

That part deserves six months of your effort.

Your future self deserves to meet who you could become.

Turn the page only if you're ready to begin.

Otherwise, gift this book to someone who is.

Because transformation isn't for everyone.

But if you're still reading, maybe—just maybe—it's for you.

Let's find out.

Mark Loudermilk New York 2025

CONTENTS

CHAPTER ONE

THE CRISIS OF MODERN IDENTITY

"THE TRAGEDY OF LIFE IS NOT THAT IT ENDS SO SOON, BUT THAT WE WAIT SO LONG TO BEGIN IT."

The Corner Office Prison

Michelle Wong's heels click against the marble floor of the construction company's headquarters at 7:15 AM, the same sound at the same time for the past six years. She badges in—employee number 3847—and the security guard doesn't look up. He doesn't need to. Michelle arrives at 7:15 every morning, takes the elevator to the fourteenth floor, walks past the same seventeen cubicles, and settles into her office with its partial view of downtown Phoenix.

At 34, Michelle is the youngest senior engineer in the company's history. Her business cards say "Senior Project Manager," her LinkedIn says "Building Tomorrow's Infrastructure Today," but her soul says nothing at all anymore.

She sets down her coffee—oat milk latte, half pump vanilla, same order for three years—and opens her laptop to the same spreadsheet she closed yesterday. Another strip mall. Another client who wants "innovative design" but really means "cheap and fast." Another day of reviewing other people's uninspired work while her own designs collect digital dust in a folder she hasn't opened in two years. The folder is labeled "Future Projects," but it might as well be labeled "Past Dreams."

Those dreams used to keep her up at night in the best way. During college at ASU, she'd spend entire weekends designing sustainable communities, sketching eco-friendly housing that could change how people lived. Her professor had called her thesis project—affordable green housing that actually looked beautiful—"revolutionary." Her boyfriend at the time, Marcus, used to joke that she was going to "save the world one building at a time."

Marcus is married now. To someone else. She saw the wedding photos on Instagram last month—a sustainable venue in Sedona, of course. The bride wore vintage. They're probably composting their wedding flowers as she sits here approving plans for another beige box that will blight the landscape for fifty years.

Michelle's phone buzzes. A text from her mother: "How's my successful daughter? Dad wants to know if you're bringing anyone to Amy's wedding."

Amy. Her younger sister. Getting married at 28 to someone she's known for eighteen months. Meanwhile, Michelle, the "successful" one, will attend alone, fielding questions about when it's her turn while internally screaming that she can't even commit to a houseplant, much less a human being.
She types back: "Still confirming. Busy week ahead."

Busy. That's her default excuse for everything now. Too busy to date. Too busy to see friends. Too busy to explain that she's not actually busy—she's empty, filling time with tasks that feel like moving through thick syrup, each action requiring enormous effort for minimal result.

Her assistant knocks. "The 8 AM meeting is ready for you."

Michelle nods, gathers her materials for a presentation she could give in her sleep. Six slides about cost projections. Four slides about timeline optimization. Zero slides about why any of this matters.

As she walks to the conference room, she passes the bathroom mirror and catches her reflection. Professional blazer, pressed perfectly. Hair in the same low bun she's worn for three years. Makeup that says "competent" but never "creative." She looks successful. She looks appropriate. She looks nothing like the girl who once stayed up until 4 AM building models of vertical gardens, hands covered in glue and hope.

Groundhog Day Syndrome

Michelle is living in her own personal Groundhog Day, except Bill Murray eventually learned and grew. Michelle just repeats.

Every morning: same arrival time, same coffee, same route to her office. She even sits in the same spot in meetings—third chair from the head of the table, far enough to avoid direct attention, close enough to seem engaged.

Every lunch: salad from the place downstairs. Dressing on the side. Eaten at her desk while scrolling through LinkedIn, watching former classmates announce promotions, new ventures, bold moves to other cities. She likes their posts. She feels nothing.

Every evening: leave at 6:30 PM, tell herself she'll go to the gym (she won't), pick up takeout from one of four restaurants in rotation, eat while watching Netflix shows she's already seen because new ones require too much attention. In bed by 10:30, scroll phone until 11:30, wonder where the day went, promise tomorrow will be different, knowing it won't.

Weekends are weekdays without the structure. Saturday: errands that could wait, laundry that isn't urgent, cleaning that's really just reorganizing the same items. Sunday: brunch with friends where everyone complains about work but no one changes anything, afternoon Netflix, evening anxiety about Monday, sleep that doesn't restore.

She's not living 365 days a year. She's living the same day 365 times.

Across the city, millions are trapped in the same temporal loop:

David Kim, 29, wakes up in his childhood bedroom, the same Pokemon posters on the wall, except now they mock him instead of inspire. Every day he tells himself he'll start applying for real jobs. Every night he goes to bed having applied for none. His computer science degree gathers dust while he works retail, each day identical to the last—clock in, zone out, clock out, game until 3 AM to avoid thinking about how he's living the same day his 19-year-old self would have lived, except now it's pathetic instead of potential.

Jennifer Martinez, 42, runs her morning routine like a military operation. 5:45 AM workout (same seven exercises), protein shake (same recipe), meditation app (same guided session), gratitude journal (struggling to find three new things, usually recycling last week's list). She's optimized everything except meaning. Her days are efficiently empty, each one a perfect copy of the last, like a printer stuck on repeat, churning out identical pages of a life that looks good on paper but feels like fiction.

Thomas Chen, 51, has been having the same Tuesday for fifteen years. It just happens to occur seven days a week. Wake tired, commute in silence, work without passion, return home depleted, watch TV, sleep poorly, repeat. He can predict every hour of his next decade because it will be identical to the last. When his daughter asks what he did at work, he says "same as always" because it's true. When his wife asks how his day was, he says "fine" because distinguishing between identical days seems pointless.

Maria Rodriguez, 38, opens her laptop every Saturday at the same coffee shop, orders the same vanilla latte, opens the same novel file, stares at the same paragraph she's been trying to fix for six months, writes nothing, tells herself she's "thinking through plot problems," leaves after two hours having changed nothing except the date on her procrastination.

They're all stuck in temporal loops of their own creation, living Groundhog Days without the growth, without the learning, without the eventual breakthrough to a new tomorrow.

The Mathematics of Modern Misery

"Most people die at 25 and aren't buried until 75."

This observation, often attributed to Benjamin Franklin, has never been more relevant. We are witnessing an epidemic of what Henry David Thoreau called "quiet desperation," but with a modern twist that would have horrified even him.

Consider the mathematics of modern misery. According to the American Psychological Association, anxiety levels have increased by 1,200% since 1980. The World Health Organization reports that depression is now the leading cause of disability worldwide, affecting more than 300 million people. Suicide rates in the United States have increased by 35% since 1999.

But these numbers don't capture the real pandemic: the millions who aren't clinically depressed but aren't truly living either. The ones who function but don't flourish. The ones who survive but don't thrive. The ones who wake up but never really wake up.

A recent Gallup poll found that 70% of employees are "not engaged" at work. Think about that—seven out of ten people spending the majority of their waking hours disconnected from what they're doing. That's not a statistic; it's a tragedy. That's millions of human beings trading their life force for a paycheck, their dreams for security, their authenticity for acceptance.

Here's what the numbers don't tell you: We have more access to information about happiness than any generation in history, yet we are measurably less happy than our grandparents.

We can access the wisdom of every philosophy, the insights of every psychology, the practices of every spiritual tradition—all from the device in our pocket. We have apps for meditation, platforms for learning, communities for growth. We have life coaches and wellness retreats and self-help books that promise transformation in seven steps or your money back.

Yet we scroll through inspirational quotes while feeling uninspired. We read about mindfulness while remaining mindless. We collect life hacks while our lives fall apart. We consume content about living authentically while living completely inauthentically.

The average modern human wakes up and immediately reaches for their phone—not to connect with their own thoughts and intentions for the day, but to connect with the thoughts and intentions of algorithm-driven corporations whose business model depends on harvesting their attention.

They consume news designed to trigger anxiety and outrage because anxious, outraged people click more links. They scroll through social media feeds curated to show them everyone else's apparent success while highlighting their own inadequacy. They listen to podcasts about productivity while being profoundly unproductive. They read articles about authentic living while living completely inauthentically.

By the time they arrive at work, they've already handed their mental state over to forces that profit from their distraction, their insecurity, and their disconnection from their own authentic desires.

The modern human has become a stranger to themselves.

This isn't an accident. It's the predictable result of a culture that profits from keeping you disconnected from your own authentic self. The more scattered your attention, the more uncertain your identity, the more you'll consume trying to fill the void. Confused people buy more. Insecure people scroll more. Disconnected people consume more.

"The person who knows themselves cannot be sold a false identity."

The Real Problem: Misalignment

After years of studying human behavior, coaching hundreds of individuals, and examining my own journey from unconscious living to authentic alignment, I've discovered something crucial: The source of quiet desperation isn't that life is meaningless—it's that people are living lives that are misaligned with their authentic selves.

You wake up tired not because you didn't sleep enough, but because your sleep patterns don't serve your natural rhythms. You're forcing yourself to be a morning person when your biology says otherwise, or staying up late scrolling when your body craves rest.

You feel unfulfilled at work not because work is inherently unfulfilling, but because your daily activities don't align with your deeper values. You're building someone else's dream while your own vision atrophies from neglect.

You feel anxious about the future not because the future is uncertain (it always has been), but because you're serving purposes that were imposed on you rather than chosen by you. You're climbing a ladder you didn't choose against a wall you didn't select, and some part of you knows that even if you reach the top, you'll have climbed to the wrong place.

You feel like you're living someone else's life because, in many ways, you are.

The crisis of modern identity is a crisis of misalignment.

Think about the last time you felt truly alive, truly yourself, truly engaged with life. Not happy necessarily—happiness is fleeting—but alive. Present. Engaged. Real.

What were you doing? How were you being? What made that moment different from the routine experience of your daily existence?

Maybe it was creating something without concern for its commercial value. Maybe it was having a conversation that went past surface pleasantries into real truth. Maybe it was solving a problem that mattered, helping someone who needed it, or simply being in nature without your phone.

I'm willing to bet that in that moment, three things were happening simultaneously:

1. Your **patterns**—your behaviors, habits, and ways of being—were serving your highest self rather than your scared self

2. Your **stories**—your beliefs about yourself and the world—were empowering rather than limiting

3. Your **purposes**—the aims and intentions guiding your actions—were authentic to who you really are rather than who you think you should be

When these three elements align, you experience what philosophers have called "eudaimonia"—not just happiness, but the deep satisfaction that comes from living in accordance with your authentic nature.

When they misalign, you experience what I call the Identity Disconnect—the gap between who you are and who you're living as.

The Architecture of Self

Every human being operates with three fundamental components that, together, create what we experience as identity. Understanding these three components—really understanding them, not just intellectually but experientially—is the key to moving from quiet desperation to conscious alignment.

The Patterns You Repeat Daily

These are your habits, routines, and consistent behaviors. They're what you do when you're on autopilot. They're the morning coffee ritual, the route you take to work, the way you respond to stress, the things you do to relax. But they're more than just behaviors—they're the physical manifestation of who you are. Your patterns are your identity made visible through action.

Consider Michael's patterns: snooze button (avoidance), phone scrolling (distraction), same breakfast (unconscious routine), passive commute (disconnection), desk lunch (isolation), evening Netflix (numbing), weekend procrastination (cycle repetition). These patterns don't just reflect his resignation—they create and reinforce it. Every repetition is a vote for the person he's becoming, and he's voting for someone he doesn't want to be.

Or Jennifer's patterns: early alarm (forcing), meditation app (performing wellness), intense workout (punishing), protein shake (optimizing), gratitude journal (manufactured positivity). These patterns look successful from the outside but feel like prison from the inside because they're not chosen from authenticity—they're performed from anxiety.

Your patterns are powerful because they're automatic. They run without conscious thought, which means they can either serve you or sabotage you without you even noticing. They're the difference between who you think you are and who you actually are. You might think you're a writer, but if your patterns don't include writing, you're not a writer—you're someone who wants to be a writer.

The Stories That Guide

These are the narratives you tell yourself about who you are, what's possible for you, and how the world works. They're the internal monologue that runs constantly in the background, the voice in your head that comments on everything you do, everything that happens to you, everything you want.

Stories are more than thoughts—they're the lens through which you interpret reality. Two people can experience the exact same event and have completely different experiences based on the stories they tell about it. One sees failure; another sees learning. One sees rejection; another sees redirection. One sees endings; another sees beginnings.

Michael's stories sound like: "This is just how adult life is," "I should be grateful for what I have," "Dreams are for people who can afford them," "It's too late to change careers," "I'm not the kind of person who takes risks," "Everyone feels this way," "I need to be responsible," "Security is more important than satisfaction."

Jennifer's stories are different but equally limiting: "I have to be perfect to be worthy," "Success means never showing weakness," "If I slow down, I'll fall behind," "Everyone is watching and judging," "I can't afford to fail," "My value is my productivity," "Vulnerability is dangerous."

These stories didn't come from nowhere. They were inherited from parents, absorbed from culture, concluded from experiences. But here's the crucial truth: just because you've been telling a story doesn't mean it's true. Just because you believe something doesn't mean it's real. Just because everyone else seems to agree doesn't mean it's right.

The Purposes You Serve

These are the missions, meanings, and motivations that drive your actions. They're what you're living for, whether you've chosen them consciously or inherited them unconsciously. They're the "why" behind your "what." They're the difference between motion and progress, between busy and productive, between existing and living.

Purposes can be authentic (chosen by you) or imposed (given to you by others). Most people are serving purposes they never chose: their parents' unfulfilled dreams, society's definition of success, their peer group's values, their culture's expectations.

Michael's current purposes, if we're honest, are: avoid discomfort, maintain security, meet others' expectations, survive until the weekend. These aren't the purposes he would choose if he felt free to choose. They're the purposes that chose him when he stopped choosing for himself.

Jennifer's purposes are: prove worth through achievement, avoid vulnerability, maintain image, outrun inadequacy. These purposes drive her relentlessly, but they never deliver what they promise because they're not connected to who she really is.

When your purposes are imposed rather than chosen, when they're about avoiding rather than creating, when they're about proving rather than being, you can achieve them perfectly and still feel empty. You can win the race and realize you were running in the wrong direction.

The Misalignment Cascade

When these three components are in discord—when your patterns don't serve your purposes, when your stories don't support your patterns, when your purposes don't inspire your stories—you experience a cascade of symptoms that most people accept as "normal adult life."

Physical Symptoms:

Your body keeps the score of your misalignment. That chronic fatigue despite adequate sleep? That's your body's way of saying it doesn't want to participate in your patterns anymore. The tension headaches that appear Sunday evening and don't leave until Friday night? That's your nervous system bracing for another week of pretending. The digestive issues that no diet seems to fix? That's your gut—your second brain—rejecting the life you're swallowing.

The lower back pain that no chiropractor can permanently adjust? You're literally carrying the weight of living out of alignment. The insomnia that keeps you scrolling at 2 AM? Your mind won't let you rest because it knows you're not living your truth. The mysterious aches that doctors can't diagnose? Your body is trying to tell you what your mind won't admit: something is fundamentally wrong with how you're living.

Emotional Symptoms:

The emotions of misalignment are so common we've normalized them. Sunday night dread is treated as a cultural joke rather than a crisis signal. Morning anxiety is managed with coffee rather than addressed at its root. Afternoon numbness is accepted as the post-lunch slump rather than recognized as soul exhaustion.

You feel irritable at minor inconveniences because you're tolerating major misalignments. You feel envious of others' lives because you're not living your own. You feel nostalgic for the past because it contained more possibility than your present. You feel anxious about the future because you know your current trajectory doesn't lead anywhere you want to go.

Mental Symptoms:

Your cognitive function reflects your alignment. When you're living in alignment, your mind is clear, focused, creative. When you're misaligned, you experience mental fog, difficulty concentrating, forgetfulness about things that should matter.

You can remember every word of an argument from three years ago but can't remember why you walked into a room. You can focus for hours on a video game or social media but can't concentrate for five minutes on work that pays your bills. You have brilliant ideas in the shower but can't access creativity when you need it.

This isn't ADD or aging or "just how brains work." This is your mind protecting you from fully engaging with a life that doesn't feel like yours.

Spiritual Symptoms:

These are the deepest and most dismissed symptoms. A sense that you're wasting your life—not dramatically, but slowly, quietly, one compromised day at a time. Fear that it's too late to change, coupled with fear that if you don't change, you'll die having never really lived.

You feel disconnected from any sense of meaning or purpose. You go through the motions of religious or spiritual practices but feel nothing. You read about awakening and transformation but feel stuck in permanent sleep. You know there must be more to life but can't access it.

You experience what I call "existential homesickness"—a longing for a life you've never lived but somehow remember, a self you've never been but somehow miss.

The Choice Point

Michael will wake up again tomorrow morning at 6:00 AM. So will Jennifer at 5:45. So will David, whenever he finally falls asleep. So will Maria, with the best intentions of writing before work. So will you.

And in that moment between sleep and consciousness, before the weight of routine descends, before the stories start their commentary, before the patterns take control, you have a choice.

You can hit snooze on your life, continuing patterns that don't serve you, believing stories that limit you, pursuing purposes that aren't yours. You can accept quiet desperation as your sentence, join the Walking Unconscious, and wait for retirement or death—whichever comes first.

Or you can wake up. Really wake up.

Not to positive thinking that denies negative reality. Not to life hacks that optimize a life you don't want. Not to motivational quotes that inspire for thirty seconds then evaporate.

But to the fundamental architecture of who you are and how to rebuild it consciously.

The mass of humanity may lead lives of quiet desperation, but you picked up this book. That means some part of you refuses to accept that sentence. Some part of you knows what Michael is starting to suspect, what Jennifer is beginning to feel, what David fears might be true, what Maria desperately hopes: that the tragedy isn't that life ends, but that most people never truly begin living.

Your patterns are not your destiny—they're your practice. Your stories are not your truth—they're your interpretation. Your purposes are not set in stone—they're your choice.

You are not condemned to quiet desperation. You are one conscious integration away from authentic living.

"Every morning, you wake up with the power to continue your performance or begin your life. Most mornings, most people choose performance. But every morning, the other choice remains available. The question isn't whether you can change. The question is whether today is the day you will."

Chapter Summary

You've met Michelle Wong, starting her day not in bed with a snooze button, but walking into her corner office prison at 7:15 AM—the youngest senior engineer in her company's history who feels dead inside despite external success. Her sustainable building dreams have been buried under strip mall spreadsheets for six years.

You've discovered the Groundhog Day Syndrome—how millions like Michelle aren't living 365 days a year but the same day 365 times. David Kim wakes in his childhood bedroom with a computer science degree gathering dust, Jennifer Martinez runs her optimized but empty morning routine, Thomas Chen has been living the same Tuesday for fifteen years, and Maria Rodriguez opens the same novel paragraph every Saturday without writing a word.

You've seen the mathematics of modern misery—anxiety up 1,200% since 1980, 70% of employees disengaged at work, and despite having access to all the world's wisdom through our devices, we're measurably less happy than our grandparents. The modern human has become a stranger to themselves.

You've learned that the real problem isn't meaninglessness but misalignment between three core components of identity:

- Patterns: Your daily habits and behaviors that vote for who you're becoming

- Stories: The narratives you tell yourself that become the lens through which you interpret reality

- Purposes: The missions and meanings driving your actions, whether consciously chosen or unconsciously inherited

You've felt the cascade of misalignment symptoms—physical (chronic fatigue, unexplained pain), emotional (Sunday dread, afternoon numbness), mental (brain fog, selective focus), and spiritual (existential homesickness, feeling you're wasting your life).

The chapter ends at a choice point: continue living in quiet desperation and temporal loops, or wake up to the fundamental architecture of who you are and rebuild it consciously. Your patterns are not destiny but practice. Your stories are not truth but interpretation. Your purposes are not fixed but chosen.

In Chapter 2, you'll discover someone who escaped this trap through understanding how these three components work together, learning that the prison door may have been unlocked all along.

CHAPTER TWO

INTRODUCING THE TRICHOTOMY

"YOU BECOME WHAT YOU REPEATEDLY DO, BELIEVE, AND SERVE—CHOOSE ALL THREE CONSCIOUSLY."

The Mirror Doesn't Lie

I need to tell you about the question that shattered my entire world and rebuilt it from the ground up.

I wasn't exactly what you'd call a "good guy" growing up. There's an old saying: "You are the average of the five people you spend the most time with." Well, for me, those five people were gang members—narcissistic, Machiavellian, psychopathic individuals who were literal killers. Most of them ended up either dead or serving life sentences in prison. As you can imagine, I wasn't developing the finest character traits.

This was Los Angeles in the '80s and '90s—the murder capital of America. I made the horrendous life decisions that followed the typical pathway of gang members in that environment. I spent most of my teenage years incarcerated, learning lessons that no classroom could teach and developing skills that no resume should list.

The psychology of that world is hard to explain to someone who hasn't lived it. You become someone else—someone you don't recognize, someone your mother doesn't recognize. You develop a different walk, a different look, a different way of being in the world. Everything becomes about survival and reputation. Weakness isn't just dangerous;

it's potentially fatal. Empathy becomes a luxury you can't afford. Violence becomes a language you speak fluently.

I won't glorify it or detail it. Some darkness doesn't deserve daylight. But understand this: when you're raised in that environment, when those are your teachers and your curriculum, you don't just do bad things—you become someone capable of doing bad things without feeling bad about them. That's the real tragedy. Not the actions themselves, but the transformation of your character, the numbing of your conscience, the death of who you might have been.

But here's the thing about rock bottom—it gives you a solid foundation to build on if you're smart enough to start digging up instead of down.

I made one intelligent decision: I got out of California. I pursued education like a man possessed, becoming a respiratory therapist, then an RN, then studying computer science. I was collecting degrees like some people collect baseball cards, not because I knew what I wanted to do when I grew up, but because I was running from who I had been.

Education was supposed to be my transformation. Every degree was supposed to be another layer of distance between me and that kid from the streets. Every certification was supposed to prove I was someone different now. I thought if I could just accumulate enough credentials, I could bury my past under achievements.
But you can't outrun yourself.

Despite all the educational achievements, despite the professional credentials, I was still drawn to the criminal element and connections. My twenties were spent living as what I now call "an educated serpent"—someone everyone would have been better off avoiding, despite my impressive resume.

Think about what that means. I had the knowledge to heal but was still choosing to harm. I had the education to build but was still drawn to destroy. I could work in a hospital saving lives by day while destroying my own life—and others'—by night. The degrees hadn't changed me; they'd just made me a more sophisticated version of my worst self.

"The most dangerous person is the one who has knowledge but lacks wisdom, education but no character."

I was that person. Educated, ambitious, professionally successful on paper, but morally bankrupt in practice. I was like a well-dressed criminal with a stethoscope. The kind of person who could discuss medical ethics in a classroom while violating every ethical principle in real life.

Then came the question that changed everything.

The Question That Changes Everything

I was in my early thirties when my mother asked me something that seemed so simple, yet hit me like a sledgehammer to the soul:
"Son, are you happy?"
I couldn't answer her.

The question took me completely by surprise. I had no idea how to respond because I had never really thought about it. I had been so busy performing the role of "successful professional" that I had never stopped to ask myself if I was actually living a life worth living.

Think about how profound that moment was. Here I was, a grown man with multiple degrees, a professional career, all the external markers of success, and I couldn't answer the simplest question in the world. I couldn't tell my own mother if I was happy because I had never asked myself. I had been so focused on appearing successful that I'd never considered whether I was actually fulfilled.

My mother waited. The silence between us grew heavy with all the unspoken truths we both knew. She had watched me transform from a troubled youth into what looked like a successful adult, but mothers see past the performance. She knew something was still wrong. She could see it in my eyes—the same emptiness that had been there since my teenage years, just hidden now behind professional accomplishments.
"I don't know," I finally said.

Those three words were the first honest thing I'd said in years. They were an admission that despite all my education, I was ignorant about the most important subject: my own life. Despite all my achievements, I had failed at the most fundamental task: knowing myself.

That night, alone with my thoughts, I began to examine my life with the kind of brutal honesty that most people spend their entire lives avoiding. What I discovered horrified me.

I was making good money but felt poor. I had degrees but no wisdom. I had a professional reputation but no self-respect. I saved lives at work while wasting my own. I was successful by every external measure and dying by every internal one.

I realized I was living a complete lie. Actually, three lies, all fighting each other for control of my life.

The Three-Part Architecture of Human Identity

That night began my real education—not in classrooms or textbooks, but in understanding the fundamental architecture of human identity.

Through years of subsequent study, therapy, and ruthless self-examination, I discovered that human beings are created and sustained by three fundamental elements that operate whether we're conscious of them or not:

Element One: The Patterns You Repeat Daily

These are your actual behaviors, not your intended ones. The things you do when you're on autopilot. Your morning routine, your stress responses, your evening rituals. These patterns are your identity made physical—who you are when you're not trying to be anyone.

My patterns at the time were a complete contradiction. I was disciplined at work but chaotic in personal life. I was healing others while harming myself. I was building a career while destroying my character. Every day, I was reinforcing patterns that kept me stuck in a life that looked successful but felt empty.

Patterns are powerful because they're automatic. They run without conscious thought, which means they can either serve you or sabotage you without you even noticing. They're the difference between who you think you are and who you actually are. You might think you value health, but if your patterns don't include healthy behaviors, then you don't actually value health—you value the idea of health.

Element Two: The Stories That Guide

These are the narratives running constantly in your mind. The beliefs about who you are, what you deserve, what's possible. Not just thoughts—the lens through which you interpret everything that happens to you.

My stories were poison: "Once a gang member, always a gang member." "People like me don't really change." "I'm fooling everyone with this professional act." "If they knew who I really was, they'd run." These stories shaped every decision, filtered every opportunity, sabotaged every chance at genuine connection.

Stories are more than just thoughts—they're the operating system of your life. They determine what you see as possible or impossible, what you deserve or don't deserve, what you're capable of or limited by. Change your stories, and you change your reality. But I hadn't learned that yet.

But as I progressed in life and started taking on bigger challenges—starting businesses, pursuing meaningful goals—I discovered something was still missing. My motivation would flee at crucial moments. I would start projects with great enthusiasm, then constantly stop what I started. I saw this pattern over and over and knew something was still wrong.

I was changing my patterns slowly. I was beginning to rewrite my stories. But there was a third component I hadn't identified yet—the missing piece that would make everything else click into place.

The Viktor Frankl Revelation

Then I read Viktor Frankl's "Man's Search for Meaning," and the final piece of the puzzle revealed itself.

Frankl was a psychiatrist who survived the Nazi concentration camps—Auschwitz, Dachau, and others. Places where human beings were systematically stripped of everything: possessions, dignity, family, identity, hope. Places designed to reduce people to nothing.

But Frankl observed something profound that changed how I understood human nature. In the camps, it wasn't necessarily the physically strongest who survived. It wasn't the youngest or the healthiest. The survivors were those who maintained a sense of purpose—something to live for beyond their current suffering.

He watched people who had every reason to give up continue fighting for life because they had unfinished work, someone to return to, or a message to deliver to the world. He watched others, younger and stronger, simply give up and die once they lost their sense of purpose.

Frankl himself survived by imagining giving lectures after the war about the psychology of the camps. While suffering unimaginable horrors, he would mentally compose the talks he would give, the book he would write, the insights he would share. His purpose transcended his circumstances.

One passage hit me like lightning:

"Everything can be taken from a man but one thing: the last of the human freedoms—to choose one's attitude in any given set of circumstances, to choose one's own way."

But it was this line that changed everything for me:

"Those who have a 'why' to live, can bear with almost any 'how.'"

That's when it dawned on me with the force of revelation: I had been working on my patterns (the "how" of my daily life) and my stories (my beliefs about what was possible), but I had never identified my authentic "why"—my purpose.

Element Three: The Purposes You Serve

These are your driving motivations, the "why" behind your "what." Not what you say matters to you, but what your actions prove matters to you. Your purposes can be conscious or unconscious, chosen or inherited, authentic or imposed.

My purposes at the time were purely survival-based: avoid pain, seek pleasure, accumulate resources, maintain image. These weren't purposes that inspired—they were purposes that imprisoned. I was serving goals that had been assigned to me by my environment, not chosen by my authentic self.

Frankl showed me that humans need purpose like they need oxygen. Without it, we suffocate spiritually even if we're breathing physically. But not just any purpose—an authentic purpose that connects our individual existence to something larger than ourselves.

I realized that my transformation had been incomplete because I had only been working with two of the three elements. I had changed my daily patterns and was rewriting my stories, but I had never identified authentic purposes that were truly mine. I was like a car with an engine and wheels but no destination—capable of movement but not progress.

When these three elements harmonize, you become unstoppable. Your patterns reinforce your stories, your stories inspire your purposes, your purposes motivate your patterns. You create a positive feedback loop that generates momentum, confidence, and deep satisfaction.

When they're in discord—as mine were—you become your own worst enemy. You create internal civil war that drains energy and generates that persistent feeling that something essential is missing from your life.

This is the Trichotomy of self—not just a framework for understanding identity, but the actual architecture of human transformation.

The Tale of Two Destinies

Let me show you how this works through two men whose parallel stories reveal exactly why these three elements matter more than talent, luck, or circumstances.

Thomas Mitchell. MBA from Northwestern. Started at a prestigious investment firm in Chicago at 26, making $85,000 in 1995—excellent money for his age. Smart, ambitious, all the right credentials.

Thomas had patterns of a high achiever: first one in the office, last one to leave, weekends spent networking or studying market trends. His patterns looked successful from the outside.

But his stories were toxic: "I'm not as smart as my colleagues." "I'm one mistake away from being exposed." "Everyone here has advantages I don't." "I have to work twice as hard just to keep up."

And his purposes? They weren't even his. He was serving his father's dream of having a son on Wall Street, his mother's need to brag about her successful boy, his own fear of being ordinary. He was climbing a ladder someone else had placed against a wall he didn't choose.

For ten years, Thomas maintained this misalignment through sheer willpower. But willpower is finite. By 36, he was taking Xanax for anxiety, Ambien for sleep, Adderall for focus. By 40, his marriage had ended. By 45, despite being a senior partner making $400,000 a year, he was profoundly depressed.

David Martinez. High school dropout. Started as a janitor at the same investment firm, also in 1995, making $18,000 a year. No credentials, no connections, just a mop and a dream.

But David had something Thomas didn't: alignment.

David's patterns were learning patterns. While cleaning offices at night, he read every investment book in executives' offices. He studied annual reports in recycling bins. He listened to traders' conversations while emptying their trash. He took free online courses during breaks. Every pattern served his growth.

His stories were empowering: "I'm in the perfect position to learn without pressure." "Every successful person started somewhere." "Knowledge is free if you're hungry enough." "This janitor job is my Harvard Business School."

And his purposes were authentic and clear: Learn everything about financial markets. Build expertise from the ground up. Create opportunities through competence. Prove that hunger beats pedigree.

But most importantly, David had a transcendent purpose: to model for his two young sons that you could build a life around authentic gifts rather than fear. He wanted them to see that security came from developing yourself, not from depending on others.

David didn't just work hard—he worked with enthusiasm. He didn't just pursue goals—he pursued meaning. He didn't just want to be successful—he wanted to be useful.

One night, a trader found David reading a complex derivatives textbook. Instead of being angry, he was intrigued. They started talking. David's insights—gained from thousands of hours of self-study—impressed him. The trader became a mentor. David moved from janitor to mail room, mail room to assistant, assistant to junior analyst.

By 36, David was managing his own portfolio. By 40, he'd started his own fund. By 45, he was managing $50 million in assets, had a strong marriage, and two sons who watched their father build something from nothing through aligned effort.

The contrast was stark. Thomas had every advantage but lived in discord. He achieved what looked like success but felt like failure. David had every disadvantage but lived in harmony. He built what felt like success and happened to look like it too.

"Purpose is what transforms effort into fulfillment, work into calling, success into significance."

My Own Transformation

After my mother's question exposed my internal discord, and Frankl's book revealed what was missing, I had to make a choice: continue living three conflicting lives, or do the hard work of integration.

I started with patterns. I eliminated every behavior that connected me to my criminal past. Changed my phone number. Moved cities. Started working out for health, not intimidation. Began reading philosophy instead of plotting schemes. Simple changes at first, but patterns compound.

Then I rewrote my stories. Instead of "once a gang member, always a gang member," I began telling myself, "I'm someone who learned from mistakes and chose growth." Instead of "people like me don't change," I started believing, "people like me are proof that anyone can transform."

But the hardest part was finding authentic purposes. For so long, my only purpose had been survival. I needed something bigger, something that could transform my past from a source of shame into a source of strength.

I found it in service—helping others escape the traps that nearly killed me. My criminal past became my credential for reaching people no traditional counselor could reach. My education became tools for articulating what I'd learned in the streets. My story became medicine for others who thought they were too far gone to change.

Suddenly, my three elements started working together instead of against each other:

- My patterns of learning and growth supported...

- My stories of transformation and possibility, which inspired...

- My purposes of service and redemption, which motivated...

- Even better patterns of learning and growth.

The civil war ended. The harmony began. Life stopped feeling like performance and started feeling like purpose.

The Three Questions That Determine Everything

Now let me ask you what my mother's question eventually led me to discover—the three questions that reveal whether you're living in harmony or drift:

Question One: Are your daily patterns serving your highest potential, or keeping you stuck?

Look at your actual behaviors, not your intentions. Track yourself for one typical day. Write down what you do in fifteen-minute increments. Be ruthlessly honest. How do you spend your mornings? What do you do when stressed? How do you spend your evenings? What do you do when no one's watching?

Your patterns reveal your true priorities. You might say you value health, but if your patterns include poor eating and no exercise, then convenience is your actual priority. You might claim you value growth, but if you consume entertainment instead of education, then comfort is your real priority.

The gap between stated values and actual patterns is where quiet desperation lives.

Question Two: Do your deepest beliefs expand your possibilities or contract them?

What story plays in your head when you wake up? When you face challenges? When opportunities appear? When you look in the mirror? Are these stories based on evidence of what's possible, or fears about what could go wrong?

Your stories create your world. If you believe success requires sacrificing happiness, you'll unconsciously choose between them. If you believe you're "not that kind of person," you won't even see opportunities meant for you. If you believe change is dangerous, you'll stay trapped even when the cage door is open.

Write down your core beliefs about yourself, money, relationships, success, and happiness. Look at these beliefs objectively. Are these beliefs you'd want your child to have? If not, why are you keeping them?

Question Three: Are you serving purposes that feel genuinely yours?

What actually drives your daily choices—not what you tell people, but what your patterns reveal? Are you working toward goals that excite you, or goals you think you should want? Do your purposes connect to something larger than yourself, or are they focused only on survival and image?

Purposes based on fear or obligation will motivate you temporarily, but they'll drain you ultimately. Purposes based on authentic values and meaningful contribution will not only motivate you—they'll energize you. They'll make Monday morning feel like opportunity instead of obligation.

Like Frankl in the concentration camps, finding a "why" that transcends your circumstances transforms suffering into meaning, obstacles into growth, mere existence into purposeful life.

The Promise of Conscious Integration

If you answered these questions honestly, you now know where you stand. You know whether your trichotomy is harmonized or at war with itself. You know whether your current trajectory leads where you actually want to go or just where you think you should go.

Here's the truth that changes everything: discord is fixable, but only through conscious choice.

You can continue letting patterns run on autopilot, accepting limiting stories as truth, and serving empty purposes. Or you can do what I did after my mother's question, what Frankl did in the camps, what David did while mopping floors, what thousands have done when they discovered the Trichotomy of Self: you can choose conscious integration.

When you learn to harmonize your patterns, stories, and purposes:

- Decision-making becomes clearer because you have a framework for evaluation

- Change becomes sustainable because you're working with identity's architecture, not against it

- Growth accelerates because all three elements reinforce each other

- Life becomes satisfying because you're living as yourself, not as who others expect

"Harmony is not perfection—it's the conscious choice to live as the person you actually are rather than the person others expect you to be."

What's Coming Next

Understanding the Trichotomy is just the beginning. In the chapters ahead, you'll learn:

- The neuroscience behind why this framework works at the deepest levels (Chapter 3)

- How to identify and redesign your current patterns (Chapter 4)

- How to recognize and rewrite limiting stories (Chapter 5)

- How to discover and serve authentic purposes (Chapter 6)

- How to align all three elements into a coherent identity (Chapter 7)

- How to make changes that last (Chapter 8)

The question isn't whether you have patterns, stories, and purposes—you do. The question is whether you're choosing them consciously or letting them choose you unconsciously.

The answer to that question determines everything.

Just like it did for that gang member in Los Angeles who discovered that the person he was didn't have to be the person he remained. Just like it did for David Martinez who chose to see his maintenance job as business school. Just like it can for you, starting right now.

Your mother probably won't ask you if you're happy. So I'm asking you instead: Are you living in harmony, or are you at war with yourself?

The mirror doesn't lie. But the story it tells can be rewritten.

"Every day you are building the person you will become tomorrow. Build consciously."

Chapter Summary

You've just met someone who transformed from gang member to healer through discovering the three-part architecture of identity: patterns, stories, and purposes—the last revealed through Viktor Frankl's profound insights from the concentration camps.

You've seen how two men with different advantages but opposite alignment created vastly different destinies—proving that alignment matters more than circumstances.

You've answered three questions that reveal whether your own trichotomy is working together or against itself.

In Chapter 3, you'll discover why this framework isn't just philosophy—it's biology. You'll learn how your brain literally rewires itself based on your patterns, how your stories shape your neurochemistry, and how your purposes affect everything from your immune system to your lifespan.

The transformation isn't magical. It's mechanical. And once you understand the mechanism, you can operate it consciously.

CHAPTER THREE

THE SCIENCE BEHIND THE FRAMEWORK

"THE BRAIN YOU WERE BORN WITH IS NOT THE BRAIN YOU HAVE TO DIE WITH." —DR. MICHAEL MERZENICH

The Man Who Rewired His Mind

In 1998, a 62-year-old stroke victim named Paul Bach-y-Rita lay in a hospital bed, the left side of his body completely paralyzed. The doctors were frank with his family: the damage to his brain was extensive and permanent. Paul would never walk again, never regain use of his left arm, never live independently. They recommended a nursing home.

But Paul's son George, a psychiatrist, refused to accept this verdict. Against medical advice, he took his father home and began an unconventional rehabilitation program. Instead of accepting that his father's brain could not change, George operated from a radical premise: the brain remained capable of rewiring itself throughout life.

For months, George worked with his father on seemingly impossible tasks. They started with crawling—yes, crawling—across the floor for hours each day. Then wall exercises where Paul would lean against surfaces and slowly shift his weight. George treated his father's 62-year-old brain like a child's brain, assuming it could learn new patterns if given the right conditions.

The medical establishment called it foolish. Neurologists of that era believed in what they called "neurological nihilism"—the idea that adult brains were fixed, hardwired, incapable of significant change. Once damaged, always damaged. Once formed, never reformed.

But something extraordinary began to happen.

After months of repetitive exercises, Paul began to recover movement. First tiny improvements—a slight twitch in his fingers, a barely perceptible shift in his leg. Then larger gains. Within a year, he was walking. Within two years, he was hiking in the mountains of California. By his seventies, he was traveling the world, fully independent, his brain having literally rewired itself around the damaged areas.

Paul Bach-y-Rita lived 30 more years, dying at age 94 not from his stroke, but from a heart attack while hiking at 9,000 feet in the Colombian mountains. His recovery became one of the foundational cases that launched the field of neuroplasticity—the science that would revolutionize our understanding of human potential and validate everything the Trichotomy of Self represents.

Here's why Paul's story matters for your life: If a 62-year-old stroke victim can rewire his brain to overcome "permanent" paralysis, what excuse do any of us have for believing we're stuck with patterns, stories, or purposes that no longer serve us?

The Three Pillars of Human Transformation

Paul's recovery didn't happen by accident. It followed three principles that, unknown to George at the time, would later be validated by decades of neuroscience research. These same three principles explain why the Trichotomy of Self works at the deepest biological level:

Principle 1: Repetition Rewires Reality (The Pattern Principle)

Principle 2: Meaning Shapes Perception (The Story Principle)

Principle 3: Purpose Provides Power (The Purpose Principle)

Let me show you how cutting-edge science validates each component of your TOS, and why aligning them creates changes that go far beyond positive thinking or willpower.

Principle 1: How Patterns Physically Reshape Your Brain
"Cells that fire together wire together." —Donald Hebb

Dr. Alvaro Pascual-Leone stands before a room of skeptical neuroscientists at Harvard Medical School, about to demonstrate something that will change how we think about human potential forever. In his hand, he holds the brain scans of two groups of people: pianists and non-musicians.

"Look at this," he says, pointing to the motor cortex region of the pianist's brain scans. "The area that controls finger movement is significantly larger in professional pianists than in non-musicians. But here's what's fascinating—we can create this same change in just five days."

The room grows quiet. Pascual-Leone explains his experiment: he took people who had never played piano and divided them into three groups. The first group practiced a simple five-finger piano exercise for two hours daily. The second group simply imagined practicing the same exercise for two hours daily—they never touched a piano. The third group did nothing.

After five days, brain scans revealed something extraordinary. Both the physical practice group and the mental practice group showed measurable increases in the motor cortex regions associated with finger movement. The control group showed no changes.

Think about the implications: In just five days, repetitive patterns—whether physical or mental—literally rewired the structure of the human brain. The pianists' brains weren't different because they were born with "musical brains"—their brains became musical through pattern repetition.

Your daily patterns are not just habits—they are literally sculpting your neural architecture.

The Michael Phelps Phenomenon

Consider Michael Phelps, the most decorated Olympian in history with 28 medals, 23 of them gold. Sports scientists have studied his physique extensively—yes, he has physical advantages. But here's what most people don't know: Phelps's greatest advantage wasn't his body—it was his brain.

From age 7, Phelps practiced swimming patterns six hours a day, 365 days a year. By the time he reached Olympic competition, he had repeated perfect swimming motions over 10 million times. Brain scans of elite athletes like Phelps show something remarkable:

their motor cortex regions are so developed that their movements require less conscious thought than an average person needs to tie their shoes.

But here's the key insight: Phelps didn't just practice swimming. His coach, Bob Bowman, had him visualize perfect races every night before sleep and every morning upon waking. Phelps would mentally swim each race stroke by stroke, seeing the pool, feeling the water, hearing the crowd. He called it "watching his videotape."

During the 2008 Beijing Olympics, Phelps's goggles filled with water during the 200-meter butterfly final. He couldn't see anything. But his patterns were so deeply encoded that he swam the race blind, counting strokes exactly as he'd visualized thousands of times. He won gold and set a world record—blind.

This is the power of patterns. They become who you are at such a fundamental level that they operate even when consciousness fails.

The Four Laws of Neural Change

Dr. Jeffrey Schwartz, a psychiatrist at UCLA, has used pattern-based neuroplasticity to help people overcome obsessive-compulsive disorder without medication. His research has revealed four laws that govern how patterns reshape your brain:

Law 1: Use It or Lose It Neural pathways that aren't used regularly begin to weaken and disappear. This is why skills you don't practice deteriorate, but it's also why limiting patterns lose their power when you stop feeding them. Every day you don't engage in a negative pattern, it literally becomes weaker in your brain.

Law 2: Use It and Improve It Neural pathways that are used frequently become stronger, faster, and more automatic. This is why practiced skills become effortless, but it's also why repeated negative patterns become increasingly difficult to break. Your brain doesn't distinguish between helpful and harmful patterns—it just strengthens whatever you repeat.

Law 3: Specificity Matters Your brain strengthens exactly what you practice, nothing more, nothing less. If you practice anxiety patterns, you become better at anxiety. If you practice confidence patterns, you become better at confidence. There's no general "improvement"—only specific neural pathway development.

Law 4: Repetition and Intensity Drive Change The more frequently and intensely you repeat a pattern, the faster your brain adapts. This is why traumatic events can create instant neural changes, but it's also why consistent daily practice creates lasting transformation.

Principle 2: How Stories Literally Create Your Reality

"The stories we tell ourselves about our lives become our lives." —Dr. Dan McAdams

In 2007, researchers at Harvard conducted an experiment that seemed to defy the laws of physics. They took 84 hotel maids—women who cleaned rooms all day, engaging in significant physical activity—and discovered something puzzling: despite their physically demanding jobs, most were overweight and had the health markers of sedentary individuals.

The researchers divided the maids into two groups. They told one group: "Your daily work qualifies as the surgeon general's recommended amount of exercise. Cleaning rooms is excellent physical activity that burns calories and improves fitness." They explained how vacuuming worked the arms, how making beds engaged the core, how walking between rooms provided cardio.

The control group received no such information.

Four weeks later, without any change in actual behavior, the informed group had lost an average of 2 pounds, reduced their blood pressure by 10%, and decreased their body fat percentage. The control group showed no changes.

The only difference? The story the maids told themselves about their daily activities.

This is the power of stories. They don't just describe your reality—they create it.

The Placebo Effect on Steroids

Dr. Alia Crum, the researcher behind the hotel maid study, has spent her career demonstrating what she calls "the mindset effect"—how our stories about experiences change the experiences themselves at a biological level.

In another study, she gave participants identical milkshakes but labeled them differently. One was labeled "Indulgence: 620 calories of decadent pleasure." The other: "Sensi-Shake: 140 calories of guilt-free satisfaction."

The shakes were identical—380 calories each. But here's what happened: Those who drank the "indulgent" shake showed a dramatic drop in ghrelin (the hunger hormone), feeling satisfied for hours. Those who drank the "diet" shake showed minimal ghrelin suppression and felt hungry again quickly.

The story about the shake literally changed how their bodies processed it.

Crum's research extends further:

- People told that stress is enhancing perform better than those told stress is debilitating

- Patients told that a treatment will be highly effective show better outcomes than those given neutral expectations

- Athletes told they have a "gene for endurance" outperform their previous records

Your stories aren't just psychological—they're physiological. They change your hormones, your immune response, your cellular function.

The Narrative Identity Theory

Dr. Dan McAdams at Northwestern University has spent 30 years studying what he calls "narrative identity"—the internalized story of who you are. His research reveals that humans don't just have stories; we ARE our stories.

McAdams found that people who tell redemptive stories about their lives—stories where suffering leads to growth—show:

- Better mental health outcomes

- Greater resilience to stress

- Higher levels of generativity (contributing to future generations)

- Improved physical health markers

- Greater life satisfaction

Conversely, people who tell contamination stories—where good things are spoiled by negative events—show opposite patterns, regardless of their actual life circumstances.

Two people can experience identical events and have completely different life outcomes based solely on the stories they tell about those events.

Principle 3: How Purpose Transforms Biology

"He who has a why to live can bear almost any how." —Friedrich Nietzsche

In 2009, researchers at Rush University Medical Center in Chicago published results from a study that followed 1,238 older adults for up to five years. They measured each participant's sense of purpose using validated psychological assessments, then tracked their health outcomes.

The results were staggering: People with a strong sense of purpose were 2.4 times less likely to develop Alzheimer's disease. They showed slower cognitive decline, better immune function, and lived significantly longer. The protective effect of purpose was greater than that of exercise, social connection, or education level.

But here's what makes this finding revolutionary: The protective effects remained even after accounting for depression, social connections, physical health, and dozens of other variables. Purpose itself—independent of all other factors—was transforming biology.

The Telomere Connection

Dr. Elizabeth Blackburn won the Nobel Prize for discovering telomerase, the enzyme that protects telomeres—the protective caps on our chromosomes that determine cellular aging. Longer telomeres mean slower aging and longer life.

In collaboration with Dr. Elissa Epel, Blackburn discovered something remarkable: People with a strong sense of purpose have longer telomeres and higher telomerase activity. Their cells are literally aging more slowly.

But it gets more specific. Not all purposes are created equal:

- **Self-focused purposes** (wealth, fame, image) showed no protective effect

- **Self-transcendent purposes** (contributing to something beyond yourself) showed significant protective effects

- **Prosocial purposes** (helping others, making a difference) showed the strongest effects

Your purpose doesn't just motivate you—it changes you at the cellular level.

The Blue Zones Revelation

Dan Buettner spent years studying the Blue Zones—five regions where people routinely live past 100: Okinawa, Japan; Sardinia, Italy; Nicoya, Costa Rica; Ikaria, Greece; and Loma Linda, California.

Despite different cultures, diets, and lifestyles, all Blue Zone communities share one characteristic: a cultural emphasis on purpose. In Okinawa, they call it "ikigai"—your reason for waking up in the morning. In Costa Rica, it's "plan de vida"—your life plan.

Researchers found that Blue Zone centenarians don't retire in the Western sense. They maintain their sense of purpose throughout life:

- The 102-year-old Sardinian shepherd still tending his flock

- The 95-year-old Okinawan woman still maintaining her garden to feed her family

- The 98-year-old Ikarian man still making wine for his community

When researchers asked these centenarians about their longevity secrets, they rarely mentioned diet or exercise first. They talked about purpose—having something important to wake up for every morning.

The Integration Effect: When All Three Harmonize

Now here's where the science becomes truly remarkable. When patterns, stories, and purposes harmonize, they create what researchers call "synergistic effects"—outcomes greater than the sum of their parts.

Dr. Martin Seligman at the University of Pennsylvania has demonstrated this through his work on flourishing. People who score high on all three dimensions—engagement (patterns), meaning (stories), and purpose—show:

- 23% reduction in cortisol (stress hormone) levels

- 30% improvement in immune function markers

- 50% reduction in depression risk

- 60% increase in life satisfaction scores

- Improved cardiovascular health equivalent to being 10 years younger

But here's the crucial finding: People who excel in just one or two dimensions don't show these benefits. It's the harmony of all three that creates transformation.

The Stanford Transformation Study

In 2018, researchers at Stanford conducted a study that perfectly demonstrates the integration effect. They took 240 adults struggling with various life challenges and divided them into four groups:

Group 1: Pattern Change Only Taught new behavioral habits and daily routines. Result: 15% improvement in wellbeing.

Group 2: Story Change Only Cognitive therapy to reframe beliefs and narratives. Result: 18% improvement in wellbeing.

Group 3: Purpose Work Only Values clarification and meaning-making exercises. Result: 12% improvement in wellbeing.

Group 4: Integrated Approach Simultaneous work on patterns, stories, and purposes. Result: 67% improvement in wellbeing.

The integrated group didn't just add the benefits—they multiplied them. Participants reported feeling like "completely different people" after just 12 weeks.

The Neuroscience of Harmony

Dr. Richard Davidson at the University of Wisconsin has spent decades studying the brains of people who've achieved what he calls "wellbeing"—sustainable happiness and life satisfaction. Using advanced brain imaging, he's identified four neural circuits that correspond to wellbeing:

1. **The Attention Circuit** (strengthened by pattern work)

2. **The Resilience Circuit** (strengthened by story work)

3. **The Outlook Circuit** (strengthened by purpose work)

4. **The Generosity Circuit** (strengthened when all three harmonize)

When these circuits work together, Davidson observes what he calls "whole brain integration"—a state where different brain regions communicate optimally, creating the subjective experience of flow, presence, and deep satisfaction.

This is exactly what happens when you harmonize your Trichotomy of Self. Your brain literally integrates, creating a biological foundation for sustainable transformation.

Your Brain on Discord

Conversely, when your patterns, stories, and purposes are in discord, your brain shows signs of what researchers call "neural conflict":

- Increased activation in the anterior cingulate cortex (the brain's conflict detector)

- Elevated amygdala activity (fear and stress response)

- Decreased prefrontal cortex function (decision-making and self-control)

- Disrupted default mode network (sense of self)

This neural conflict doesn't just feel bad—it is bad for you. Chronic discord is associated with:

- Accelerated cellular aging

- Increased inflammation markers

- Compromised immune function

- Higher risk of depression and anxiety

- Reduced cognitive performance

- Shorter lifespan

Your brain and body know when you're living out of harmony, even if your conscious mind denies it.

The Choice Point

Every scientific discovery in this chapter points to the same liberating truth: You have far more control over who you become than you've been led to believe.

Your brain remains plastic throughout life, capable of rewiring based on the patterns you choose to repeat. Your reality is actively shaped by the stories you tell, and these stories can be examined and rewritten. Your sense of purpose can enhance your health, extend your life, and transform your daily experience.

The question isn't whether you can change—the science proves you can. The question is whether you will choose to change consciously.

Most people allow their patterns to run on autopilot, shaped by habit rather than intention. They accept their stories as fixed truths rather than editable narratives. They serve purposes assigned by others rather than chosen by their authentic selves.

But now you know the science. You understand the mechanisms. You've seen the evidence.

The brain you have today is not the brain you have to keep. The stories you tell today are not the stories you have to believe tomorrow. The purposes you serve today are not the purposes you have to serve forever.

The Bridge to Practice

In the next section of this book, we'll move from understanding to application. We'll dive deep into each component of your TOS, exploring how to assess your current patterns, stories, and purposes, and how to align them consciously.

But before we continue, pause and absorb the magnitude of what you've just learned. The framework you're about to master isn't just another self-help system—it's a scientifically validated approach to human flourishing that bridges ancient wisdom with cutting-edge research.

Paul Bach-y-Rita didn't know the neuroscience when he learned to walk again, but he proved it with every step. The hotel maids didn't understand narrative psychology, but their bodies responded to new stories anyway. The Blue Zone centenarians don't read scientific journals, but they live the evidence of purpose every day.

You now have something they didn't: conscious understanding of the mechanisms. You know not just that transformation is possible, but how it works at the deepest biological level.

"The most important decision you make is who you become. The second most important is harmonizing your daily patterns, guiding stories, and driving purposes with that decision. Science has proven this harmony doesn't just change your life—it changes your brain, your cells, your very biology."

In the next chapter, we begin the practical work of transformation by examining the first component of your TOS: the patterns you repeat daily.

The journey from unconscious living to authentic coherence starts with understanding the science. Now that you understand, it's time to apply.

Chapter Summary

You've discovered how a stroke victim's recovery launched the neuroplasticity revolution, proving brains can rewire at any age through conscious pattern repetition.

You've learned that your stories don't just describe reality—they create it, changing everything from hunger hormones to immune function based on the narratives you believe.

You've seen how purpose transforms biology, protecting against disease, slowing cellular aging, and extending life when that purpose transcends the self.

Most importantly, you've discovered the integration effect—how harmonizing patterns, stories, and purposes creates synergistic transformation far beyond what any component achieves alone.

In Chapter 4, you'll learn to identify and redesign your current patterns, beginning the practical work of rewiring your brain for the life you choose rather than the life you inherited.

The science is clear. The mechanism is proven. The only question remaining is: What will you do with this knowledge?

CHAPTER FOUR

THE PATTERNS YOU REPEAT DAILY

"WE ARE WHAT WE REPEATEDLY DO. EXCELLENCE, THEN, IS NOT AN ACT, BUT A HABIT." —ARISTOTLE

The Man Who Became His Schedule

At 4:27 AM, before his alarm even rings, Tim Cook's eyes open. The CEO of Apple doesn't need an alarm clock—his patterns are so deeply encoded that his body knows exactly when to wake. By 4:30, he's reading customer emails. By 5:00, he's at the gym. By 6:30, he's in the office. Every. Single. Day.

This isn't discipline. This is identity.

Cook doesn't decide each morning whether to wake early or exercise or dive into work. These patterns have become so automatic that NOT doing them would require more effort than doing them. His patterns aren't something he does—they're who he is.

Now consider Sarah, a marketing manager who also sets her alarm for 4:30 AM. She read about Cook's routine in a productivity blog and decided to copy it. Day one, she forces herself out of bed, exercises halfheartedly, and drags herself to work early. By day three, she's hitting snooze. By day five, she's abandoned the experiment entirely, feeling worse about herself than before she started.

What's the difference between Cook and Sarah? It's not willpower. It's not motivation. It's not even desire for success. The difference is that Cook's patterns emerged from his identity, while Sarah was trying to paste someone else's patterns onto hers.

"Your patterns are not your habits. Your patterns are your character made visible, your values made physical, your beliefs made manifest. Every repetition is a vote for the person you're becoming."

The Ancient Wisdom of Repetition

The Greeks understood something we've forgotten: that character—ethos—was not something you possessed but something you practiced. Aristotle didn't speak of habits as mere behaviors but as the architecture of virtue itself. Each repeated action was a stone laid in the foundation of who you were becoming.

The Stoics took this further. Marcus Aurelius wrote his Meditations not as philosophy for others, but as daily practice for himself—patterns of thought repeated until they became patterns of being. He understood that the emperor who could command legions meant nothing if he couldn't command himself.

"The universe is change; our life is what our thoughts make it. But thoughts without patterns remain merely wishes whispered to the wind."

Patterns are the bridge between intention and transformation, between who you hope to be and who you actually become.

The Janitor Who Changed Everything

Let me tell you about Maria Santos, because her story reveals something profound about patterns that most people never see.

Maria worked the night shift as a janitor at Jefferson Middle School in East Los Angeles. Every morning at 3 AM, she'd wake up in her small apartment, kiss her sleeping children goodbye, and drive through empty streets to clean the halls where other people's children would learn.

For the first year, Maria followed the same routine: Clock in at 4 AM. Clean 30 classrooms. Empty 200 trash cans. Mop 15,000 square feet of hallway. Clock out at noon. Sleep until her own kids came home from school.

But Maria had grown up in these same neighborhoods. She'd been one of these kids—the ones who came to school hungry, who moved through the halls like ghosts, who learned early that invisibility was safety. And as she cleaned, she began to see patterns within patterns.

She noticed which desks were covered with doodles of rockets and spaceships—always the same boy, Carlos, who sat in the back corner of Mrs. Rodriguez's class. She saw the crumpled math tests in Jennifer's trash—all F's, but with work that showed understanding, just unfinished because time ran out. She found the love notes Stephanie wrote to herself and threw away—"You matter. You're smart. Don't give up"—a fifteen-year-old trying to parent herself through ink and paper.

Most people would have emptied the trash and moved on. But Maria began developing what I call patterns of recognition—the sacred practice of seeing the unseen, honoring the unhonored.

She learned every student's name from the papers left in desks. She memorized which teachers stayed late helping struggling students. She observed which kids ate lunch alone, which ones showed up without supplies, which ones carried invisible weights on their small shoulders.

And Maria began to leave traces—not just clean classrooms, but acts of witness. A favorite pencil placed on Carlos's desk with a note: "Para el astronauta." Extra time spent erasing Jennifer's board work slowly, giving the girl time to copy notes. Books about space exploration left on Carlos's desk. A pack of mechanical pencils in Stephanie's backpack with a note in Spanish: "Para la escritora brillante." (For the brilliant writer.)

Nobody asked Maria to notice these things. Nobody paid her to care. But Maria understood something profound: The sacred lives not in grand gestures but in the consecration of ordinary moments through conscious attention.

After two years of these patterns of care, something remarkable happened. The academic performance at Jefferson began to improve. Disciplinary problems decreased. Attendance rates climbed. Teacher morale soared.

The administration brought in consultants to study their "miraculous turnaround." They analyzed data, surveyed students, interviewed teachers. But they never looked at the patterns of the woman who worked while they slept.

Carlos became the first person in his family to graduate high school and got a scholarship to study aerospace engineering. Jennifer discovered she had a learning difference, got accommodations, and became a math tutor. Stephanie started a peer counseling group and is now a social worker.

Years later, at Carlos's college graduation, he found Maria in the crowd. "Mrs. Santos," he said, tears in his eyes, "you probably don't remember, but you left me pencils and books when I was in middle school. Nobody had ever noticed what I loved before."

Maria smiled. "Mijo, I remember everything. I saw the astronaut in you before you saw it in yourself."

"We do not need a different life to live meaningfully. We need to live our current life differently. The transformation happens not in changing our circumstances, but in changing how we show up within them."

The Philosophy of Becoming Through Repetition

Here lies one of life's great paradoxes: Freedom comes not from unlimited choices, but from choosing limitations consciously.

Think of a river. Its power comes not from spreading aimlessly across the landscape, but from the constraints of its banks. Those banks—seemingly restrictive—actually create the conditions for the river to carve canyons, move mountains, and flow toward the sea.

Your patterns are the banks of your life's river. Chosen unconsciously, they become prisons. Chosen consciously, they become the very source of your power to transform yourself and your world.

The philosopher William James understood this when he wrote: "All our life, so far as it has definite form, is but a mass of habits." But he meant something deeper than routine. He meant that the self we experience as continuous, as "me," is actually a collection of patterns repeated so consistently that they create the illusion of a fixed identity.

"You are not a noun but a verb—not a thing but a process of becoming. Your patterns are the grammar of your becoming."

The Teacher Who Lost Her Voice

Before we explore where patterns come from, let me tell you about Dr. Amanda Richardson, because her story illustrates how patterns can betray us without our awareness.

Amanda had been a beloved high school English teacher for fifteen years. Students sought her out for advice, parents requested her specifically, administrators relied on her wisdom. She lived for those moments when a struggling student's eyes would light up with understanding.

But somewhere along the way, Amanda had developed what she didn't recognize as a pattern of self-silencing. In faculty meetings, she'd prepare thoughtful contributions but rarely share them. When administrators made decisions she disagreed with, she'd voice her concerns to colleagues in private but remain silent in official settings. When budget cuts threatened programs she believed in, she'd worry and complain but wouldn't speak up publicly.

Amanda told herself she was being diplomatic, professional, respectful of hierarchy. But the truth was more complex: she had developed patterns of avoiding conflict, even when that conflict could serve her students.

The breaking point came during a budget meeting where the district proposed cutting the creative writing program—Amanda's pride and joy, the class where she'd watched shy students find their voices, where future poets and novelists first discovered their gifts.

Amanda sat through the entire meeting with her hands folded, her mouth shut, her heart breaking. She had pages of notes about the program's impact, statistics about student engagement, testimonials from parents. She had everything she needed to make a compelling case.

But her pattern was stronger than her passion. Her habit of silence overruled her love for her students.

The program was cut. Amanda went home that night and wept—not just for the lost program, but for her own lost voice. She realized she'd been practicing self-betrayal so consistently that it had become her default response to situations that mattered most.

"The cruelest patterns are not the ones that hurt us obviously, but the ones that slowly erode our authentic self while whispering that this erosion is wisdom, maturity, or keeping the peace."

Amanda's story teaches us something crucial: patterns don't just shape what we do—they shape what we don't do. They don't just create our actions—they limit our possibilities. They don't just reflect who we are—they determine who we're not allowed to become.

The Archaeology of Your Automatic Behaviors

Before you can consciously reshape your patterns, you must understand their origins. Every pattern you practice has a story, a genealogy that traces back through time like roots of an ancient tree.

The Family River

Your first teachers weren't your kindergarten instructors—they were your family members, teaching you through their own patterns what it meant to be human in this world.

Consider Rebecca, a 35-year-old architect, who couldn't understand why she felt anxious every time she sat down to eat—even alone. Through what I call pattern archaeology—the practice of tracing behaviors back to their origins—she discovered that family dinners in her childhood were tense interrogations where her father would quiz her about school performance while her mother sat silent, managing his moods.

Forty years later, her nervous system still associated eating with evaluation and conflict. The child's survival response had become the adult's limitation. She was living not her own patterns, but the emotional residue of her family's dysfunction, passed down like an heirloom she never asked to inherit.

Or consider Michael, a successful surgeon who never finished a cup of coffee while hot. He'd always abandon it halfway through to attend to something "more important." Tracing this back, he discovered his mother did the exact same thing—constantly sacrificing her own small pleasures for others' immediate needs, never quite believing her own comfort mattered.

Michael had inherited not just a coffee-drinking pattern, but an entire philosophy of existence: that his own needs were always secondary, his own pleasure always negotiable. He was living his mother's story of noble self-sacrifice without ever choosing whether it was his own.

"We are all archaeological sites, layers upon layers of inherited patterns waiting to be excavated and examined in the light of conscious choice."

The Survival Adaptations

Some patterns formed as brilliant adaptations to situations you no longer face. The human psyche is remarkably creative when it comes to survival—it will develop whatever patterns keep you safe, even if those patterns eventually become the very thing that limits your growth.

After devastating public humiliation in seventh grade, Jennifer developed patterns of invisibility—speaking quietly, avoiding eye contact, deflecting any attention. At twelve, these patterns protected her from further humiliation. At thirty-two, they were preventing her from advancing in her career, speaking up in meetings, or forming deep friendships.

The hypervigilance that once kept her safe now kept her small. The protective patterns had become a prison whose walls were made of her own fear.

This reveals something profound about human adaptation: We are meaning-making creatures who will sacrifice almost anything—including our own growth—to maintain consistency with the story we've told ourselves about who we are and what the world requires.

The Cultural Inheritance

Beyond family, you inherited patterns from your broader culture—patterns so normalized they feel like natural law rather than human convention.

David grew up in a culture that equated busyness with importance, motion with progress, achievement with worth. He absorbed patterns of constant activity without ever questioning whether activity and accomplishment were the same thing. Even on vacation, he'd pack every moment with experiences to photograph and share. Sitting still felt like laziness. Doing nothing felt like dying.

He didn't realize he was performing productivity rather than experiencing life, mistaking the shadow of accomplishment for its substance. He was living not his own rhythm, but his culture's anxious tempo, dancing to music he'd never chosen to play.

The Accidental Accumulations

Many patterns simply drifted into existence through what seems like chance but is actually the result of unconscious choices compounded over time.

Lisa started checking her phone first thing in the morning simply because it served as her alarm. This convenient choice became an entrenched pattern that hijacked the first thirty minutes of every day, flooding her system with other people's agendas before she'd even connected with her own intentions.

What began as practicality became prison. She was living not her own morning, but the urgent demands of a connected world that never sleeps, never pauses, never asks permission to colonize her consciousness.

"The patterns we drift into by accident become the channels through which our life force flows. Choose your channels consciously, or they will choose you unconsciously."

The Executive Who Disappeared

Let me tell you about James Morrison, because his story reveals how patterns can slowly erase our authentic selves while convincing us we're being successful.

James was a rising star at a consulting firm—brilliant, ambitious, tireless. But over five years, he had developed what he didn't recognize as patterns of self-abandonment in service to others' expectations.

He'd developed a pattern of saying yes to every request, no matter how unreasonable or poorly timed. He'd developed a pattern of working weekends without being asked, sending emails at midnight to prove his dedication. He'd developed a pattern of minimizing his own ideas while amplifying others', especially those of senior partners.

James thought he was being strategic, professional, a team player. But really, he was practicing erasure. Every yes to others' priorities was a no to his own. Every weekend at the office was time not spent discovering what he actually valued. Every brilliant idea he credited to someone else was a small act of self-betrayal.

The pattern revealed itself when James was passed over for promotion—again. The partners told him he was "indispensable in his current role" but lacked "executive presence." The very patterns he'd developed to advance his career had made his advancement impossible.

James sat in his car after that meeting and realized something terrifying: he couldn't remember the last time he'd expressed an authentic opinion, defended an original idea, or said no to a request. He'd become so skilled at reading and meeting others' expectations that he'd lost touch with his own.

"The most dangerous patterns are not the ones that make us obviously unhappy, but the ones that make us successful at being someone we never chose to become."

The Four Sacred Domains of Pattern Work

Physical Patterns: The Body as Teacher

Your body doesn't just carry you through life—it is the foundation upon which every other experience rests. The ancient Greeks understood this: mens sana in corpore sano—a sound mind in a sound body. But they meant something deeper than physical fitness.

They understood that how you inhabit your body teaches you how to inhabit your life.

Take Dr. Sarah Kim, an emergency room physician who discovered her chronic anxiety wasn't psychological—it was respiratory. Years of shallow chest breathing had kept her nervous system in a constant state of fight-or-flight. When she learned to breathe deeply into her belly, activating her parasympathetic nervous system, her anxiety decreased by 60% within two weeks.

Your posture is a daily vote for confidence or defeat. Your breathing patterns create the internal weather of your emotional life. Your movement patterns determine whether you experience your body as ally or burden.

Amy Cuddy's research revealed that holding an expansive posture for just two minutes changes your hormone levels—increasing testosterone and decreasing cortisol. But this isn't just about biochemistry. It's about the profound truth that how you carry yourself literally shapes who you become.

"Your body is not a machine you operate but a sacred text you write with every gesture, every breath, every choice about how to move through space."

Mental Patterns: The Architecture of Consciousness

In our fragmented age, your attention patterns don't just determine productivity—they determine the very quality of your consciousness.

The mystics understood this. Buddhist meditation is fundamentally attention training. The Stoics practiced prosoche—continuous attention to the present moment. They knew that where attention goes, identity follows.

Consider Rachel Thompson, a writer who felt constantly scattered until she tracked her attention for a week. She discovered she was switching tasks every six minutes, creating what researchers call "attention residue"—part of her mind always stuck on the previous task.

But the real discovery was deeper: She was living in a constant state of partial presence, never fully here, never fully anywhere. She was missing her own life, distracted from the very experiences she was living.

Rachel implemented "attention batching"—dedicating specific time blocks to specific types of work. Her writing quality improved dramatically, but more importantly, she began experiencing what she'd lost: the deep satisfaction of sustained focus.

Information Processing Patterns: How do you consume information? Do you seek out diverse perspectives and challenging ideas, or do you stay within comfortable echo chambers? Do you engage with difficult material that requires sustained thinking, or do you consume only easily digestible content?

Your information diet shapes your mental fitness as surely as your food diet shapes your physical fitness. People who consistently consume shallow, reactive content develop shallow, reactive thinking patterns. Those who engage with deep, thoughtful material develop deeper, more nuanced cognitive abilities.

"In a world designed to scatter your attention, the ability to focus becomes not just a skill but a form of resistance, a declaration that your consciousness belongs to you."

Emotional Patterns: The Inner Weather

Your emotional patterns create the climate in which everything else in your life must live and grow.

Some people practice what I call patterns of resilience—pausing when triggered, breathing through difficulty, choosing responses rather than reactions. Others live in patterns of reactivity—immediate emotional discharge, rumination cycles, blame patterns that keep them trapped in stories that don't serve.

Marcus Chen, a project manager, realized his stress patterns were like emotional weather systems that affected everyone around him. When deadlines approached, he'd become a storm system—irritable, snappish, demanding. His team would batten down the hatches, his family would take shelter, and he'd feel isolated and misunderstood.

Marcus learned to recognize his stress signals—shallow breathing, tight shoulders, rushed speech—as early warning systems. When he noticed these, he'd take what he called "strategic pauses"—two minutes of deep breathing and intention-setting.

This wasn't just stress management. It was leadership through emotional modeling. He was showing others that storms could be weathered, that intensity didn't require reactivity, that pressure could be met with presence.

Gratitude and Appreciation Patterns: What do you focus on throughout your day? Do you practice noticing and appreciating positive experiences, or do you practice dwelling on problems and complaints? Do you express gratitude to others regularly, or do you take their contributions for granted?

Research shows that people who practice regular appreciation develop measurably better mental health, stronger relationships, and greater life satisfaction. Gratitude isn't just a nice sentiment—it's a pattern that rewires your consciousness for abundance rather than scarcity.

"Your emotional patterns are not just personal—they are environmental. You create the emotional weather in which everyone around you must live."

Social Patterns: The Web of Connection

Every interaction is practice. You're either practicing patterns that weave you deeper into the web of human connection, or patterns that isolate you within the prison of your own perspective.

David Park, a software engineer, wondered why his relationships felt superficial until he discovered his patterns of conversational hijacking. When others shared problems, he'd immediately offer solutions rather than presence. When they shared successes, he'd relate it back to his own experiences rather than celebrating theirs.

These patterns seemed helpful, even generous. But they were actually forms of control—ways of managing his discomfort with others' emotions by redirecting the conversation back to familiar territory.

David practiced new patterns: asking follow-up questions that showed he was truly listening, reflecting back what he heard before offering anything, sitting with others' emotions rather than trying to fix or redirect them.

His relationships deepened dramatically, but the most profound change was internal. For the first time, he began experiencing genuine intimacy—the rare and precious experience of being known and accepted for who he truly was.

Communication Patterns: How do you interact with others throughout your day? Do you practice active listening and genuine curiosity, or do you practice waiting for your turn to speak? Do you ask thoughtful questions, or do you make assumptions? Do you express yourself clearly and honestly, or do you hide behind ambiguity and people-pleasing?

Boundary Patterns: How do you protect your time, energy, and values? Do you practice saying no to requests that don't align with your priorities, or do you say yes to everything and become overwhelmed? Do you communicate your needs clearly, or do you expect others to read your mind?

Healthy boundary patterns aren't selfish—they're essential for sustainable relationships and authentic living.

"Connection is not something you achieve but something you practice. Every interaction is an opportunity to weave yourself more deeply into the fabric of human community or to retreat further into the fortress of the self."

The Mirror Week: Seeing Your Invisible Self

Before transformation comes recognition. Most people live in a strange unconsciousness about their own patterns—they know their intentions but remain blind to their actions.

The ancient Greek maxim "Know thyself" wasn't philosophical advice—it was practical instruction. You cannot change what you cannot see. You cannot choose consciously what you practice unconsciously.

Set five random alarms throughout each day for one week. When they ring, become an anthropologist of your own existence:

- What are you doing in this exact moment?

- How are you holding your body?

- What's the quality of your breathing?

- What's your emotional state?

- How are you relating to whatever or whoever is present?

- What does this moment reveal about what you truly value?

Don't judge—just witness. The goal is not evaluation but revelation.

Jennifer, a marketing executive, was shocked to discover she checked her phone 127 times per day—every 7.5 minutes during waking hours. She thought she used technology intentionally, but the data revealed a pattern of constant distraction she'd been unconscious of.

More profound was the recognition that she was living in a state of perpetual anxiety—not about anything specific, but about the possibility of missing something, being left out, falling behind. Her phone wasn't just a device; it was a security blanket against the fundamental uncertainty of being alive.

The Honesty Audit

Before completing the energy audit, you need to practice radical honesty with yourself:

- What patterns am I currently practicing that I don't want to admit?

- Where am I lying to myself about my actual behaviors versus my intended behaviors?

- What stories am I telling myself to justify patterns that don't serve me?

- How is my relationship with myself (in terms of honesty and follow-through) affecting my relationships with others?

- If someone could only know me by observing my patterns for a month, what would they conclude about my character?

The goal isn't self-judgment—it's self-honesty. You can't change patterns you won't acknowledge, and you can't build authentic relationships on a foundation of self-deception.

"The unexamined life is not worth living, but the examined life—truly examined, without flinching from what we discover—is the beginning of all transformation."

The Four Stages of Conscious Becoming

Stage 1: Unconscious Incompetence (The Sleepwalk) You're practicing patterns that don't serve your authentic becoming, but you're unaware of them. You hit snooze without thinking, scroll social media mindlessly, eat while distracted, interrupt others without realizing it. Your patterns live you rather than you living your patterns.

Change is impossible because you don't see what needs to change.

Stage 2: Conscious Incompetence (The Awakening) You become aware that your patterns don't match your intentions, but you don't yet know how to bridge the gap. You see the distance between who you are and who you want to become. This brings frustration, but awakening—even painful awakening—is progress, not failure.

This stage is often accompanied by frustration and self-judgment. You know better, but you're not yet doing better. The key is to treat this awareness as progress, not failure. Consciousness is the first step toward change.

Stage 3: Conscious Competence (The Practice) You begin choosing new patterns consciously and consistently. This requires effort, attention, and patience with yourself.

You're practicing new ways of being, but they don't feel natural yet. New patterns feel awkward while old ones remain seductively familiar.

This stage is where most people give up because it requires sustained effort without immediate gratification. The new patterns feel awkward and effortful while the old patterns still feel comfortable and automatic.

Stage 4: Unconscious Competence (The Integration) New patterns that serve your authentic self become automatic and effortless. You no longer have to think about choosing the better response—it becomes your natural way of being. You're no longer someone who practices healthy patterns—you've become someone for whom healthy patterns are natural. The new patterns have woven themselves into the fabric of your identity.

"Transformation is not an event but a process—not a destination but a way of traveling through life with increasing consciousness and decreasing resistance to your own becoming."

The Pattern Change Protocol

Based on decades of research in neuroscience and behavioral psychology, here's a proven process for transforming any pattern:

Step 1: Start Impossibly Small

The biggest mistake people make when changing patterns is starting too big. They try to transform their entire morning routine, overhaul their diet completely, or revolutionize their work habits all at once.

True change begins not with grand gestures but with what I call ridiculous specificity—changes so small they seem almost silly, yet so precise they slip beneath your resistance like water finding cracks in stone.

Dr. BJ Fogg at Stanford discovered that the smaller the change, the more likely it is to stick. But this isn't just about psychology—it's about honoring the profound truth that all great transformations begin with humble beginnings.

Lisa wanted to exercise but kept failing at ambitious workout plans. She started with one push-up per day after brushing her teeth. "It felt ridiculous," she admits. "But after a week, I was someone who exercised daily. That identity shift changed everything."

The power wasn't in the push-up—it was in the daily practice of keeping a promise to herself, of proving that she could be trusted with her own transformation.

The goal isn't immediate transformation—it's to prove to your brain that change is possible and safe.

Step 2: Stack the New Pattern

Research by Stanford's BJ Fogg reveals that new habits are most likely to stick when they're "stacked" onto existing routines. Your brain already has automatic sequences throughout the day—use these as anchors for new patterns.

"After I pour my morning coffee, I will take three deep breaths." "After I sit down at my desk, I will write one sentence about my priorities for the day." "After I park my car, I will take a moment to appreciate something I'm grateful for."

This isn't just practical—it's philosophical. You're not adding to your life but consecrating what already exists. You're not changing everything but transforming anything through the alchemy of conscious attention.

This leverages the existing neural pathways rather than trying to create entirely new ones.

Step 3: Design Environmental Support

Your environment is constantly influencing your patterns, usually unconsciously. Take control of this influence by designing your surroundings to support the patterns you want.

Want to read more? Put books in every room and hide your phone in a drawer. Want to exercise? Lay out your workout clothes the night before. Want to eat healthier? Stock your kitchen with healthy options and remove tempting junk food.

Make the desired pattern easier and the undesired pattern harder.

This isn't just about convenience—it's about honoring the truth that we are shaped by our surroundings as much as we shape them.

Step 4: Track the Process, Not the Outcome

Most people track outcomes—pounds lost, money saved, books read. But outcomes are often delayed and influenced by factors outside your control. Instead, track the patterns themselves.

"Did I do my new morning routine today? Yes or no." "Did I practice my new communication pattern in that difficult conversation? Yes or no." "Did I choose the new response to stress today? Yes or no."

This focuses your attention on what you can control and builds intrinsic motivation for the process itself.

Track not outcomes but process. "Did I practice my new pattern today? Yes or no." This focuses attention on what you control—your choices—rather than what you cannot control—the results of those choices.

This isn't just about data—it's about developing what the Buddhists call right mindfulness: clear awareness of what is actually happening rather than what you wish were happening or fear might happen.

Step 5: Celebrate Small Wins

Every time you choose the new pattern, pause for a moment and acknowledge what you just did. Say "Yes!" Give yourself a mental high-five. Feel the satisfaction of following through on your commitment to yourself.

This isn't self-indulgence—it's neuroscience. Your brain releases dopamine when you celebrate, which strengthens the neural pathway you just used and makes you more likely to choose that pattern again.

But celebration is more than neuroscience—it's recognition that every conscious choice is a small miracle worth honoring.

"Every moment you choose consciousness over habit, intention over reaction, growth over comfort, you participate in the ancient and ongoing miracle of human transformation."

Step 6: Plan for Obstacles

You will face moments when choosing the new pattern feels difficult or impossible. Plan for these moments in advance by asking yourself:

- What situations will make it harder to choose my new pattern?

- What stories will my mind tell me to justify reverting to the old pattern?

- What specific strategy will I use when I feel resistance?

- Who can I ask for support when I'm struggling?

Having a plan for obstacles prevents temporary setbacks from becoming permanent relapses.

The Most Common Pattern Traps

After working with hundreds of people on pattern transformation, I've identified the most common ways people sabotage their own progress:

Trap 1: The Perfection Prison

"I missed one day, so I've failed. I might as well give up."

This all-or-nothing thinking destroys more pattern change attempts than any other factor. Progress is not perfection. A single missed day doesn't erase weeks of progress—unless you decide it does.

Recovery strategy: Treat missed days as data, not failure. What caused the lapse? How can you adjust your approach? What would you tell a good friend who experienced the same setback?

Trap 2: The Motivation Myth

"I don't feel motivated today, so I'll wait until I feel like doing it."

Here's the analogy that changes everything: Motivation is like the starter in your car—it gets the engine turning, but it's not what takes you from point A to point B. Discipline is the engine that actually moves you forward.

Most people spend their entire lives waiting for the starter to kick in, not realizing they already have a perfectly good engine. They say things like "I'll start my diet when I feel motivated" or "I'll begin exercising when I get inspired." But motivation is just the initial spark. What gets you to your destination is the disciplined choice to keep the engine running, mile after mile, regardless of how you feel.

Think about it: professional athletes don't train only when they feel motivated. Successful writers don't write only when inspiration strikes. Devoted parents don't care for their children only when it feels easy. They've learned to separate the decision to act from the feeling of wanting to act.

"Motivation gets you started. Discipline gets you finished. But patterns get you there automatically."

Recovery strategy: The Engine Check Method. When you don't feel motivated, run through this quick check: (1) Acknowledge that motivation isn't required for your next choice. (2) Ask: "What's the smallest version of this pattern I can do right now?" (3) Take that action regardless of how you feel. (4) Celebrate that you just proved your discipline engine works perfectly. Remember: "Motivation is optional. Action is available. Patterns create momentum."

Trap 3: The Complexity Trap

"I need to optimize everything perfectly before I start."

This is perfectionism disguised as preparation. You don't need the perfect morning routine, the ideal workout plan, or the optimal productivity system. You need to start with something simple and improve it through experience.

Recovery strategy: Choose one pattern, make it simple, and start today. You can optimize later, but you can't optimize something that doesn't exist.

Trap 4: The External Validation Trap

"No one notices or appreciates my changes, so why bother?"

Your pattern changes are primarily for you, not for others to notice or applaud. If you're changing patterns to impress others, you're building your identity on a foundation of external validation that will ultimately disappoint you.

Recovery strategy: Find intrinsic reasons for your pattern changes. How do they make you feel? How do they serve your authentic values? How do they contribute to the person you're becoming?

Pattern Transformation Stories: The Evidence of Possibility

Sarah: The Revolution of Attention Sarah Kim was a software engineer who felt constantly scattered and anxious. Despite being successful in her career, she couldn't shake the feeling that she was always behind, always reacting, never in control of her own attention.

The breakthrough came when she tracked her phone usage for a week and discovered she was checking it 127 times per day—every 7.5 minutes during waking hours. She was practicing patterns of distraction and reactivity without realizing it.

Her transformation began with one environmental change: moving her phone charger from bedside to kitchen. This eliminated the pattern of beginning and ending each day in service to other people's agendas.

Within weeks, her scattered attention began to gather itself. Her anxiety decreased. Her relationships deepened. But the most profound change was philosophical: She realized she'd been living as if urgency were the same as importance, as if being busy were the same as being alive.

"I didn't realize how much my phone was controlling my thoughts and emotions until I took control of when and how I used it," Sarah reflects. "Changing that one pattern changed everything else."

Marcus: The Exercise Identity Shift Marcus Thompson was a 45-year-old accountant who had tried and failed to establish an exercise routine dozens of times. He would start ambitious workout programs, maintain them for a few weeks, then quit when life got busy or motivation waned.

The problem wasn't his programs—it was his identity. Marcus saw himself as "not an exercise person" and was trying to force himself to act like someone he wasn't.

His transformation began with one push-up per day. Not a workout routine, not a fitness program—just one push-up, every day, right after brushing his teeth.

"It felt ridiculous," Marcus admits. "One push-up doesn't do anything for your fitness. But after a week, I realized I was someone who exercises every day. That was a bigger shift than I expected."

After a month of one push-up per day, Marcus naturally wanted to do more. He added a second push-up, then five, then ten. Within three months, he was doing a complete bodyweight routine. Within six months, he had joined a gym and was exercising five days per week.

But the real transformation was in his identity. Marcus no longer saw himself as someone trying to become fit—he was a fit person who happened to be in the process of developing his fitness. The pattern had changed his self-concept, which made maintaining the pattern effortless.

"I used to think I needed motivation to exercise," Marcus explains. "Now I realize I needed identity. Once I became someone who exercises, the motivation took care of itself."

Rachel: The Communication Pattern Breakthrough Rachel Martinez was a talented teacher whose career was stalled by her communication patterns. In faculty meetings, she would stay quiet even when she had valuable insights. In one-on-one conversations, she would agree with others even when she disagreed. In conflicts, she would avoid difficult conversations until problems became crises.

Her breakthrough came when she recognized that her silence wasn't protecting her—it was limiting her impact and contribution. She decided to practice a new pattern: sharing one insight in every meeting, no matter how small.

The first few times felt terrifying. Rachel's heart would race, her voice would shake, and she worried constantly about saying something stupid. But gradually, she noticed that her contributions were welcomed and often valuable. More importantly, she began seeing herself as someone who had something worthwhile to contribute.

As her confidence grew, Rachel's communication patterns evolved. She started asking thoughtful questions, proposing new ideas, and eventually leading project discussions. Her career accelerated, but more importantly, she began feeling authentic in her professional relationships.

"I spent years being frustrated that no one recognized my potential," Rachel reflects. "But I was hiding my potential behind patterns of silence and agreement. When I changed how I communicated, everything else changed too."

The Pattern Paradox

Here's something that might surprise you: the goal of pattern development isn't to become more disciplined or controlled. It's to become more free.

When you consciously choose patterns that serve your authentic self, they become automatic and effortless. You don't have to use willpower to choose healthy responses—they become your natural way of being. You don't have to force yourself to act according to your values—your patterns embody your values automatically.

True freedom comes not from having unlimited options, but from having patterns that consistently lead you toward what you truly want.

Think about master musicians. They spend years practicing scales, exercises, and techniques until they become automatic. But this discipline doesn't limit their creativity—it liberates it. Because the technical skills are automatic, they can focus entirely on artistic expression.

The same principle applies to life patterns. When healthy responses become automatic, you're free to focus on meaning, creativity, and contribution. When you no longer have to think about basic self-care, you can direct your attention toward your deepest purposes.

"Discipline is not the enemy of freedom but its prerequisite. Structure is not the opposite of creativity but its foundation. Patterns are not limitations but the very source of your power to transcend limitations."

The Daily Choice Architecture

Every day presents you with thousands of micro-choices that either reinforce or reshape your identity. Most people make these choices unconsciously, which means they're allowing random circumstances to determine who they become.

But when you understand that patterns create identity, you can approach each day as an opportunity to consciously craft your character.

Morning Patterns: How you start your day sets the tone for everything that follows. Do you begin with reactive patterns (checking phone, hitting snooze, rushing) or intentional patterns (reflection, movement, preparation)?

Transition Patterns: How do you move between different parts of your day? Do you practice patterns of presence and intention, or patterns of hurry and distraction?

Challenge Patterns: When you face difficulties, do you practice patterns of avoidance and complaint, or patterns of curiosity and growth?

Evening Patterns: How you end your day determines the quality of your rest and your preparation for tomorrow. Do you practice patterns of reflection and gratitude, or patterns of consumption and worry?

The Compound Identity Effect

Small patterns seem insignificant in isolation, but they compound over time to create profound transformations. One push-up per day becomes an identity as someone who exercises. One conscious breath per day becomes an identity as someone who practices mindfulness. One kind word per day becomes an identity as someone who contributes positively to others' lives.

James Clear, author of "Atomic Habits," describes this as the "identity-based habit" approach: instead of focusing on what you want to achieve, focus on who you want to become. Then ask yourself: what would that person do in this situation?

This shift from outcome-based to identity-based thinking makes pattern change easier and more sustainable. You're not forcing yourself to act differently—you're allowing your authentic self to emerge through conscious choice.

"Every repetition is an act of faith—faith that small actions matter, that consistency creates transformation, that who you are becoming is more important than who you have been."

The Pattern Revolution

Understanding the true power of patterns changes everything about how you approach personal development. You stop trying to motivate yourself into temporary behavior changes and start crafting sustainable identity transformations.

You stop hoping for inspiration and start relying on preparation. You stop waiting for the perfect moment and start creating better moments through conscious choice. You stop being a victim of your circumstances and start being the architect of your character.

Every moment is a choice point. Every pattern is a vote for the type of person you want to become. Every day is an opportunity to align your actions with your authentic self.

The person you were born to be isn't hiding somewhere waiting to be discovered—they're waiting to be practiced into existence through the accumulation of conscious patterns.

Your patterns are your prayers. Your consistency is your character. Your daily choices are your destiny.

But remember: this power only becomes available when you stop lying to yourself about your current patterns and start aligning your actual behaviors with your stated values. The gap between who you say you are and what you actually do is the gap between potential and reality, between dreams and destiny.

The most important relationship you'll ever have is the one with yourself. Make it an honest one. Make it a trustworthy one. Make it one that serves your highest potential.

"Excellence is not a single act, but a collection of daily patterns. Authenticity is not a destination, but a practice. Character is not inherited—it's built, one conscious choice at a time."

In the next chapter, we'll explore the second component of your TOS: the stories that guide your decisions and shape your reality. You'll discover how your interpretive frameworks can either limit your potential or unleash your possibilities—and how to consciously rewrite any story that no longer serves your authentic self.

But for now, the work is simple: choose one pattern that would serve your highest self. Make it small. Start today. Let your transformation begin with your next conscious choice.

Chapter Five

THE STORIES THAT GUIDE

"WE DON'T SEE THE WORLD AS IT IS. WE SEE THE WORLD AS WE ARE."

The Two Brothers and the Broken Window

Let me tell you about two brothers I knew growing up in Phoenix. Same parents, same house, same schools, same tough neighborhood where police sirens were more common than ice cream trucks. Their father was an alcoholic who disappeared when they were young. Their mother worked three jobs trying to keep food on the table.

By any measure, these boys had every excuse to fail.

Today, one brother runs a successful construction company and mentors at-risk youth every weekend. The other died of an overdose at 34, leaving behind two kids and a mountain of regrets.

I asked the successful brother, Marcus, how he explained the different paths they took.

"Everyone thinks we had the same childhood," he said, pouring coffee in his office overlooking downtown Phoenix. "But we didn't. We lived in the same house, but we lived in completely different worlds."

He leaned back in his chair. "See, when our dad left, I told myself a story: 'This is my chance to become the man he never was.' But my brother Tommy? He told himself: 'Even our own father didn't want us. We're worthless.'"

Marcus continued, "When Mom worked those three jobs, I saw a warrior showing me what determination looked like. Tommy saw abandonment—proof that everyone leaves eventually. When the electricity got cut off, I saw it as training for toughness. Tommy saw it as evidence that we'd never escape poverty."

"Same events. Different stories. Different lives."

Then Marcus said something that stopped me cold: "The most important conversation you'll ever have is the one you have with yourself. Because that conversation becomes your life."

The Story You Tell Becomes the Life You Live

Here's what most people don't understand: **You're not living your life. You're living your story about your life.**

And the scariest part? Most of us don't even know we're telling ourselves a story. We think we're just observing "reality." We think we're just seeing "what is." But we're not. We're seeing what we've trained ourselves to see, interpreting everything through the lens of stories we've been telling ourselves for so long that we've forgotten they're just stories. Let me prove it to you with something that happens to everyone.

The Restaurant Story

You're at a restaurant with friends. The server seems short with you, barely makes eye contact, doesn't smile. What's the story you tell yourself?

Person A thinks: "I must have done something wrong. Maybe I'm not dressed nice enough for this place. They probably think I don't belong here."

Person B thinks: "What terrible service! This person clearly doesn't care about their job. I'm going to speak to the manager."

Person C thinks: "This server seems overwhelmed. They're probably having a rough day. We all have those days."

Person D thinks: "This is perfect—less interruption means more time with my friends."

Same server. Same behavior. Four completely different stories. And here's the kicker—each person's story determines their entire experience of that meal. Person A feels small and self-conscious. Person B feels angry and righteous. Person C feels compassionate. Person D feels grateful.

But it goes deeper than just feelings. Each story leads to different actions. Person A might leave a bigger tip, trying to prove they belong. Person B might leave no tip and write a bad review. Person C might leave an encouraging note with their normal tip. Person D might not even remember the server an hour later.

The server's behavior was just data. The story each person told turned that data into their reality.

Why Your Stories Matter More Than Your Circumstances

Jim Rohn used to say, "It's not what happens to you, but what you do with what happens to you that makes the difference." But I want to take it one step further: It's not even what you DO with what happens—it's the STORY you tell yourself about what happens that determines what you'll do.

Your stories are the invisible directors of your life. They determine:

- What opportunities you see (or don't see)

- What actions you take (or don't take)

- What you believe is possible (or impossible)

- Who you become (or don't become)

Think about it. Have you ever noticed how two people can have the exact same experience and come away with completely different lessons?

Two people get laid off from the same company on the same day:

- One says: "This is the push I needed to finally start my own business."

- The other says: "This proves the economy is rigged against people like me."

Two people go through a difficult divorce:

- One says: "I learned so much about myself. I'll be a better partner next time."

- The other says: "I'll never trust anyone again."

Two people grow up in poverty:

- One says: "I've seen what I don't want. Now I know what to work toward."

- The other says: "People like us don't get ahead. Why even try?"

Same circumstances. Different stories. Completely different futures.

The Girl Who Refused to Be a Victim

Let me tell you about one of the most powerful story transformations I've ever witnessed. It came from an unexpected place—a jiujitsu mat.

There was a woman in my training group, Ana, who had an almost supernatural ability to escape from chokes. You could have a deep choke locked in—the kind where most men twice her size would tap out immediately—and somehow she'd find a way out. It was like watching water slip through your fingers.

After months of training together, rolling after class to improve our techniques, I finally asked her over lunch: "How did you get so good at escaping? What's your secret?"

She set down her water bottle and looked at me for a long moment. "Do you really want to know?"

What she told me next changed how I think about stories forever.

"Four years ago, my ex-boyfriend took me camping with two of his friends. During the night, they took turns choking me unconscious and assaulting me. Over and over. I thought I was going to die in those mountains. Somehow, I convinced them to let me go—promised I wouldn't tell anyone."

My heart stopped. I started to apologize for asking, but she held up her hand.

"The first thing I did when I got to safety was call the cops. All three went to prison. But that's not the important part of the story."

She continued, "For weeks after, I was destroyed. Couldn't sleep. Couldn't eat. Couldn't leave my apartment. I had two choices for my story. I could be a victim—'Why me? I'll never be safe. The world is full of monsters. I'm broken forever.' Or..."
She paused, and when she spoke again, her voice was steel.

"Or I could tell myself a different story: 'This happened because I was unprepared and untrained. Never again. I will become so capable, so aware, so strong that no one will ever make me feel powerless again.'"

"So I walked into a jiujitsu gym. Could barely get through the door, I was shaking so hard. But every time I learned to escape a choke, I was rewriting my story. Every time I got stronger, I was choosing who I would become. Not a victim. A warrior."

She smiled then, a smile that held both pain and power. "Don't apologize for asking. Talking about it reminds me how far I've come. That girl in the mountains? She was weak and unprepared. But she's not me anymore. I chose a different story. I chose to let that experience forge me instead of break me."

Ana didn't just survive—she transformed. Not by denying what happened, not by pretending it was okay, but by choosing what it would mean in her life story.

This is the ultimate power we all possess: We can't always choose what happens to us, but we can always choose the story we tell about what happens to us.

The Stoic Secret: Response Is Everything

Twenty centuries ago, the Roman Emperor Marcus Aurelius wrote something in his personal journal that he never intended to publish: "You have power over your mind—not outside events. Realize this, and you will find strength."

He was leading an empire, fighting wars, dealing with plague, facing betrayal—and yet he understood that his only true power was in choosing his response, in choosing his story.

The Stoics had a word for this: "premeditatio malorum"—the premeditation of evils. But they weren't being pessimistic. They were preparing their stories in advance. "If I lose my wealth, I'll tell myself this story: Now I get to discover who my real friends are. If I face illness, I'll tell myself: This is my chance to develop courage. If someone betrays me, I'll tell myself: Their actions reveal their character, not mine."

They understood what Ana understood: **The event is neutral. The story makes it heaven or hell.**⬚

Think about it. Rain falls.

- The farmer says: "Thank God, my crops are saved!"

- The bride says: "My wedding is ruined!"

- The child says: "Puddles to jump in!" Same rain. Different stories. Different realities.

You can tell a lot about people by the stories they tell about the same events:

- "Traffic is horrible, this city is falling apart" vs. "Extra time to listen to that podcast"

- "My boss is so demanding" vs. "I'm being prepared for bigger responsibilities"

- "Everything always goes wrong for me" vs. "I'm gathering interesting experiences"

Here's the radical truth: Maybe it's not the world that's horrible. Maybe it's your story about the world that's horrible.

The Judgment Trap

Here's something that will free you: You don't have a moral obligation to judge everything that happens. You don't need a story about everything.

We've become addicted to having opinions, to judging everything as good or bad, right or wrong, fair or unfair. But this constant storytelling is exhausting. It's like being a film critic who can't just watch a movie—you're so busy analyzing and judging that you miss the actual experience.

Sometimes rain is just rain. Sometimes a delay is just a delay. Sometimes a mistake is just a mistake. Not everything needs a story. Not everything needs to mean something about you, about others, about life.

The Buddhists call this "beginner's mind"—seeing things as they are, not through the filter of our stories. Children have this naturally. A child doesn't see a "broken" toy—they see a toy that works differently now. They don't see a "ruined" drawing—they see new possibilities.

What if you could choose when to apply stories and when to simply experience life without the constant narration?

The Elephant and the Rope

In India, they train elephants using a simple method that reveals everything about the power of stories.

When an elephant is young and small, trainers tie it to a post with a heavy rope. The baby elephant pulls and pulls, but the rope is too strong. After days of trying, the elephant learns a story: "When this rope is on my leg, I cannot break free."

Years pass. The elephant grows massive—strong enough to uproot trees, to carry enormous loads, to break any rope ever made. But the trainers only need a thin rope, sometimes just a piece of twine, to keep this powerful creature in place.

Why doesn't the elephant break free?

It's not living in reality. It's living in a story—a story learned so long ago that the elephant has forgotten it's just a story. The rope isn't keeping the elephant captive. The story about the rope is.

How many thin ropes are keeping you captive right now?

- "I'm not smart enough for that promotion"

- "People like me don't start businesses"

- "I'm too old to change careers"

- "I'm not the relationship type"

- "I've always been bad with money"

- "I don't have what it takes"

These aren't facts. They're stories. And like that elephant, you've told them to yourself so many times that you've forgotten they're just stories.

The Three Types of Stories That Run Your Life

After years of listening to people's stories—the ones they tell others and the ones they tell themselves—I've discovered that we all carry three types of stories that shape our destiny:

1. The Stories About Ourselves (Identity Stories)

These are the stories about who we are, what we're capable of, what we deserve. They usually start with "I am..." or "I'm not..." or "I always..." or "I never..."

- "I'm just not a morning person"

- "I've always been shy"

- "I'm bad at public speaking"

- "I'm not creative"

- "I'm a perfectionist"

Here's the trap: We think we're describing ourselves, but we're actually prescribing ourselves. Every time you say "I'm not a morning person," you're giving yourself permission to hit snooze. Every time you say "I'm bad at public speaking," you're excusing yourself from opportunities to improve.

You're not reporting the news about yourself. You're writing the script for yourself.

2. The Stories About Others (Relationship Stories)

These are the stories about what other people are like, what they want from us, whether they can be trusted.

- "People only care about themselves"

- "You can't trust anyone these days"

- "Everyone's just trying to use you"

- "Rich people are greedy"

- "My family doesn't understand me"

A woman once told me, "All men are liars." She'd been married three times, and sure enough, all three husbands had lied to her. "See?" she said. "I told you—all men are liars."

But here's what she didn't see: Her story became a filter. When she met honest men, she didn't notice them—they didn't fit her story, so they were invisible to her. But when she met men who were deceptive, her radar went off. "That's the one!" her subconscious said. She was unconsciously seeking evidence to confirm her story.

Your stories about others become self-fulfilling prophecies. You find what you're looking for, and you're always looking for evidence that your stories are true.

3. The Stories About How Life Works (World Stories)

These are the big-picture stories about how the world operates, what's possible, what's fair.

- "Life is hard"

- "You have to struggle to succeed"

- "Money doesn't grow on trees"

- "It's not what you know, it's who you know"

- "The deck is stacked against people like me"

I knew a man who believed "You have to work hard for money." So he did. He turned down profitable opportunities that seemed "too easy." He complicated simple solutions. He worked 70-hour weeks when 40 would have been plenty. Why? Because easy money didn't fit his story about how life works.

Meanwhile, his neighbor believed "Money flows to value." So she focused on creating value, solving problems, serving others. She worked smart, not hard. She made twice as much in half the time.

Same economy. Same opportunities. Different stories. Different results.

The Story That Almost Killed Me

Let me share something personal. For years, I told myself a story: "I have to do everything myself. Asking for help is weakness."

Where did this story come from? My father. He was a proud man, a self-made man. Never asked anyone for anything. "A man handles his own business," he'd say. I absorbed that story like scripture.

That story served me well in some ways. It made me self-reliant, resourceful, determined. But it also nearly destroyed me.

When my business was struggling, I didn't ask for advice. When my marriage was falling apart, I didn't seek counseling. When depression crept in like fog, I didn't reach out for support. Why? Because my story said asking for help meant I was weak, and being weak meant I wasn't a real man.

I was drowning in six feet of water, too proud to stand up and ask for a hand.

The breakthrough came when a friend asked me a simple question: "What if your story is wrong? What if asking for help isn't weakness, but wisdom? What if the strongest people are the ones who know when they need support?"

That question cracked my story open like an egg. For the first time, I saw it for what it was—not truth, but interpretation. Not fact, but fiction. A story I'd inherited from my father, who'd inherited it from his father, passed down like a family heirloom that no one ever questioned.

Changing that one story changed everything. I asked for help with my business and it thrived. I sought counseling and saved my marriage. I reached out during dark moments and found light.

The story "I must do everything alone" almost killed me. The story "Seeking support is strength" saved my life.

Where Your Stories Come From

You weren't born with your stories. You collected them, inherited them, absorbed them. Understanding where they came from is the first step to changing them.

The Hand-Me-Down Stories

Just like you inherited your eye color and your height, you inherited stories from your family. But unlike genetics, these stories can be changed.

Your parents didn't sit you down and say, "Here are the stories you should believe." They lived their stories in front of you, and you absorbed them like a sponge.

Maybe your mother always said, "We can't afford that," and now you have a scarcity story about money. Maybe your father always worked weekends, and now you have a story that "successful people sacrifice family for work." Maybe your grandmother always warned, "Don't get too happy—something bad is bound to happen," and now you have a story that happiness is dangerous.

These aren't your stories. They're your family's stories living through you.

The Scar Tissue Stories

Some stories form around wounds, like scar tissue around an injury. Something painful happened, and you created a story to make sense of it, to protect yourself from it happening again.

- You got bullied, so you created the story "I need to be invisible to be safe"

- You failed publicly, so you created the story "It's better not to try than to fail"

- Someone you loved left, so you created the story "Everyone leaves eventually"

- You were criticized, so you created the story "I'm not good enough"

These stories might have protected you once. But now they're prison walls built from old pain.

The Cultural Programming Stories

You also absorbed stories from your culture, your community, your generation. These stories are so common, so "normal," that you don't even recognize them as stories—they just feel like "the way things are."

- "You need a college degree to succeed"

- "Follow your passion and the money will follow"

- "Good things come to those who wait"

- "Life begins at 40" (or 30, or 50, or retirement)

Every culture has its stories, and they seep into your consciousness like water into soil. You don't choose them; they choose you—unless you become conscious of them.

The Explanation Stories

These are the stories you created to explain why things happened the way they did. Your brain hates uncertainty, so when something doesn't make sense, it creates a story to fill the gap.

- "I didn't get the job because I'm too old"

- "She broke up with me because I'm not successful enough"

- "My business failed because the economy was bad"

- "I'm overweight because of my genetics"

Here's the thing: You might be right. Or you might be completely wrong. But once you've created an explanation story, you stop looking for other possibilities. The story becomes "the truth," and you build your future on it.

The Story Detox Process

Just like your body sometimes needs a detox from unhealthy foods, your mind sometimes needs a detox from unhealthy stories. Here's a powerful process I call the Story Detox:

Day 1-3: The Story Fast (The Most Powerful Tool You'll Ever Learn)

Let me tell you why this first step might be the most transformative thing you do. For three days, you're going to practice something that sounds simple but is revolutionary: describing without reacting.

Here's what happens in your brain when something occurs: An event triggers your amygdala—the emotional center—which immediately starts creating a story. "They disrespected me!" "This is unfair!" "I'm going to fail!" These emotional stories flood your system with stress hormones before your logical brain even has a chance to assess what actually happened.

But when you force yourself to just describe—to state only facts without interpretation—something miraculous happens. You bypass the amygdala and engage your prefrontal cortex, the logical part of your brain. This isn't just calming; it's literally rewiring your neural pathways from reactive to responsive.

Here's how to do it:

Something happens—your partner forgets to call, you hit traffic, you make a mistake—and instead of immediately creating a story, you become a court reporter. Just the facts.

- NOT: "They don't care about me" → INSTEAD: "Partner didn't call. Period."

- NOT: "This always happens to me!" → INSTEAD: "Traffic is moving at 5 mph. Period."

- NOT: "I'm such an idiot" → INSTEAD: "I sent the email to the wrong person. Period."

Why this works: When you describe instead of react, you're literally changing which part of your brain is in charge. The emotional brain screams stories. The logical brain states facts. And here's the magic—when you're in your logical brain, you make better decisions, see more options, and maintain your power.

I had a client, Robert, who tried this after his business partner betrayed him. Instead of spiraling into "I can't trust anyone" or "I'm ruined," he practiced the Story Fast: "My partner moved money without telling me. He started a competing company. I have six months of runway left."

Just facts. No drama. And from that calm, logical place, Robert saw options he would have missed in emotional chaos. He restructured, found new partners, and built a stronger business. He told me later, "The Story Fast saved my company. When I stopped telling myself horror stories, I could see the actual situation clearly."

The challenge: For three days, every time you catch yourself adding emotion or interpretation to an event, stop. Describe it like you're a camera, not a critic. You'll be amazed how much mental energy you reclaim when you stop turning every event into a drama.

This isn't about becoming emotionless. It's about choosing when to engage emotions rather than being hijacked by them. It's the difference between watching a storm and being swept away by it.

Day 4-5: The Story Flip

For two days, practice flipping every negative story into its opposite—not because the opposite is true, but to reveal that stories are just choices.

- "This is terrible" becomes "This is perfect"

- "I can't handle this" becomes "I was made for this"

- "Why me?" becomes "Why not me?"

Don't believe the flipped stories. Just notice how arbitrary all stories are.

Day 6-7: The Story Choice

For the final two days, consciously choose stories that serve you. Not fake positive stories, but useful ones.

- "This is challenging" becomes "This is developing my strength"

- "I don't know how" becomes "I'm learning how"

- "This isn't what I planned" becomes "I'm discovering new possibilities"

The Story Compass: Finding Your True North

When you're lost in the wilderness, a compass doesn't tell you where to go—it just shows you which direction is north. From there, you choose your path. I want to give you a Story Compass—a tool to quickly recognize when your stories are leading you astray.

The Four Directions of Story

North: Growth Stories These stories point toward expansion, learning, possibility.

- "I haven't learned this yet"

- "This is developing my character"

- "I'm becoming someone who can handle this"

South: Protection Stories These stories keep you safe but small.

- "Better safe than sorry"

- "I should just be grateful for what I have"

- "This is good enough"

East: Connection Stories These stories build bridges to others.

- "They're doing their best with what they know"

- "We're all fighting battles"

- "How can I help?"

West: Separation Stories These stories create walls between you and the world.

- "No one understands me"

- "I have to do everything myself"

- "People always disappoint you"

Throughout your day, check your compass. Which direction are your stories taking you? Are you stuck going one direction? Remember—sometimes you need to go south for safety, or west for boundaries. But if you only travel in one direction, you go in circles.

The Story Archaeologist's Toolkit

Become an archaeologist of your own mind. Here are the tools for excavating and examining your stories:

Tool 1: The Origin Dig

When you catch a limiting story, dig for its origin:
- Who said this first? (Sometimes it was you, sometimes someone else)

- How old were you when you first believed this?

- What were the circumstances?

- Would you tell a child this story today?

Tool 2: The Evidence Inventory

For any story you tell yourself regularly, do an honest inventory:
- What evidence supports this story?

- What evidence contradicts it?

- What evidence am I ignoring?

- What evidence am I exaggerating?

Tool 3: The Story Stress Test

Test your stories like engineers test bridges:

- Is this story making me stronger or weaker?

- Is this story opening doors or closing them?

- Would I want my child to inherit this story?

- Will this story matter on my deathbed?

Tool 4: The Reframe Practice

Every story can be told differently. Practice reframing:

- The Victim Frame: "This happened to me"

- The Student Frame: "This happened for me"

- The Teacher Frame: "This happened through me"

- The Creator Frame: "This happened by me"

Same event. Four different levels of power.

The Story of Stories: Why We're Wired This Way

Your brain is a meaning-making machine. It can't help but create stories—it's how humans survived for millions of years.

See a rustling in the bushes? Your ancestors who created the story "That's a predator" and ran survived more often than those who created the story "That's just the wind" and stayed. We're descended from the worried storytellers, the ones who created cautionary tales, the ones who saw danger in shadows.

But here's what's changed: Most of the rustling bushes in your life aren't tigers. They're opportunities dressed in uncertainty. They're growth dressed in discomfort. They're breakthroughs dressed in breakdowns.

Your ancient story-making brain is trying to keep you safe from tigers that no longer exist.

The stories that kept your ancestors alive—"Don't stand out," "New things are dangerous," "Different people are threats"—these stories are killing your potential in a world that rewards innovation, connection, and courage.

The Master Story: Who's the Hero?

Here's the most important story question you'll ever answer: In the story of your life, are you the hero or are you a supporting character?

Too many people cast themselves as supporting characters in their own life story:

- "I'm here to support my kids"

- "My role is to make others happy"

- "I don't matter as much as..."

Or they cast themselves as the victim:

- "Life happens to me"

- "I never get breaks"

- "If only things were different"

But what if you rewrote your story with you as the hero? Not the perfect hero—the human hero. The one who struggles, falls, gets back up, learns, grows, and ultimately triumphs not by defeating others but by becoming who they were meant to be.

Joseph Campbell studied thousands of stories across all cultures and found they all follow the same pattern—the Hero's Journey:

1. The ordinary world (where you are now)

2. The call to adventure (the change you're resisting)

3. Refusing the call (your current stories keeping you stuck)

4. Meeting the mentor (wisdom that changes your perspective)

5. Crossing the threshold (choosing a new story)

6. Tests and trials (living your new story despite challenges)

7. Death and rebirth (letting your old identity die)

8. Return with the elixir (sharing your transformation with others)

Where are you in your Hero's Journey? Are you still refusing the call, held back by old stories? Or are you ready to cross the threshold?

The Story Emergency Kit

Sometimes you need to change your story RIGHT NOW. In moments of crisis, panic, or despair, you need emergency story intervention. Here's your kit:

The Pattern Interrupt

When a destructive story starts spiraling, physically interrupt it:
- Clap your hands three times, hard

- Say out loud: "That's a story, not a fact"

- Ask yourself: "What else could this mean?"

The Story Switch

Have these emergency replacement stories ready:
- Instead of "Why is this happening to me?" → "What is this here to teach me?"

- Instead of "I can't handle this" → "I've handled difficult things before"

- Instead of "Everything is falling apart" → "Everything is falling into place"

- Instead of "It's too late" → "It's the perfect time"

The Future Story

Jump forward in time:
- "How will I tell this story in five years?"

- "What will this teach me that I'll be grateful for?"

- "How will this struggle become part of my strength?"

Ana, the woman from my jiujitsu class, used this. In her darkest moments, she would imagine telling her future daughter: "This is how your mother became unbreakable."

The Story Upgrade Process

Now here's the good news—the liberating, life-changing, destiny-altering news: **You can change your stories.**

Not through positive thinking. Not through affirmations you don't believe. But through a process I call Story Archaeology—digging up your old stories, examining them in the light, and consciously choosing which ones to keep and which ones to rewrite.

Step 1: Catch Your Stories in Action

For the next week, become a detective of your own mind. When something happens—good or bad—ask yourself: "What story am I telling myself about this?"

- Your boss criticizes your work. What's your story?

- You see someone successful. What's your story?

- You face a new opportunity. What's your story?

- Something goes wrong. What's your story?

Don't judge the stories. Just notice them. Write them down. See them for what they are—not truth, but interpretation.

Step 2: Question Your Stories

For each story you catch, ask yourself:

- Is this actually true, or is it just familiar?

- Where did this story come from?

- How is this story serving me?

- How is this story limiting me?

- What would be possible if this story wasn't true?

Step 3: Look for Evidence Against Your Story

Your brain is constantly looking for evidence to support your existing stories. It's time to become a lawyer for the opposition.

If your story is "I'm not good with money," look for evidence that contradicts it:

- Times you made smart financial decisions

- Times you saved successfully

- Times you learned something new about finances

The evidence is there. You just haven't been looking for it because it didn't fit your story.

Step 4: Write a Better Story

Don't try to jump from "I'm terrible with money" to "I'm a financial genius." Your brain won't buy it. Instead, write what I call a Bridge Story—something believable that moves you in the right direction:

- Old Story: "I'm terrible with money"

- Bridge Story: "I'm learning to make better financial decisions"

- Future Story: "I'm someone who manages money wisely"

The bridge story is believable AND helpful. It acknowledges where you are while pointing toward where you're going.

Step 5: Live Your New Story

Stories become true through repetition and evidence. So start living as if your new story is true, and collect evidence that supports it.

If your new story is "I'm learning to make better financial decisions":

- Read one article about personal finance

- Save $5 this week

- Track your spending for three days

- Ask someone good with money for one piece of advice

Small actions that support your new story. Evidence that your new story is true. Repetition that makes your new story feel real.

The Story of the Two Wolves

An old Cherokee grandfather was teaching his grandson about life.

"A fight is going on inside me," he said to the boy. "It's a terrible fight between two wolves. One wolf is evil—he is anger, envy, sorrow, regret, greed, arrogance, self-pity, guilt, resentment, lies, and ego. The other wolf is good—he is joy, peace, love, hope, serenity, humility, kindness, empathy, generosity, truth, and faith. The same fight is going on inside you—and inside every person."

The grandson thought for a minute and then asked, "Which wolf wins?"
The grandfather replied, "The one you feed."

But here's what the grandfather didn't say, the part most people miss: **You feed the wolves with stories.**

Every story of resentment feeds the angry wolf. Every story of gratitude feeds the peaceful wolf. Every story of limitation feeds the fearful wolf. Every story of possibility feeds the courageous wolf.

The wolves are always hungry. The question is: Which one are your stories feeding?

The Million-Dollar Story

Let me tell you about Sarah, a single mom from Detroit who changed her family's destiny by changing one story.

Sarah grew up hearing, "People like us don't go to college." Her parents hadn't gone. Her grandparents hadn't gone. College was for "other people"—smarter people, richer people, luckier people.

Sarah believed this story so completely that she didn't even take the SAT in high school. Why bother? People like her didn't go to college.

But when her daughter turned five and asked, "Mommy, will I go to college?" something shifted in Sarah. She heard herself starting to say, "People like us..." and she stopped. She saw the story for what it was—a chain, passed down through generations, each link forged from limitation and fear.

"Yes, baby," she told her daughter. "You'll go to college."

But her daughter was smart: "Will you go with me, Mommy?"

That night, Sarah made a decision that terrified her: She would break the chain. She would change the story.

She started with one community college class. Just one. "I'm someone who takes college classes," she told herself, even though the story felt like a costume that didn't fit.

That one class led to another. Then another. Some nights she studied while her daughter slept. Some mornings she was so tired she could barely see straight. The old story kept whispering: "People like you don't finish college. You're going to fail. You're wasting time and money."

But Sarah had learned something powerful: Stories aren't facts. They're choices.

She graduated with her associate degree, then her bachelor's. Her daughter watched her walk across that stage, and in that moment, the old story died forever. Not just for Sarah, but for her daughter, and her daughter's children, and every generation that would follow.

Sarah now runs a nonprofit that helps first-generation college students. Last year, her daughter graduated from medical school. At the graduation, her daughter said, "My mom didn't just change her story. She changed our family's story. She changed our DNA."

One story. Changed. Everything.

The Story That Never Ends

Here's a truth that might disturb you: You will tell yourself stories until the day you die. You can't stop it. It's how human consciousness works. But you can become conscious of your stories. You can become the author instead of the audience.

The Zen masters have a saying: "Before enlightenment, chop wood, carry water. After enlightenment, chop wood, carry water." The activities don't change. But the story about the activities transforms everything.

Before: "I have to chop wood. This is tedious. Why is this my life?" After: "I get to chop wood. Each swing is meditation. This is my life."
Same axe. Same wood. Revolutionary difference.

Your Story Assignment

Before we move on to exploring the purposes you serve, I want you to do something that might change your life:

Write three versions of your life story. Same events, three different narratives:

Version 1: The Victim Story Write your life as if you're the victim. Everything that went wrong. Everyone who hurt you. Every disadvantage you faced. Every unfairness. Really lean into it. Make it dramatic. Make yourself the most unfortunate person alive.

Version 2: The Hero Story Write your life as if you're the hero. Every challenge was a training ground. Every setback was a setup for comeback. Every loss taught you something valuable. Every person who hurt you was a teacher in disguise. Make yourself the protagonist who overcomes everything.

Version 3: The True Story Write your life with nuance. You were sometimes the victim, sometimes the hero, sometimes the villain in someone else's story. Some things were unfair, some were deserved. Some people helped you, some hurt you, most did both. This is the complex, human story.

Now ask yourself: Which story have you been telling? Which story serves you? Which story would you want to pass on to someone you love?

The Final Truth About Stories

That day at lunch, after Ana told me her story, she said something I'll never forget:

"You know what the strangest part is? If I could go back and erase that night from my history, I'm not sure I would. I hate what happened. I hate what they did. But I love who I became because of how I chose to respond. My story isn't about what they did to me. It's about what I did with what they did to me."

She paused, then added: "We all have our mountains to climb. Some people's mountains are abuse. Some are poverty. Some are addiction. Some are loss. The mountain isn't the story. How you climb it—that's the story."

Your mountain is in front of you. Your old stories got you to the base. But they won't get you to the summit. You need new stories for new altitudes.

The Three Questions That Change Everything

Before we move on to explore the third component of your Trichotomy—the purposes you serve—I want you to ask yourself three questions:

1. **What's the most limiting story you tell yourself?** The one that stops you from pursuing what you really want. The one that makes you say "I can't" before you even try.

2. **Where did that story come from?** Who gave it to you? When did you first believe it? What evidence have you been collecting to support it?

3. **What would be possible if that story wasn't true?** If you woke up tomorrow and that story had evaporated like morning mist, what would you do differently? Who would you become?

Sit with these questions. Don't rush past them. Because hidden in your answers is the key to your transformation.

Your Story Starts Now

Remember Sarah's daughter at that medical school graduation? She said something else that day, something that applies to every person reading these words:

"We all inherit stories. But we don't have to live them. We can honor where we came from while choosing where we're going. We can love the people who gave us limiting stories while writing liberating ones. We can be grateful for the past while being the authors of our future."

The pen is in your hand. The page is blank. Your old stories got you here, but they don't have to take you where you're going.

What story will you tell yourself tomorrow morning when you wake up? What story will you tell yourself when you face your next challenge? What story will you tell yourself about what's possible for someone like you?

Because here's the truth that changes everything: **You're not living your life. You're living your story about your life. Change the story, change your life.**

The most important conversation you'll ever have is the one you're having with yourself right now. Make it a good one. Make it one that opens doors instead of closing them. Make it one that feeds the wolf you want to win.

Your new story starts with the very next thought you think.

What's it going to be?

"You are the author of your own life story. You have the power to write a tragedy or a triumph, a comedy or a drama. The story you tell yourself becomes the life you live. Choose wisely. Choose consciously. Choose courageously."

In the next chapter, we'll explore the third and final component of your Trichotomy of Self: the purposes you serve. You'll discover how having a compelling "why" can transform any "how," and why the quality of your purpose determines the quality of your life.

But for now, remember this: Every giant was once a child who told themselves a story about what was possible. Every success was once a failure who changed their story about what failure means. Every hero was once afraid but told themselves a story about courage.

What story will you tell?

CHAPTER SIX

THE PURPOSES YOU SERVE

"HE WHO HAS A WHY TO LIVE CAN BEAR ALMOST ANY HOW." ---FRIEDRICH NIETZSCHE

The Man Who Should Have Died

In the winter of 1944, in a Nazi concentration camp, a skeletal man named Viktor Frankl made an observation that would change how we understand human resilience forever.

By every measure, Frankl should have been among the first to die. He was a psychiatrist, not a laborer---his hands were soft, unused to the brutal physical work the Nazis demanded. He was older than many prisoners. He had no special connections, no extra food, no advantages whatsoever.

Yet Frankl survived when stronger, younger, better-connected prisoners died all around him.

Years later, when asked how he endured what no human should have to endure, Frankl's answer was simple but profound: "I had something to live for that was bigger than my suffering."

His purpose? To survive so he could share with the world what he'd learned about finding meaning in the midst of hell. Every day in that camp, while his body starved and froze, Frankl took mental notes. He observed which prisoners gave up and which ones persevered. He studied the invisible difference between those who survived and those who didn't.

What he discovered contradicts everything we think we know about survival.

The survivors weren't necessarily the physically strongest. They weren't the youngest or the healthiest. They weren't even the most optimistic. The survivors were those who had found a purpose that transcended their immediate suffering---a reason to endure that was bigger than their pain.

Some lived to reunite with a child who needed them. Others lived to bear witness, to ensure the world would know what happened. Some lived to finish a scientific work, others to return to a spouse, others simply to prove that the human spirit could not be broken.

The specific purpose didn't matter. What mattered was having one.

Frankl watched a fellow prisoner, a scientist, survive on nothing but the thought of finishing his manuscript. Another man endured unspeakable torture sustained by the image of his wife's face and his determination to see her again. A young woman found strength in her purpose to care for her elderly father after the war.

Meanwhile, prisoners who had no purpose beyond their own survival---no mission bigger than themselves---often died within days of arriving, even when they were young and strong.

"Those who have a 'why' to live," Frankl would later write, "can bear with almost any 'how.'"

The Three Deaths

There's an old saying that everyone dies three deaths:

1. The first is when your body stops functioning

2. The second is when you're buried or cremated

3. The third is when your name is spoken for the last time

But I believe there's a death that comes before all of these---a death far more tragic than physical death. It's the death that happens when you stop having a reason to get up in the morning. When you no longer serve any purpose that matters to you. When you're still breathing but you've stopped truly living.

I see this death everywhere I look.

I see it in the executive making $500,000 a year who can't remember why he wanted success in the first place. I see it in the mother who's so lost in serving everyone else's purposes that she's forgotten she's allowed to have her own. I see it in the retiree who worked forty years for "someday" only to discover that someday feels empty when it finally arrives.

These people aren't depressed in the clinical sense. They're not mentally ill. They're experiencing something far more common and rarely diagnosed: **Purpose Deficit Disorder**---the quiet agony of having no compelling reason to exist beyond mere existence.

The Paycheck Prison

Let me tell you about Tom, a man I met at a conference in Denver. Tom had what most people would call a dream life. Senior partner at a law firm. Seven-figure income. House in the suburbs, another in Aspen. Kids in private schools. The whole package.

But when I asked Tom what he was working toward, his eyes went dead.

"Working toward?" he repeated, like the question was in a foreign language. "I guess... retirement?"

"And what will you do when you retire?"

Long pause. "I don't know. Travel, I suppose. Play golf."

"And after you've traveled and played golf?"

Even longer pause. Then, in a voice I'll never forget, Tom said: "I honestly have no fucking idea why I do any of this anymore."

Here was a man who'd climbed to the top of the mountain only to discover the view was of another mountain, then another, then another---an endless range of achievements that led nowhere he actually wanted to go.

Tom was serving purposes, but they weren't his purposes. He was serving:

- His father's purpose (who always wanted a lawyer in the family)

- His wife's purpose (who enjoyed the lifestyle his income provided)

- Society's purpose (which said success meant money and status)

- His ego's purpose (which needed to win, to be important, to matter)

But Tom himself? He had no idea what Tom wanted. He'd been so busy serving everyone else's purposes that he'd never asked himself the most important question: **What do I want my life to be about?**

The Purpose Hierarchy

After years of studying human motivation, I've discovered that purposes exist in a hierarchy. Not all purposes are created equal. Some will sustain you through anything. Others will abandon you the moment things get difficult.

Level 1: Survival Purposes

At the bottom are survival purposes---avoiding pain, securing basic needs, making it through another day. These purposes will keep you alive, but they won't make you feel alive.

People operating from survival purposes ask:

- "How do I avoid pain?"

- "How do I pay the bills?"

- "How do I get through this?"

There's no shame in survival purposes when you're actually in survival mode. But too many people remain stuck here long after the real danger has passed, living their entire lives in emergency mode, never moving beyond "just getting by."

Level 2: Comfort Purposes

Next come comfort purposes---seeking pleasure, accumulating resources, making life easier. These feel better than survival, but they're ultimately empty calories for the soul.

People here ask:

- "How can I be more comfortable?"

- "What would make me happy?"

- "How can I have more fun?"

The problem with comfort purposes is what philosophers call the "hedonic treadmill"---you adapt to each new level of comfort and need more to feel the same satisfaction. The third car doesn't bring the joy of the first. The tenth vacation feels routine. The bigger house just means more rooms to fill with things you don't need.

Level 3: Achievement Purposes

Higher up are achievement purposes---accomplishing goals, proving yourself, winning recognition. These generate real energy and drive, but they're fragile. They depend on external validation and comparison to others.

People here ask:

- "How can I succeed?"

- "How can I be the best?"

- "What will make me important?"

Achievement purposes can create extraordinary results, but they have a dark side. Every achievement is followed by the question, "What's next?" Every summit reached reveals another, higher summit. You become addicted to accomplishment, but the high gets shorter each time.

Level 4: Service Purposes

Here's where purpose becomes powerful---when it extends beyond yourself to serve others. These purposes tap into something fundamental in human nature: we're wired to contribute, to matter, to make a difference.

People here ask:

- "How can I help?"

- "What does the world need?"

- "How can I contribute?"

Service purposes have sustained people through the darkest circumstances imaginable. They're what kept Frankl alive in the concentration camps. They're what drives teachers in underfunded schools, doctors in war zones, parents caring for special needs children.

When you're serving something bigger than yourself, your suffering has meaning. Your struggles have purpose. Your life has significance beyond your own happiness or success.

Level 5: Transcendent Purposes

At the highest level are transcendent purposes---those connected to universal truths, spiritual callings, or eternal impacts. These purposes make you feel connected to the fabric of existence itself.

People here ask:

- "What is my calling?"

- "How do I align with truth/God/the universe?"

- "What legacy will outlast my life?"

Transcendent purposes are rare but unmistakable. You see them in the eyes of the monk who's found enlightenment, the scientist pursuing truth regardless of recognition, the artist creating beauty because beauty must exist, the parent raising children to be good humans because that's what the world needs.

The Empty Trophy Case

I knew a woman named Jennifer who'd built her entire life around achievement purposes. By 35, she'd checked every box:

- Harvard MBA □

- VP at Fortune 500 company □

- Million-dollar net worth □

- Ran three marathons □

- Climbed Kilimanjaro □

Her apartment was literally filled with trophies, certificates, and photos of her achievements. But Jennifer came to me because she felt dead inside.

"I keep achieving things," she said, "but each achievement feels emptier than the last. It's like I'm addicted to a drug that stopped working, but I keep taking it anyway."

Jennifer was suffering from what I call **Achievement Exhaustion**---the inevitable burnout that comes from pursuing purposes that impress others but don't inspire you.

The breakthrough came when I asked her a simple question: "If you could only be remembered for one thing, what would it be?"

She started to give me her resume---"Well, I was the youngest VP in my company's history..."

"No," I interrupted. "Not what you've done. What would you want to be remembered FOR? What difference would you want to have made?"

Jennifer sat in silence for so long I thought she might leave. Then, barely above a whisper: "I want to be remembered as someone who helped girls believe they could do anything."

That was it. Hidden under all those achievement trophies was a service purpose waiting to emerge.

Today, Jennifer still has her corporate job, but she also runs a nonprofit that mentors young women in STEM fields. Same skills, same talents, completely different purpose. The exhaustion is gone. In its place is energy that seems inexhaustible because it comes from serving something that truly matters to her.

The Purpose Audit

Before we go any further, I want you to do something that might be uncomfortable: audit your current purposes. Not the purposes you tell people you have. Not the purposes you think you should have. The purposes actually driving your daily decisions.

Look at your calendar for the last month. Where did you spend your time? Look at your bank statement. Where did you spend your money? Look at your thoughts. Where did you spend your mental energy?

Now ask yourself: What purposes are these serving?

- Are you serving survival purposes? (Just trying to make it through)

- Are you serving comfort purposes? (Trying to make life easier)

- Are you serving achievement purposes? (Trying to prove something)

- Are you serving service purposes? (Trying to contribute)

- Are you serving transcendent purposes? (Trying to align with something eternal)

There's no judgment here. Just awareness. You can't change what you don't acknowledge.

The Borrowed Purpose Trap

Most people are living out purposes they never consciously chose. They inherited them, absorbed them, or had them assigned by others. They're like actors who showed up to a play and started reading whatever script was handed to them, never asking, "Is this the role I want to play?"

The Family Purpose

Maybe your purpose came from your family:

- "Our family serves God"

- "Our family builds wealth"

- "Our family serves the community"

- "Our family achieves excellence"

These aren't necessarily bad purposes, but are they YOUR purposes? Or are you just playing out a script written by previous generations?

The Cultural Purpose

Maybe your purpose came from your culture:

- "Make money"

- "Be happy"

- "Leave your mark"

- "Find yourself"

Again, not necessarily wrong, but chosen for you by societal programming rather than conscious decision.

The Trauma Purpose

Sometimes our purposes are reactions to pain:

- "I'll never be poor like my parents" (running from poverty)

- "I'll never be powerless again" (running from vulnerability)

- "I'll never let anyone down" (running from abandonment)

- "I'll never fail" (running from shame)

These reactive purposes can generate tremendous energy, but they're exhausting because you're running FROM something rather than TO something. You're playing defense instead of offense with your life.

The Mother Teresa Moment

In 1946, a 36-year-old nun named Agnes was riding a train to Darjeeling when she experienced what she would later call her "call within a call." She'd been a nun for years, serving the purpose of her religious order, teaching at a girls' school in Calcutta.

But on that train, looking out at the slums of India, Agnes heard a different calling: to serve "the poorest of the poor." Not from the safety of a convent, but in the streets, among the dying and abandoned.

Her superiors thought she was crazy. Leave the convent? Work in the slums? This wasn't what nuns did. But Agnes---who would become Mother Teresa---knew she'd found her true purpose. Not the purpose assigned to her by her order, not the purpose expected by her family, but the purpose that made her soul come alive.

For the next 50 years, she served that purpose with a dedication that seemed superhuman. When asked how she could bear the suffering she witnessed daily, she said something remarkable: "I see Jesus in every dying person."

Her purpose wasn't just to serve the poor. It was to serve God by serving the poor. This transcendent purpose transformed unbearable work into sacred calling.

The Purpose Test

How do you know if a purpose is truly yours? Here's a simple test:

Energy Test: Does thinking about this purpose energize you or drain you? Real purposes give energy; false purposes take it.

Monday Morning Test: When you wake up Monday morning, does this purpose make you want to get out of bed or stay in it?

Suffering Test: Would you suffer for this purpose? Not masochistically, but would you endure difficulty because the purpose matters more than the comfort?

Death Bed Test: On your death bed, will you be proud you served this purpose, or will you regret the time spent on it?

Legacy Test: Do you want to be remembered for serving this purpose?

Autonomy Test: Did you choose this purpose, or was it chosen for you?

The Father's Day Realization

Let me tell you about my own purpose transformation. For years, my purpose was achievement. Build businesses. Make money. Be important. Prove I mattered.

Then one Father's Day, my eight-year-old daughter gave me a handmade card. Inside, she'd written: "Dad, thank you for working so hard. *Maybe someday we can play.*"

Maybe someday we can play.

Those five words shattered me. I'd been so busy serving the purpose of success that I'd forgotten the purpose of being a father. I was providing for my family financially but failing them relationally. I was winning in business but losing at home.

That night, I asked myself: "Twenty years from now, what will matter more---that I built another business or that I built a relationship with my daughter?"

The answer was obvious. But living that answer required completely restructuring my life around a different purpose. Not the purpose of achievement, but the purpose of presence. Not the purpose of success, but the purpose of significance.

I didn't quit my job or abandon my responsibilities. But I changed why I did them. I stopped working to build my empire and started working to build my family's future. I stopped measuring success by revenue and started measuring it by relationships.

Same activities, different purpose, completely different life.

The Purpose Discovery Process

If you're realizing your current purposes aren't really yours, don't panic. Purpose can be discovered at any age, in any circumstance. Here's a process that's helped thousands find their authentic purpose:

Step 1: The Death Meditation

Imagine you're at your own funeral. Someone is giving your eulogy. What do you want them to say? Not what achievements you accumulated, but what difference you made? What lives did you touch? What changed because you existed?

Write that eulogy. Be specific. Be honest. Be ambitious about the impact you want to have had.

Step 2: The Child Question

What did you want to be when you grew up, before the world told you what was "realistic"? Not the job title, but the essence. If you wanted to be a firefighter, was it about saving people? Being brave? Being a hero?

That childhood dream contains clues about your authentic purpose.

Step 3: The Anger Analysis

What makes you genuinely angry about the world? Not annoyed, but deeply, morally angry? Injustice? Waste? Suffering? Ignorance?

Your anger points to your values, and your values point to your purpose. We get angry when something we care about is threatened or violated.

Step 4: The Envy Examination

Who do you envy and why? Not their money or status, but their impact, their life's work, their contribution?

Envy is your soul's way of showing you what it wants. If you envy someone who's educating children, maybe your purpose involves education. If you envy someone who's creating beauty, maybe your purpose involves art.

Step 5: The Flow Finder

When do you lose track of time? What activities make you forget to eat, forget to check your phone, forget your problems?

These flow states indicate alignment with purpose. You lose yourself because you've found yourself.

The Man Who Found His Purpose at 67

Robert had been an accountant for 40 years. Good at it, but never loved it. It was a job, a way to pay bills, nothing more. He retired at 67 with a nice pension and absolutely no idea what to do with himself.

Golf got boring after three months. Travel felt aimless. His wife was getting tired of him moping around the house.

Then his grandson asked him to help with a school project about World War II. Robert's father had served in the war but never talked about it. Robert started researching, trying to understand his father's experience.

That research led him to the local veterans' home, where he met men who'd served with his father. Their stories captivated him. But what struck him most was how many of these stories were dying with their tellers---never recorded, never preserved, soon to be lost forever.

Robert found his purpose at 67: recording the stories of veterans before they were lost. He bought recording equipment, learned to edit video, started a YouTube channel. In the next five years, he recorded over 300 veterans' stories.

When Robert died at 74, his funeral was standing room only---filled with veterans whose stories he'd preserved and families who finally understood what their fathers and grandfathers had experienced.

Robert spent 40 years serving someone else's purpose (making money for a corporation) and 7 years serving his own purpose (preserving history). Guess which years he said were the best of his life?

The Purpose Progression

Purpose isn't static. It evolves as you evolve. The purpose that drives you at 20 might not be the purpose that drives you at 40 or 60. This isn't failure or inconsistency---it's growth.

The Seasons of Purpose

Spring (Youth): Your purpose is often about discovering yourself, developing capabilities, exploring possibilities. The question is "What can I become?"

Summer (Young Adulthood): Your purpose shifts to establishing yourself, proving yourself, achieving goals. The question is "What can I accomplish?"

Autumn (Middle Age): Your purpose often transitions to contributing, mentoring, building things that last. The question is "What can I give?"

Winter (Later Life): Your purpose becomes about wisdom, legacy, preparing the next generation. The question is "What can I leave behind?"

Each season has its own beauty, its own purpose. The mistake is trying to live in the wrong season---the 50-year-old still trying to prove himself like he's 25, the 30-year-old trying to leave a legacy before he's built anything to leave.

The Purpose Partnership

Your purpose doesn't exist in isolation. It connects to other people's purposes, creating what I call Purpose Partnerships---relationships where individual purposes align and amplify each other.

The best marriages are Purpose Partnerships. Not two people serving the same purpose, but two people whose individual purposes complement and strengthen each other.

I know a couple where the husband's purpose is to create financial security for his family, and the wife's purpose is to raise children who contribute positively to the world. Different purposes, but perfectly aligned. His purpose supports hers, hers gives meaning to his.

The best businesses are Purpose Partnerships too. When individual purposes align with organizational purpose, you get extraordinary results. Everyone's rowing in the same direction, not because they have to, but because they want to.

The Purpose Without a Name

Sometimes the most powerful purposes can't be easily labeled. They're too personal, too specific, too unique to fit in a category.

I knew a man whose purpose was to make his autistic son laugh at least once every day. That's it. That was his driving purpose. It influenced every decision---where they lived (near a park the son loved), what job he took (one with flexible hours), what skills he developed (he became an amateur magician).

Was this a small purpose? Some might think so. But it transformed not just his son's life but his own. It gave him a reason to be creative every day, to be present, to find joy in small moments.

Your purpose doesn't have to be grand. It doesn't have to save the world. It just has to matter to you.

The Warning

Here's what nobody tells you about finding your authentic purpose: it might cost you everything you've built serving false purposes.

When you discover your real purpose, you might realize:

- Your career is aligned with someone else's purpose

- Your relationships are based on old purposes you've outgrown

- Your lifestyle serves purposes that no longer matter to you

This is the Purpose Crisis---the moment when you see clearly that your life is built on foundations that aren't truly yours.

Some people see this and retreat, choosing the familiar prison over the unknown freedom. Others have the courage to rebuild, even if it means starting over.

The CEO Who Became a Teacher

Michael was CEO of a tech company worth $50 million. By every external measure, he'd won. But when he did the purpose audit, he realized his true purpose had nothing to do with building companies.

His purpose was to help young people find their path---the same way a teacher had helped him when he was a lost teenager.

At 45, Michael sold his company, went back to school to get his teaching certificate, and became a high school computer science teacher in an inner-city school. His salary went from $500,000 to $45,000.

His friends thought he'd lost his mind. His ex-wife (who'd enjoyed the CEO lifestyle) definitely thought so. But Michael?

"I wake up excited every day," he told me. "I go to bed satisfied every night. I make in a year what I used to make in a month, but I'm richer than I've ever been."

Last year, one of Michael's students got accepted to MIT with a full scholarship. The kid was from a single-parent home, first in his family to go to college. At graduation, he said, "Mr. Mitchell saved my life. He showed me what was possible."

That's what serving your true purpose looks like. It might not make you rich. It might not make you famous. But it will make you come alive.

The Purpose Equation

After years of studying purpose, I've distilled it down to a simple equation:

Your Purpose = Your Gifts + Your Passion + The World's Need

Your Gifts: What you're naturally good at, what comes easily to you, what others struggle with but you find simple.

Your Passion: What you care about deeply, what makes you angry when it's done wrong, what you'd do for free.

The World's Need: What problems need solving, what pain needs healing, what beauty needs creating.

When these three circles overlap, you find your purpose sweet spot. Miss any one element and purpose feels forced:

- Gifts + Passion without Need = Self-indulgent hobby

- Passion + Need without Gifts = Frustrating struggle

- Gifts + Need without Passion = Soul-crushing work

The Daily Purpose Practice

Purpose isn't just a grand vision---it's a daily practice. Every morning, before the chaos of the day begins, ask yourself:

"What purpose will I serve today?"

Not what tasks will you complete or what goals will you achieve, but what purpose will guide your actions?

Maybe today your purpose is to be fully present with your family. Maybe it's to solve a problem that's been plaguing your team. Maybe it's to create something beautiful. Maybe it's simply to be kind to everyone you meet.

The specific purpose matters less than the practice of consciously choosing it.

The Purpose Revolution

We're living in what I call the Purpose Revolution. For the first time in history, millions of people have the luxury of choosing their purpose rather than having it dictated by survival needs.

Your grandparents didn't ask, "What's my purpose?" Their purpose was survival---feed the family, keep a roof overhead, make it through. Purpose was a luxury they couldn't afford.

But you? You have the freedom---and therefore the responsibility---to choose your purpose consciously. This is both a blessing and a burden. A blessing because you can align your life with what truly matters to you. A burden because you can't blame circumstances for a purposeless life.

The Three Questions

As we prepare to integrate all three components of your Trichotomy of Self, I want you to answer three questions about purpose:

1. **What purposes are you currently serving?** Be honest. Look at where you spend your time, energy, and resources. What purposes do these serve?

2. **Whose purposes are they?** Did you choose them consciously, or were they inherited, assigned, or absorbed? Are you the author of your purposes or just an actor?

3. **What would you serve if you knew you couldn't fail?** If resources were unlimited, if success were guaranteed, if judgment didn't exist---what purpose would call to your soul?

Your Purpose Awaits

Remember Viktor Frankl in that concentration camp, taking mental notes while his body starved. He survived because he had a purpose that transcended his suffering. His purpose gave him power over circumstances that should have destroyed him.

You may never face a concentration camp, but you face your own challenges, your own suffering, your own dark nights of the soul. The question is: Do you have a purpose powerful enough to sustain you?

Not a purpose someone else gave you. Not a purpose you think you should have. A purpose that makes your soul say YES. A purpose that makes Monday morning feel like opportunity rather than obligation. A purpose that transforms suffering from meaningless pain into meaningful growth.

Your authentic purpose is waiting for you. It's been there all along, buried perhaps under others' expectations, society's programming, or your own fears. But it's there, as unique as your fingerprint, as essential as your heartbeat.

The question isn't whether you have a purpose. The question is whether you have the courage to claim it, to serve it, to let it transform your life from mere existence into meaningful contribution.

What will you serve?

"The two most important days in your life are the day you are born and the day you find out why." ---Often attributed to Mark Twain

In the next chapter, we'll explore how to align all three components of your Trichotomy---your patterns, your stories, and your purposes---into a coherent whole that creates authentic, purposeful living. You'll discover why alignment, not perfection, is the key to a life well-lived.

But for now, sit with this truth: You are here for a reason. Your life has purpose. The only question is whether you'll discover it, claim it, and serve it with everything you have. Your purpose is calling. Will you answer?

CHAPTER SEVEN

WHEN YOU STOP FIGHTING YOURSELF

"THE GREATEST TRAGEDY ISN'T LIVING THE WRONG LIFE---IT'S LIVING THREE DIFFERENT LIVES AT THE SAME TIME AND WONDERING WHY YOU'RE EXHAUSTED."

The Day Everything Fell Apart

Jennifer Martinez had built the perfect life. Every morning at 5 AM, she'd spring out of bed for her workout---not because she loved it, but because "successful people exercise before dawn." She'd told herself this story so many times it felt like truth: "I'm someone who has their shit together."

But on this particular Tuesday, at 5 AM, Jennifer couldn't move.
Not wouldn't. Couldn't.

Her body---the same body she'd disciplined into submission for fifteen years---had finally said no. Not a dramatic no. Not a heart attack or stroke. Just a quiet, firm refusal to participate in the lie anymore.

She lay there in the dark, her husband sleeping beside her, and felt something she'd never felt before: the complete collapse of her internal architecture. The patterns she'd perfected, the stories she'd polished, the purposes she'd pursued---none of them were talking to each other anymore. They were three strangers living in the same body, pulling in different directions, tearing her apart from the inside.

Her patterns said: "Get up, workout, achieve, produce, perform." Her stories said: "You're tired, you're failing, you're not who you pretend to be." Her purposes said: "None of this matters anyway."

This is **The Breaking Point**---the moment when the three components of your Trichotomy of Self stop cooperating and start competing. It's not depression, though it can feel like it. It's not burnout, though it resembles it. It's something more fundamental: it's when the patterns you repeat daily, the stories that guide you, and the purposes you serve declare war on each other.

Jennifer was living proof of a truth most people never discover: **You can have all three components of your TOS functioning perfectly and still have them destroying each other.**

Think about that for a moment. It's not enough to have good patterns. It's not enough to have empowering stories. It's not enough to have meaningful purposes. If they're not working together---if they're not in conversation with each other, supporting each other, amplifying each other---you're not living one life. You're living three lives simultaneously, and the friction between them is burning you alive from the inside.

The Hidden Civil War

Right now, as you read this, there's likely a civil war raging inside you that you've gotten so used to, you think it's peace.

Let me show you what I mean. Think about your last Monday morning:

Your alarm goes off. Your patterns want to hit snooze---that's what you've trained them to do. But your stories start their assault: "Lazy people hit snooze. You're not lazy, are you?" Meanwhile, your purposes are screaming: "What's the point of getting up? Another day of meaningless work?"

Three components. Three different agendas. One exhausted you caught in the crossfire.

This is the hidden tragedy of modern life. We've been taught to develop good habits, think positive thoughts, and find our purpose---but nobody taught us how to make them work together. It's like having three members of a band where the drummer is playing rock, the guitarist is playing jazz, and the singer is performing opera. Each might be talented, but together they create noise, not music.

Most people aren't suffering from bad patterns, limiting stories, or weak purposes. They're suffering from internal warfare between good components that are destroying each other.

The Anatomy of Integration

Let me tell you about Marcus Chen---five years after his transformation from accountant to craftsman. You'd think someone who successfully changed careers, found his purpose, and rebuilt his life would have it all figured out.

You'd be wrong.

Marcus called me on a Sunday night, and I could hear the defeat in his voice. "I thought I'd fixed everything when I became a woodworker," he said. "I found my purpose, I changed my patterns, I rewrote my stories. So why do I feel like I'm falling apart again?"

Here's what Marcus had discovered: **Unity of self isn't found, it's practiced in constant balance.**

When Marcus first transformed his life, everything inside him was working together:

- **Patterns:** Working with his hands, creating beauty, teaching craftsmanship

- **Stories:** "I'm an artist," "Manual work has dignity," "I'm building a legacy"

- **Purposes:** Preserving traditional skills, creating heirlooms, mentoring youth

But over five years, things had shifted. His business had grown. He now spent more time managing than making. His patterns had evolved but his stories hadn't. He was still telling himself he was a craftsman while his daily patterns were those of a CEO. The disconnection was subtle but devastating.

"I wake up to emails, not wood shavings," he said. "I spend more time in QuickBooks than at my workbench. But I keep telling myself I'm still that guy who builds things with his hands. The lie is killing me."

This is **The Drift**---the slow, almost imperceptible way your components start moving in different directions, like tectonic plates creating pressure that will eventually cause an earthquake.

The Three Laws of Integration

After studying thousands of people's TOS patterns, I've discovered three laws that govern how integration works:

Law 1: The Weakest Link Principle

Your inner harmony is only as strong as the weakest relationship between components. You can have perfect pattern-story cooperation and perfect story-purpose unity, but if your patterns don't serve your purposes, the whole system collapses.

Think of it like a three-legged stool. Two strong legs mean nothing if the third is broken. You'll still fall.

I saw this with my client Robert, a recovering alcoholic with seven years of sobriety. His patterns were impeccable---meetings, meditation, exercise, service work. His purposes were clear---stay sober, help others recover, be present for his family. But his stories? His stories were killing him.

Despite seven years of sobriety, Robert still told himself the story: "I'm an alcoholic. I'm broken. I'm one drink away from losing everything." This story made him hypervigilant, anxious, unable to trust himself. His perfect patterns and noble purposes couldn't overcome the poison of that limiting story.

The breakthrough came when Robert realized he could honor his recovery while updating his story: "I'm someone who chose sobriety and continues to choose it. I'm not broken; I'm experienced. I'm not one drink from disaster; I'm one choice from continued freedom."

Same patterns. Same purposes. Revolutionary new story. Suddenly, the three components started singing in harmony instead of shouting over each other.

Law 2: The Amplification Effect

When your components work together, they don't just cooperate---they amplify each other exponentially. This is why someone with modest talents but strong inner unity often outperforms someone with extraordinary talents but internal warfare.

Sarah Rodriguez discovered this when she finally stopped fighting herself. For years, she'd been what I call **High-Functioning Chaos**---successful despite the civil war inside her.

Her patterns were those of a corporate warrior: long hours, aggressive negotiation, constant competition. Her stories were those of a nurturer: "I care about people," "Relationships matter most," "Success means everyone wins." Her purposes were confused: sometimes serving shareholder value, sometimes serving human value, never sure which mattered more.

The internal conflict was profitable but painful. Sarah made money but lost sleep. She won deals but lost friends. She climbed the ladder but descended into emptiness.

Then Sarah's daughter asked her a question that changed everything: "Mommy, why do you use your mean voice at work but your nice voice at home?"

That innocent question revealed the schizophrenia of Sarah's existence. She was literally living as two different people, switching between them based on context, exhausting herself maintaining both personas.

Sarah began the painful work of integration. She brought her nurturing stories into her work patterns. She started negotiating with empathy, competing with compassion, leading with love. She thought it would destroy her career.
Instead, it transformed it.

Her clients, shocked by her authenticity, started trusting her more. Her team, inspired by her vulnerability, started performing better. Her results, freed from the friction of internal warfare, skyrocketed.

"When I stopped fighting myself," Sarah told me, "I had so much more energy to fight for what mattered."

Law 3: The Resistance Paradox

Here's the counterintuitive truth: The closer you get to living as one person, the more resistance you'll feel. Not external resistance---internal resistance.

Why? Because integration requires the death of false identities you've invested years in maintaining.

When Jennifer (from our opening story) finally got out of bed that Tuesday morning, she began what she calls "The Great Unbecoming." She had to let die:

- The Jennifer who never missed a workout (pattern identity)

- The Jennifer who had it all together (story identity)

- The Jennifer who existed to achieve (purpose identity)

Each of these identities had served her. They'd gotten her promotions, praise, social media followers. Letting them die felt like letting parts of herself die. Because they were parts of herself---just not authentic parts.

"The resistance was incredible," Jennifer told me. "Every cell in my body wanted to go back to the old chaos. At least it was familiar. This new wholeness felt like walking naked through the world."

The Chaos Archetypes

Through years of observation, I've identified five archetypal patterns of internal chaos. Which one are you?

The Performer

The Performer has patterns that look perfect from the outside but feel empty from the inside. They do all the "right" things for all the wrong reasons.

Daniel Kim was the perfect Performer. Morning routine? Optimized. Productivity system? Bulletproof. Network? Influential. Life? Meaningless.

Daniel's patterns served the purpose of impression, not expression. His stories were all about external validation: "I am what I achieve," "Worth equals productivity," "If I slow down, I'll be exposed as a fraud."

The disconnection was sophisticated---everything looked unified if you didn't look too close. But Daniel was performing the role of a successful person rather than being one. He was method acting his own life.

The Dreamer

The Dreamer has beautiful purposes and empowering stories but patterns that betray both. They know exactly who they want to be and why, but their daily actions tell a different story.

Lisa Rodriguez was a classic Dreamer. Her purpose? To write novels that change how people see the world. Her stories? "I'm a writer," "I have important things to say," "My words matter." Her patterns? She hadn't written anything in two years.

Lisa spent her days reading about writing, talking about writing, thinking about writing---everything except writing. Her patterns were those of a consumer, not a creator. Her refrigerator was covered with inspiring quotes about creativity, but her laptop was covered with dust.

The cruelest part? Lisa knew exactly what she needed to do. But knowing and doing existed in different universes, and Lisa couldn't build a bridge between them.

The Grinder

The Grinder has disciplined patterns that serve unclear or borrowed purposes. They're highly efficient at going nowhere meaningful.

Tom Washington was grinding himself into dust. Up at 4:30 AM. Gym. Work. Network. Study. Optimize. Achieve. Repeat.

When I asked Tom what purpose all this grinding served, he looked at me like I'd asked him to explain the color blue. "Purpose? I'm building success."
"And what does success mean to you?"
Long pause. "I... I guess I never really thought about it."

Tom was like a powerful engine running without a transmission---lots of noise and heat, no forward movement. His patterns were impressive but pointless, serving a purpose he'd never consciously chosen.

The Chameleon

The Chameleon's components change based on who they're with or where they are. They have no stable identity because they have no stable self.

Rachel Foster was whoever you needed her to be. At work, her patterns were aggressive, her stories were about domination, her purpose was winning. At home, her patterns were passive, her stories were about harmony, her purpose was peace. With friends, she became someone else entirely.

Rachel wasn't consciously deceptive. She'd simply never developed her own coherent identity, so she borrowed others'. She was a different TOS with different people, exhausting herself maintaining multiple personalities.

"I don't even know which one is the real me anymore," Rachel confessed. "Maybe none of them are. Maybe I don't exist except as a reflection of what others expect."

The Zombie

The Zombie has components that once worked together but no longer do. They're running on outdated programming, living a life that made sense five years ago but doesn't anymore.

Michael Roberts was living his 35-year-old self's dream at 48. His patterns, stories, and purposes had once been perfectly unified---for an ambitious young man building his career. But Michael wasn't that man anymore.

His kids were grown. His marriage had evolved. His values had shifted. But his TOS hadn't. He was still grinding like he had something to prove, still telling himself stories about "making it," still serving purposes that had been accomplished years ago.

"I achieved everything I wanted," Michael said. "But I forgot to want new things. I'm living a life that expired, and I don't know how to update it."

The Integration Diagnostic Deep Dive

Let's get specific about where your internal warfare lives. This isn't a casual assess-ment---this is surgery. Be honest, or waste your time.

Pattern-Story Integration Analysis

When your patterns and stories work together: Your daily actions provide evidence for your beliefs about yourself. Each workout proves you're disciplined. Each creative session proves you're an artist. Each kind act proves you're compassionate. The story and the evidence dance together, each reinforcing the other.

When they're at war: You experience **Evidence Dissonance**. Your stories say one thing, your patterns prove another. You tell yourself you're a writer but you don't write. You believe you're a good parent but you're always at work. You think you're health-con-scious but your patterns are self-destructive.

The Diagnostic Questions:

- If someone watched your patterns for a month without hearing your stories, what would they conclude about you?

- What stories do you tell that your patterns don't support?

- What patterns do you practice that contradict your stories about yourself?

- Where's the biggest gap between who you say you are and what you actually do?

The Jennifer Example: Jennifer's stories: "I'm disciplined, successful, unstoppable." Jennifer's patterns: Forcing herself through exhaustion, medicating with wine, crying in bathroom stalls.

The warfare: Her patterns were screaming that she was falling apart while her stories insisted she was thriving. This created **Narrative Whiplash**---the psychological confusion of living evidence that contradicts your story.

Pattern-Purpose Integration Analysis

When your patterns and purposes work together: Every action serves your mission. Your daily behaviors are investments in what matters most. You don't need motivation because your purposes pull you forward and your patterns carry you there.

When they're at war: You experience **Purpose Drift**---working hard in directions that don't matter to you. You're efficient but not effective, productive but not purposeful.

The Diagnostic Questions:

- What percentage of your daily patterns directly serve your stated purposes?

- Which patterns actively work against your purposes?

- If your purposes are your destination, are your patterns taking you closer or further away?

- What would someone conclude your purposes are based solely on your patterns?

The Marcus Example: Marcus's purposes: Create beauty, teach craftsmanship, preserve traditions. Marcus's patterns: Emails, spreadsheets, managing employees, handling logistics.

The warfare: His patterns had evolved to serve business growth, but his purposes remained focused on craft. He was succeeding at something he didn't want while failing at what he did want.

Story-Purpose Integration Analysis

When your stories and purposes work together: Your beliefs about yourself support your mission. Your internal narrative energizes your pursuit. You have what I call **Narrative Momentum**---your stories propel you toward your purposes.

When they're at war: You experience **Story Sabotage**---your beliefs undermine your mission. You want to serve a purpose but don't believe you're capable or worthy.

The Diagnostic Questions:

- Do your stories about yourself support or sabotage your purposes?

- What do you believe about yourself that makes your purposes harder to serve?

- If you fully believed your current stories, would your purposes feel achievable or impossible?

- What story would you need to believe to naturally serve your authentic purposes?

The Lisa Example: Lisa's purposes: Write novels that change how people see the world. Lisa's stories: "I'm not good enough yet," "Real writers don't struggle like this," "Maybe I'm fooling myself."

The warfare: Her purposes required confidence and conviction, but her stories created doubt and paralysis. She was trying to drive with the emergency brake on.

The Integration Process: How Unity Actually Happens

Here's what nobody tells you about stopping the civil war inside: it doesn't happen through force. You can't wrestle your components into submission. Integration happens through conversation---getting your patterns, stories, and purposes to talk to each other.

Stage 1: The Truth Telling (Week 1-2)

Before your components can work together, they need to be honest about where they are.

Pattern Truth: Document your actual patterns, not your intended ones. Use your phone to track your real behavior. Set random alarms throughout the day. When they go off, write down exactly what you're doing. No judgment, no editing, just truth.

Story Truth: Write down the stories you tell yourself, especially the ones you don't want to admit. The victim stories. The superiority stories. The fear stories. The shame stories. Get them out of your head and onto paper where you can see them for what they are---just stories.

Purpose Truth: List what your patterns suggest your purposes are. If someone analyzed your time, energy, and resource allocation, what would they conclude matters most to you? This is your functional purpose, regardless of your stated purpose.

Stage 2: The Component Conversation (Week 3-4)

Now facilitate a conversation between your components. Literally. Write it out like a script.

Patterns speak to Stories: "Hey, I notice you keep saying we're a writer, but I haven't typed a creative word in months. What's going on?"

Stories respond to Patterns: "I'm scared if we actually write, people will see we're frauds. So I keep you busy with other things."

Purposes enter the conversation: "Both of you are missing the point. We're not here to impress anyone. We're here to express truth through words. Can we agree on that?"

This might feel silly, but it works. You're giving voice to the different parts of yourself that have been operating in isolation. You're facilitating the integration that needs to happen.

Stage 3: The Unity Negotiation (Week 5-6)

Your components need to negotiate a new relationship. They each have needs:

Patterns need: Consistency, clarity, and achievable actions. **Stories need:** Evidence, credibility, and internal coherence. **Purposes need:** Meaning, significance, and connection to something larger.

The negotiation might look like:

- "Patterns, can you commit to writing for just 15 minutes daily?"

- "Stories, can you update from 'I'm a fraud' to 'I'm learning'?"

- "Purposes, can you focus less on changing the world and more on expressing truth?"

Small adjustments that bring components into conversation rather than conflict.

Stage 4: The Living Integration (Week 7-12)

Now live the negotiated unity. Every morning, check in with all three components:
- "Patterns, what will you practice today?"

- "Stories, what will you believe today?"

- "Purposes, what will you serve today?"

Every evening, review:

- "Did you three work together or against each other?"

- "Where did harmony feel natural?"

- "Where did conflict creep in?"

Stage 5: The Dynamic Maintenance (Ongoing)

Living as one person isn't static. As you grow, your components need to renegotiate their relationship. What worked together at 30 might conflict at 40. What served you as a single person might not serve you as a parent.

This isn't failure---it's evolution. Your TOS is a living system that needs regular updates, not a machine that, once fixed, runs forever.

The Story of David's Midnight Reckoning

David Thompson was a surgeon who saved lives by day and destroyed his own by night. His case shows how internal warfare can hide behind competence.

David's patterns were those of a healer at work: precise, caring, dedicated. But at home, his patterns shifted: distant, numbed by alcohol, absent even when present.

His stories were confused: "I'm a healer" at work, "I'm a failure" at home. He couldn't reconcile saving strangers' lives while failing his own family.

His purposes were at war: serve patients, serve family, serve hospital, serve self---all competing for resources he didn't have.

The breaking point came when his 8-year-old son asked: "Dad, why do you care more about sick people than us?"

David realized he'd been living what I call a **Compartmentalized TOS**---different versions in different contexts, exhausting himself maintaining multiple identities.

The integration work was brutal. David had to admit that being a great surgeon didn't automatically make him a great father. That saving lives professionally didn't excuse destroying lives personally. That you can't have integrity if you're integrated at work but fragmented at home.

David's transformation required what he calls "surgical precision on my own soul." He had to:

- Bring his home patterns into harmony with his work patterns (presence, care, attention)

- Update his stories to include the full truth (great surgeon, learning father)

- Clarify his purposes to include both domains (heal bodies AND nurture family)

It took two years. David reduced his surgery schedule. He entered therapy. He learned that living as one person isn't about being perfect---it's about being whole.

"I used to think I was saving lives," David told me. "Now I realize I was hiding from life. True integration means you're the same person in scrubs or pajamas, in the OR or the living room. That's integrity."

The Resistance Roster: What Fights Against Unity

As you work toward living as one coherent person, you'll face predictable resistance. Know your enemies:

The Comfort Resistance

Internal warfare might be painful, but it's familiar. Your nervous system prefers familiar pain to unfamiliar health. You've built your life around your chaos---relationships, routines, identity. Integration threatens all of it.

The Identity Resistance

You've invested years in being who you are, even if who you are isn't who you want to be. Unity requires admitting you've been living as an imposter---not to others, but to yourself.

The Social Resistance

People know you as your fragmented self. They're comfortable with your performance. Your wholeness threatens their comfort. They'll unconsciously (or consciously) try to pull you back to who you were.

The Success Resistance

If your internal warfare has been profitable, integration might cost you money, status, or achievement. You have to decide: would you rather be successfully fragmented or authentically whole?

The Expertise Resistance

You've become an expert at managing your chaos. You know how to navigate the friction, manage the exhaustion, maintain the performance. Unity requires becoming a beginner again.

The Integration Accelerators

Certain practices dramatically speed up the process of living as one person:

The Morning Trinity Check

Every morning, before the world starts pulling you in different directions, connect with your TOS:

- Touch your head: "What stories will I tell myself today?"

- Touch your heart: "What purposes will I serve today?"

- Touch your hands: "What patterns will I practice today?"

This takes 30 seconds but unifies your entire day.

The Evening Integrity Scan

Before bed, scan for where the civil war erupted:

- Where did my patterns contradict my stories?

- Where did my stories undermine my purposes?

- Where did my purposes not guide my patterns?

No judgment, just awareness. You're training your consciousness to notice conflict in real-time.

The Weekly Harmony Audit

Every Sunday, review your week through the integration lens:

- What patterns moved me toward my purposes?

- What stories supported my patterns?

- What purposes inspired my stories?

Then plan the coming week:

- What pattern will I strengthen?

- What story will I update?

- What purpose will I clarify?

The Monthly Deep Dive

Once a month, go deeper:

- Are my components growing together or apart?

- What internal warfare am I tolerating?

- What unity am I ready for?

The Quarterly Revolution

Every three months, question everything:

- Are these still my authentic patterns, or am I maintaining habits?

- Are these still my empowering stories, or am I repeating old scripts?

- Are these still my meaningful purposes, or am I serving expired goals?

The Ultimate Integration Truth

Here's what I need you to understand, what Jennifer discovered on that Tuesday morning when her body refused to maintain the lie, what Marcus learned when success felt like failure, what all of us must eventually face:

You can't sustain internal warfare indefinitely. The friction will eventually create fire, and that fire will either refine you or consume you.

Your patterns, stories, and purposes aren't separate systems---they're three aspects of one system: you. When they work together, you experience what mystics call "flow," what psychologists call "integration," what I call "being fully alive."

When they work against each other, you experience what feels like being torn apart from the inside---because you are.

The Three Final Questions

Before we move to the next chapter, answer these with brutal honesty:

1. **The Friction Question:** Where do you feel the most warfare between your patterns, stories, and purposes? Where is the civil war loudest?

2. **The Fear Question:** What are you afraid will happen if you stop fighting yourself? What will you lose? Who will you disappoint? What identity will die?

3. **The Freedom Question:** What becomes possible when your patterns serve your purposes, your stories support your patterns, and your purposes inspire your stories? Who do you become when the civil war ends?

Your Integration Moment

Jennifer eventually got out of bed that Tuesday morning. But she got up different. She got up whole. She stopped practicing patterns that served others' purposes. She stopped telling stories that weren't hers. She stopped serving purposes that felt important but weren't authentic.

It cost her everything that looked successful. It gave her everything that felt meaningful.

Marcus brought his components back into harmony. He hired managers to handle business while he returned to craftsmanship. His patterns again matched his purpose. His stories again supported his patterns.

Lisa finally brought her patterns into unity with her purpose. She wrote badly for months before she wrote well. But she wrote. Her patterns finally provided evidence for her story: "I'm a writer."

David, Sarah, Tom, Rachel, Michael---they all discovered the same truth: **Living as one person isn't a luxury for the enlightened. It's a necessity for the living.**

You can continue the civil war between your patterns, stories, and purposes. You can keep living three lives simultaneously, exhausting yourself maintaining the performance, wondering why success feels empty and achievement brings no peace.

Or you can begin the sacred work of integration. Not perfect unity---that doesn't exist. But conscious harmony. Dynamic wholeness. Living integration.

Your greatest strength is unity within. Your greatest weakness is conflict within. Which one you nurture decides everything.---Mark Loudermilk

In the next chapter, we'll explore the Art of Conscious Change---how to transform your TOS without overwhelming yourself, how to work with resistance rather than against it, and how to create lasting transformation rather than temporary modification.

But for now, feel the truth of your current integration or warfare. Feel where the friction burns. Feel where the harmony sings. Feel where the work needs to be done.

Your whole life isn't somewhere else. It's right here, waiting for your components to stop fighting and start dancing.

The war can end today. The dance can begin now.

Will you let it?

Chapter Eight

BECOMING THE GUARDIAN OF YOUR SOUL

"YOU ARE NOT RESPONSIBLE FOR WHO KNOCKS AT YOUR DOOR. YOU ARE 100% RESPONSIBLE FOR WHO YOU LET IN."

The Prison Education

I was fifteen years old, locked in a cell with predators, when I learned the most valuable skill of my life: how to read people before they can hurt you.

In prison, you don't get second chances to figure out someone's true nature. The guy who approaches friendly in the yard—is he looking for an ally or sizing up a victim? The cellmate who offers to watch your back—is he building genuine trust or setting you up for leverage? The inmate who shares his story with emotional vulnerability—is he actually connecting or is he gathering intelligence to use against you later?

I spent my teenage years learning this skill not from books but from necessity. Misreading someone's patterns, stories, and purposes could cost you everything. Your safety. Your sanity. Your commissary. Sometimes more.

The predators taught me more about human nature than any psychology course ever could. I watched them work. I studied their methods. I learned to see the signs: the eyes that never quite match the smile, the story that shifts based on the audience, the kindness that always comes with a price tag attached.

But here's what I discovered when I finally got out: The outside world is full of the same predators. They just wear better suits and use more sophisticated vocabulary.

The corporate climber who befriends you over coffee then undermines you in the meeting. The romantic partner who love-bombs you with intensity then controls you with calculation. The family member who guilts you with obligation then drains you with endless demands. The business partner who smiles while positioning for betrayal.

They're all showing you exactly who they are within the first thirty days of knowing them. Usually within the first thirty minutes. The question isn't whether you can see it. The question is whether you're willing to look, whether you trust what you see, and whether you have the courage to act on that knowledge.

This chapter is about becoming the guardian of your own soul—learning to read people's true framework quickly and accurately, then making conscious decisions about who deserves access to your life and at what level.

The Sacred Responsibility

Let me be brutally clear about something most self-help books won't tell you: You don't get to blame the vampire for your blood loss if you're the one who invited them in.

This isn't victim-blaming. This is power-claiming.

The moment you accept that you're the gatekeeper of your own existence, you stop being prey and start being sovereign. You stop being a victim of toxic people and start being the conscious architect of your relationships. You stop hoping people will change and start choosing people who don't need to.

Every person you allow deep access to your life—every intimate relationship, every close friendship, every trusted advisor, every business partner—is either helping you build coherence between your patterns, stories, and purposes, or they're helping you fragment. There's no neutral ground. People are either photosynthesis or parasitism. They're either adding energy to your system or extracting it.

And here's the revolutionary part that changes everything once you understand it: They're showing you which one they are within the first thirty days. Usually within the first thirty minutes. Always within the first three interactions.

The research validates what the streets taught me. Paul Babiak and Robert Hare's studies of corporate psychopaths showed they follow predictable patterns of assessment, manipulation, and abandonment. Delroy Paulhus and Kevin Williams's research confirmed that Dark Triad personalities—narcissists, Machiavellians, and psychopaths—can't maintain their mask indefinitely. The cracks show. The patterns emerge. The truth reveals itself.

But you don't need a psychology degree to spot toxic people. You need what I call Guardian Sight—the ability to rapidly read someone's patterns, decode their stories, and recognize their purposes before they can cause damage to your life.

This isn't paranoia. This isn't being judgmental or closed-off or cynical. This is wisdom. This is discernment. This is the difference between being someone who learns from others' mistakes and being someone who has to learn everything the hard way.

Understanding Healthy Integration First

Before we learn to identify toxic frameworks, we need to understand what healthy integration actually looks like. Most people have never seen it modeled consistently, so they can't recognize its absence. They mistake intensity for authenticity, neediness for intimacy, manipulation for leadership, extraction for friendship.

The Integrated Person

Someone with genuine internal coherence—where their patterns, stories, and purposes work in harmony—shows these unmistakable characteristics.

Their patterns remain remarkably consistent across different contexts. They're recognizably the same person on Monday morning as Friday night, the same when stressed as when relaxed, the same in public as in private. Their energy level might shift, their stress level might show, but their core way of treating people, keeping commitments, and showing up in the world remains stable. You can trust them because their behavior is predictable in the best possible way.

Their stories maintain integrity across time and audience. The details don't shift to serve current advantages. They acknowledge their role in both successes and failures. They can hold complexity without needing to make someone else the villain. Past events stay in the past rather than being constantly rewritten to fit current narratives. When they tell you about their ex-wife, their former business partner, their previous employer, the story stays consistent even if you hear it three months later or hear them tell it to someone else.

Their purposes show clear demonstration in their actual lives. Their actions align with their stated values. Their time and energy investments reflect their claimed priorities. They can articulate not just what they do but why it matters to them. The sacrifices they make correspond to their expressed purposes. If they say family is their priority, you'll see it in their calendar. If they claim to value health, you'll observe it in their patterns. If they profess to care about personal growth, you'll notice it in what they read, who they spend time with, how they use their resources.

Most importantly, these three elements work in harmony. Their patterns provide evidence for their stories. Their stories support their purposes. Their purposes guide their patterns. It's a coherent system where all the parts reinforce rather than contradict each other.

And when you're around them, you feel energized rather than drained. Conversations go deeper than surface pleasantries without becoming dramatic or extractive. They ask about you as genuinely as they talk about themselves. Conflicts, when they arise, get resolved rather than recycled endlessly. Support flows in both directions naturally.

The Fragmented Person

Now contrast this with someone whose internal architecture is fundamentally fragmented—where their patterns, stories, and purposes are at war with each other.

Their patterns show dramatic inconsistency based on context. They're a different person with different people. Their public persona bears little resemblance to their private behavior. The personality they show bosses versus peers versus subordinates versus family are so distinct they might as well be different people entirely. Promises made are regularly broken. The only consistency is their inconsistency.

Their stories shift like sand based on audience and advantage. They're always either the hero or the victim, never responsible. Details change to serve manipulation. History gets rewritten whenever it's convenient. The same event gets told three different ways to three different people. Emotions appear and disappear strategically rather than authentically—tears that turn off like a faucet, anger that vanishes the moment it's served its purpose, affection that's performed for effect rather than felt.

Their purposes, when you examine their actual behavior, reveal themselves as fundamentally different from what they claim. They talk about values they don't practice, priorities they don't honor, goals they don't pursue. Their time and energy go to things they claim don't matter while the things they say are important receive no investment. The gap between stated and demonstrated purposes is where their true character lives.

Most tellingly, their three components actively fight each other. Their patterns contradict their stories. Their stories undermine their purposes. Their purposes don't guide their patterns. It's a system in civil war with itself, and you can feel the chaos when you're near them.

When you're around fragmented people, you feel consistently drained afterward, even if you can't articulate why. Conversations stay surface or turn dramatic with no middle ground. Everything becomes about them—their needs, their crises, their stories. The same conflicts recycle endlessly without resolution. Support flows in only one direction. And you leave interactions feeling somehow less than you were before, diminished in ways you struggle to define but definitely feel.

This is the difference you're learning to see. This is the distinction that will save your life, your peace, your energy, your purposes. Because once you can recognize healthy integration versus toxic fragmentation, you'll stop wasting time trying to fix the unfixable and start investing deeply in relationships that multiply rather than drain you.

The Three-Layer Reading System

After almost 3 decades in emergency medicine and decades of studying human nature in both the most dangerous and most professional environments, I've developed a system that reveals someone's true internal framework in three progressive layers of observation. Each layer takes you deeper, but even the first layer can save your life.

Layer One: The Thirty-Minute Surface Read

In the first thirty minutes of meeting someone, you can gather eighty percent of what you need to know if you know what to look for. This isn't intuition or mysticism—it's pattern recognition based on unconscious behaviors that reveal authentic character.

The Pattern Scan

Watch their micro-patterns, not their macro-performance. How do they treat the server, the receptionist, the person who can do nothing for them? This reveals their baseline treatment of human beings when there's no strategic advantage to kindness. If they're rude to the server but charming to you, understand: you're getting the performance. The server is getting the truth. And eventually, when you can no longer do something useful for them, you'll get what the server got.

Do they maintain eye contact or are they scanning for better options? Are they present with you or performing for an audience? Do they mirror your energy or impose their own? Do they respect your personal space or invade it? These micro-behaviors reveal whether they see you as a person to connect with or an object to use.

The Story Sample

Listen to the first three stories they tell about themselves. Are they the hero, victim, or villain? Do others in their stories exist as full people with motivations and complexity, or as props in their drama? Is there emotional depth or just events recounted without feeling? Do the stories serve genuine connection or carefully crafted impression?

Healthy people tell stories where they're fully human—sometimes succeeding, sometimes failing, sometimes being helped, always learning. Toxic people tell stories where they're always in the same role and everyone else exists only to serve or oppose them.

The Purpose Probe

Notice what makes their eyes light up versus what they claim to value. What do they complain about? What do they brag about? What do they actually want from this interaction—connection, information, leverage, validation, or supply?

The gap between stated values and demonstrated excitement reveals their true purposes. Someone who talks about family but gets animated about work promotions is telling you where their real energy goes.

The Thirty-Minute Mantra: *"In thirty minutes, people show you their patterns, tell you their stories, and reveal their purposes. Your job isn't to analyze—it's to observe without judgment, collect without conclusion, and trust what you see."*

Layer Two: The Thirty-Day Deep Dive

If someone passes the thirty-minute scan and you're considering letting them deeper into your life, activate the thirty-day protocol. This isn't manipulation—it's protection. You're documenting reality, not creating tests.

The Consistency Test

People's true framework emerges across different contexts. Create a simple Pattern Map in your journal tracking their behavior across different situations: Monday morning versus Friday night, stressed versus relaxed, public versus private, winning versus losing, sober versus intoxicated.

Healthy people show high-fidelity consistency. They're the same person across contexts with natural variation for circumstance. Toxic people show calculated shifting. They're charming in public, cruel in private. They're supportive when witnessed, dismissive when alone. They make promises Friday night and "forget" them Monday morning.

The Story Evolution Tracker

Liars and manipulators can't maintain narrative consistency. Track their stories over time. Do details shift based on audience? Do roles reverse based on advantage? Do emotions appear and disappear strategically? Does history get rewritten to match current needs?

When people constantly rewrite their stories, they're revealing that truth is whatever serves them in the moment. That's not someone you want close to anything that matters.

The Purpose Revelation Process

Purposes are revealed not by words but by sacrifice patterns. What do they invest in without immediate return? What do they protect even when it costs them? What do they destroy even when it benefits them? What patterns emerge in their major life decisions?

The gap between claimed purposes and demonstrated purposes reveals everything. Someone who says "family first" but works seventy hours a week and misses their kids' events is showing you their true purpose is status, not family.

The Thirty-Day Mantra: *"Thirty days of observation reveals thirty years of character. Time strips away performance and reveals essence. Trust patterns over promises. Trust consistency over claims. Trust demonstrated purposes over declared values."*

Layer Three: The Crisis Revelation

Nothing reveals someone's true internal framework faster than crisis. When some-one faces real pressure—financial stress, health scare, relationship loss, professional set-back—their authentic structure emerges from beneath whatever mask they've been maintaining.

The Pressure Patterns

Do they become more themselves or someone entirely different? Do they protect others or only themselves? Do they take responsibility or distribute blame? Do they problem-solve or problem-create? Do they stay calm or become volatile?

I've watched business partners who seemed completely integrated unravel in three days of financial pressure. The collaborative patterns became controlling. The "we're building this together" stories became "you're messing this up" blame. The noble purposes revealed themselves as pure self-protection.

The Stress Stories

Under stress, authentic people become more real—their stories include doubts, fears, un-certainty, genuine emotion. Toxic people become more theatrical—their stories become more dramatic, more absolute, more victim-focused, more manipulative.

The Crisis Purposes

What becomes non-negotiable in crisis? What gets abandoned immediately? What emerges as truly important? What was always just performance?

When someone's stated purposes collapse under the first real pressure, you're seeing their true framework. Be grateful for the revelation.

The Crisis Mantra: *"Crisis doesn't create character—it reveals it. Pressure doesn't change people—it shows you who they've always been. Trust the revelation. Honor what it teaches you. Protect yourself accordingly."*

The Dark Triad Detection Protocols

Based on research by Jones and Paulhus (2014), Jonason et al. (2012), and my own experience in environments where misreading someone was life-threatening, here are specific protocols for rapidly identifying Dark Triad personalities—narcissists, Machiavellians, and psychopaths—through observing their three-part framework.

The Predator Protocol (Covert Narcissistic and Psychopathic Blend)

Pattern Recognition: Love bombing with excessive attention, gifts, and declarations unusually early. Boundary testing where small violations escalate to larger ones. Isolation tactics through subtle criticism of your support network. Emotional temperature changes from hot to cold without explanation, creating punishment and reward cycles. You're constantly wondering what you did wrong when you didn't do anything wrong—they're creating dependency through intermittent reinforcement.

Story Recognition: Grandiose narratives where they're always exceptional. Emotion-flat recounting of what should be emotional events. Others exist only as objects that served or failed them. No genuine remorse, only regret at being caught. History littered with dramatic endings where everyone else was always the problem.

Purpose Recognition: Excitement about control and dominance. Investment in image over substance. Pursuit of power without actual purpose behind it. Need for admiration without offering reciprocation. Goals that require others' diminishment to succeed.

The Predator Mantra: *"The Predator announces themselves with intensity, reveals themselves through inconsistency, and destroys through dependency. They're not complicated—they're predictable. See them clearly. Distance yourself completely."*

The Parasite Protocol (Covert Narcissistic and Dependent Blend)

Pattern Recognition: Consistent lateness or absence when needed. Present only when extracting value. Energy depletion in their presence—you feel exhausted after every interaction. Crisis creation for attention and resources—there's always something dramatic happening. Responsibility avoidance systems where everything is always someone else's fault or someone else's job.

Story Recognition: Perpetual victim narratives where the world is always happening TO them. Others cast as perpetual disappointers who have all failed them. Success credited to luck, failure blamed on others. Emotional manipulation disguised as vulnerability. Historical pattern of being "saved" repeatedly.

Purpose Recognition: Survival through extraction. Comfort without contribution. Maximum gain with minimum investment. Attachment without accountability. Security without reciprocity.

The Parasite Mantra: *"The Parasite doesn't take your life—they take it one drop at a time until you don't notice you're empty. They're not bad people having hard times—they're professional takers wearing the costume of victims."*

The Puppeteer Protocol (Machiavellian Dominant)

Pattern Recognition: Information gathering as default mode—they always want to know more about you than you know about them. Strategic relationship building where they connect people for future leverage. Triangulation where they tell you what others think or say about you. Calculated vulnerability sharing where they reveal secrets to extract yours. Invisible string attachment where you feel obligated but can't explain why.

Story Recognition: Chess metaphors and game language about "playing the long game." Others described as pieces to be moved. Wins through manipulation celebrated as intelligence. Deception ability equated with sophistication. Relationships framed as transactions to be optimized.

Purpose Recognition: Control disguised as care—"I'm just looking out for you." Power through information asymmetry—they know more about everyone than anyone knows about them. Influence without visibility—they're never the obvious leader, always the whisper in the ear. Leverage building in all relationships. Long-term positioning for advantage.

The Puppeteer Mantra: *"The Puppeteer's strings are so light you think you're flying, until you try to leave and discover you can't. They don't control through force—they control through obligation, information, and invisible debt."*

The Bully Protocol (Power-Based Domination)

Bullying is its own distinct category of toxic behavior—it's about using power to dominate, intimidate, and control. In prison, I watched bullies operate daily. They weren't necessarily narcissists seeking admiration or Machiavellians building leverage. They were people who needed to feel powerful by making others feel powerless.

The scary part? Bullies exist everywhere—workplaces, families, social groups, even romantic relationships. And most people tolerate bullying far longer than they should because they've been taught that standing up to bullies "causes drama" or "makes things worse."

Pattern Recognition: Intimidation through volume, physical presence, or aggressive body language. Public humiliation disguised as "jokes" or "just being direct." Undermining your competence or confidence in front of others. Taking credit for your work while criticizing your contributions. Isolating you from support systems. Punishing you for successes that threaten their position. Creating fear-based compliance where people walk on eggshells around them.

In the workplace, bullies target competent people who pose a threat to their status. They'll sabotage your projects, exclude you from meetings, spread rumors about your performance, or set you up to fail with impossible deadlines or unclear expectations. They operate through fear—you comply not because you respect them but because you're afraid of what they'll do if you don't.

In families, bullies use emotional intimidation, guilt, shame, and the threat of withdrawal to control others. The parent who rages when challenged. The sibling who mocks and humiliates. The partner who uses the silent treatment as punishment. They create an atmosphere where everyone is managing their moods, walking carefully, sacrificing their own needs to avoid triggering an explosion.

Story Recognition: Narratives that frame all interactions as dominance contests—they're either winning or you're disrespecting them. Stories where they're always "just being honest" or "telling it like it is" when they're actually being cruel. Historical pattern of conflicts that escalated because others were "too sensitive" rather than because they were too aggressive. No acknowledgment of the impact of their behavior on others—if you're hurt, that's your weakness, not their responsibility.

Bullies tell stories where strength means never backing down, never apologizing, never showing vulnerability. They frame kindness as weakness and empathy as manipulation. In their narratives, the world is divided into dominators and the dominated, and they've chosen which side they'll be on.

Purpose Recognition: Need to feel superior by making others feel inferior. Identity built on power over rather than power with. Goals that require others to shrink so they can feel big. Excitement about winning conflicts rather than resolving them. Investment in maintaining hierarchy with themselves on top. Threatened by others' confidence, competence, or success.

The bully's purpose is dominance for its own sake. They don't want your resources like a Parasite. They don't want your admiration like a Predator. They don't want to manipulate you into serving their agenda like a Puppeteer. They want you to feel small so they can feel big. Your diminishment is their goal, not a means to another end.

The Prison Lesson About Bullies:
In prison, I learned three critical truths about bullies:

First truth: Bullies are fundamentally insecure. Every single one. They bully because they feel powerless in some core way, and making others feel powerless temporarily makes them feel powerful. Confident people don't need to dominate others. Secure people don't need to diminish others. The bully's aggression is always compensating for internal weakness.

Second truth: Bullies escalate until they meet resistance. They keep pushing boundaries, testing limits, increasing intensity until someone finally says "no more." Appeasement doesn't work. Trying to be nicer doesn't work. Attempting to avoid conflict doesn't work. The only thing that works is boundary enforcement with consequences.

Third truth: Bullies are cowards who target perceived weakness. In prison, they never went after people who looked like they'd fight back. They selected targets who seemed vulnerable, compliant, afraid. The moment you demonstrated you weren't an easy target—that there would be costs to bullying you—they moved on to someone else.

How to Handle Bullies Using the Guardian Protocol:

Immediate Response: The moment you identify bullying patterns, move the person to Circle 5. No second chances here. Bullying is intentional harm, and intentional harm disqualifies someone from access to your life. Period.

Document Everything: Bullies deny, minimize, and rewrite history. Keep detailed records of incidents—dates, times, what was said, who witnessed it. Screenshots of messages. Notes immediately after interactions. This isn't paranoia; it's protection. You'll need this evidence when you enforce consequences.

Set Clear Boundaries With Consequences: "When you speak to me that way, I end the conversation immediately." "If you take credit for my work again, I will cc leadership on all project communications." "The next time you humiliate me in public, I will formally report this behavior." Then follow through. Every single time. Bullies only respect boundaries backed by consequences.

Never Explain, Justify, or Defend: Bullies use your explanations as ammunition. "That's not acceptable" is a complete sentence. "I don't tolerate that treatment" needs no elaboration. "This conversation is over" requires no justification. State boundaries, enforce consequences, refuse engagement.

Get Witnesses and Allies: Bullies operate differently with an audience. They're more careful when they know others are watching and documenting. Build relationships with people who see what's happening. You're not alone—bullies leave a trail of other targets who will support you when you stand up.

Escalate When Necessary: If setting boundaries doesn't work, escalate. HR complaints for workplace bullies. Family interventions for family bullies. Legal action if needed. Bullies count on you not escalating because escalation brings consequences they want to avoid. Your willingness to escalate communicates that you're serious.

The Ultimate Bully Response: In some cases, the only effective response is complete extraction. No contact. Blocked numbers. Job changes if necessary. Family distance. Because here's the truth: some bullies won't stop until you remove yourself from their sphere of influence entirely. And that's not weakness—that's wisdom.

The Workplace Bully Specific Scenario:

You have a coworker or manager who publicly criticizes your work, takes credit for your ideas, excludes you from meetings, spreads rumors about your performance, or creates a hostile environment through intimidation and aggression.

The thirty-day protocol: Document every instance with dates, direct quotes, and witnesses. Simultaneously, begin building relationships with people outside their influence. Copy others on emails that previously were one-on-one. Create paper trails for all interactions. Start updating your resume and networking—not because you'll definitely leave, but because having options reduces their power over you.

The confrontation: Schedule a private meeting. Bring documentation. State clearly: "On [date], you [specific behavior]. On [date], you [specific behavior]. This pattern is unacceptable. Going forward, I expect [specific different behavior]. If this continues, I will [specific consequence—HR complaint, documentation to senior leadership, etc.]." Stay calm. Don't argue. Don't get emotional. State facts and consequences.

The follow-up: If behavior improves, cautiously remain in Circle 5 with high vigilance. If behavior continues or escalates, immediately execute your stated consequence. No empty threats. Bullies test whether you mean what you say.

The exit plan: Sometimes the healthiest choice is leaving. A toxic environment damages you daily. Your mental health, your confidence, your sense of self—all get eroded by sustained bullying. If the organization protects the bully or your attempts to set boundaries fail, leaving isn't giving up. It's protecting yourself. Your career will recover. Your peace of mind is invaluable.

The Family Bully Specific Scenario:

You have a family member—parent, sibling, extended relative—who uses rage, criticism, humiliation, guilt, or emotional intimidation to control family dynamics.

The recognition: Family bullies are the hardest to protect against because we're taught that family requires unconditional tolerance. "That's just how Dad is." "You know Mom has a temper." "Don't upset your brother." These narratives enable abuse by framing the bully's behavior as something everyone else must accommodate rather than something that's unacceptable.

The new narrative: "I love you AND I won't tolerate being treated this way" is a complete sentence. Love doesn't require accepting abuse. Family doesn't mean surrendering boundaries. You can honor the relationship while protecting yourself from harm.

The enforcement: Family bullies escalate when you set boundaries because they're losing control. Expect guilt trips: "After all I've done for you." Expect rage: "How dare you talk to me this way." Expect triangulation: They'll recruit other family members to pressure you. Expect punishment: Silent treatment, exclusion from events, turning others against you.

Stand firm anyway.

"I'm leaving now" when they start yelling. Following through when you say you'll hang up if they continue. Missing family events where they'll be present and hostile. Reducing contact to what you can handle emotionally. Moving them from Circle 2 to Circle 4 or 5 regardless of biology.

The long game: Some family bullies eventually respect boundaries once they realize you're serious. Others never change, and you have to decide how much contact you can maintain while protecting your peace. Both outcomes are okay. You're not responsible for teaching them how to treat people. You're only responsible for deciding what treatment you'll accept.

The Bully Mantra: *"Bullies rely on my silence, my fear, my desire to avoid conflict. The moment I document, set boundaries, and enforce consequences, their power disappears. I am not their victim. I am not their target. I am the guardian of my own peace, and bullies have no place in my life."*

The Critical Distinction:

Not all conflict is bullying. Not all criticism is bullying. Not all directness is bullying. The distinction is: Does this person want me to grow, or do they want me to shrink? Do they correct behavior to help me improve, or do they attack my character to make me feel small? Do they communicate with respect even when disagreeing, or do they use volume, intimidation, and humiliation to dominate?

Healthy people challenge you to become better. Bullies need you to feel worse so they can feel better. Once you see the difference, you'll never tolerate bullying again.

The Rapid Assessment Tools

These are practical tools you can use in real-time to assess someone's framework quickly and make informed decisions about access levels.

The PATTERNS Method (2-Minute Initial Scan)

Score each element 0-2 points:

- **P - Presence:** Are they here with you or performing for an audience? (2 = fully present, 0 = performing)

- **A - Attention:** Where does their focus consistently go? (2 = on connection, 0 = on self)

- **T - Treatment:** How do they treat those who can do nothing for them? (2 = with respect, 0 = with contempt)

- **T - Tempo:** Do they match natural rhythm or force their own? (2 = matches rhythm, 0 = imposes rhythm)

- **E - Energy:** Do you feel energized or drained in their presence? (2 = energized, 0 = drained)

- **R - Respect:** Do they honor boundaries or test them? (2 = honors, 0 = tests)

- **N - Nature:** Does their behavior feel natural or calculated? (2 = natural, 0 = calculated)

- **S - Stability:** Are they consistent or constantly shifting? (2 = consistent, 0 = shifting)

Scoring:

- 12-16 points: Potentially healthy framework, proceed with normal caution

- 8-11 points: Proceed with heightened awareness and slower access granting

- 0-7 points: Protect yourself immediately. Do not grant deeper access.

The STORIES Framework (5-Minute Story Analysis)

Listen to one story they tell and evaluate:

- **S - Self:** What role do they cast themselves in? (Hero/Victim/Villain)

- **T - Tone:** Is emotional tone appropriate to content? (Yes/No)

- **O - Others:** Do others exist as full people or props? (Full people/Props)

- **R - Responsibility:** Do they own their part or blame others? (Own/Blame)

- **I - Integrity:** Do details remain consistent? (Consistent/Shifting)

- **E - Emotion:** Is there genuine feeling or performance? (Genuine/Performed)

- **S - Service:** Do stories build connection or impression? (Connection/Impression)

Red flags in 3+ categories = Significant concern Red flags in 5+ categories = Dangerous personality

The PURPOSE Compass (10-Minute Direction Finding)

Have a conversation and observe:

- **P - Passion:** What genuinely excites them? (Creative or destructive?)

- **U - Underlying:** What need drives their behavior? (Connection or control?)

- **R - Resources:** Where do they invest time/energy/money? (Growth or extraction?)

- **P - People:** How do they use relationships? (For value or for supply?)

- **O - Outcomes:** What end results do they consistently create? (Building or burning?)

- **S - Sacrifice:** What will they give up, and for what? (Transcendent or survival?)

- **E - Endgame:** What's their ultimate destination? (Contribution or accumulation?)

This reveals whether their purposes are creative or destructive, contributive or extractive.

The Philosophy of Spiritual Sovereignty

Here's what nobody told you about dealing with toxic people: You don't need to justify your boundaries. You don't need to explain your distance. You don't need to prove their toxicity to anyone else. You only need to protect your sovereignty.

Every spiritual tradition throughout history has recognized this truth in different words:

- **Buddhism:** "Guard the doors of your senses"

- **Christianity:** "Above all else, guard your heart"

- **Islam:** "The believer is not bitten from the same hole twice"

- **Stoicism:** "You have power over your mind—not outside events"

But I'll put it in plain language: You are the bouncer at the nightclub of your soul. Your job isn't to rehabilitate the drunks—it's to keep them out.

The Four Laws of Spiritual Sovereignty

Law 1: The Permission Principle Nobody gets access to your deep self without earning it through demonstrated consistency of patterns, integrity of stories, and clarity of purposes. Access is not a right—it's a privilege. And privileges can be revoked.

Law 2: The Energy Equation Every relationship is either adding energy to your system or extracting it. There's no neutral. If you consistently feel drained after interactions, that's your soul telling you something. Listen.

Law 3: The Pattern Prophet People's patterns are prophecies of their future behavior. What they've done to others, they'll do to you. What they do in small things, they'll do in large things. Patterns don't lie—stories do.

Law 4: The Protection Priority Your first responsibility is to protect your own internal coherence. You can't save someone by letting them destroy you. You can't heal someone by letting them infect you. You can't lift someone by letting them pull you down.

The Guardian Mantras

The Morning Mantra: *"I am the guardian of my soul. I choose who enters, who stays, and who leaves. My patterns are precious, my stories are sacred, my purposes are protected. Today I will observe clearly, decide wisely, and protect courageously."*

The Boundary Mantra: *"No is a complete sentence. Distance is a valid choice. Protection is not paranoia. Discernment is not judgment. I honor my intuition."*

The Recognition Mantra: *"I see you. I see your patterns, your stories, your purposes. I honor your journey, but I protect my own. You have shown me who you are, and I believe you."*

The Release Mantra: *"I release you to your path as I protect my own. I wish you well from a distance. I choose coherence over attachment, growth over comfort, truth over harmony."*

The Five Circles of Access

Not everyone who shows concerning patterns needs complete elimination from your life. I use what I call The Five Circles of Access—a graduated system of relationship boundaries.

Circle 1 - Soul Access (2-3 people maximum) Reserved for people who've proven their integrated framework over years, through multiple crises, across many contexts. They get access to your deepest self—fears, dreams, vulnerabilities, authentic purposes.

Circle 2 - Heart Access (5-8 people) Close friends and family who've demonstrated consistent care and internal coherence. They get access to your emotions, your struggles, your authentic experience.

Circle 3 - Mind Access (15-25 people) Colleagues and community members who share your values and contribute to your purposes. They get access to your ideas, collaboration, and professional efforts.

Circle 4 - Social Access (50-100 people) Acquaintances and necessary contacts. They get your public self only—professional courtesy, surface pleasantness, but no personal information.

Circle 5 - No Access (Dark Triad individuals and energy vampires) People whose framework is fundamentally fragmented or toxic. They get nothing but minimum required by circumstance—minimal professional courtesy if absolutely necessary, otherwise complete distance.

The crucial insight: Most people assign circles randomly, giving soul access to people who've only earned social access, keeping energy vampires in Circle 2 out of guilt or obligation. This is how souls get corrupted.

The Extraction Process

When you identify someone who needs to be moved to Circle 5:

Week 1-2: The Fade: Gradually reduce response time, shorten interactions, become "busier," reduce emotional availability, stop initiating contact.

Week 3-4: The Boundary: State limits clearly but without justification: "I'm not available for that." "That doesn't work for me." "I need to focus on other priorities." Do not JADE (Justify, Argue, Defend, Explain).

Week 5-6: The Distance: Minimal required contact only, no personal information sharing, no emotional engagement, professional courtesy only, complete cutting of contact if necessary.

The Extraction Mantra: *"I don't need to explain my distance. I don't need to justify my boundaries. I don't need to prove my reasons. I need to protect my coherence. This is not cruelty—it's wisdom. This is not judgment—it's discernment. This is not selfishness—it's sovereignty."*

The Dangerous Compassion Trap

Here's something that might anger you, but I need to say it: Your compassion for toxic people is not noble if it enables their toxicity.

The most empathetic people are the favorite food of Dark Triad personalities. Your empathy is their weapon. Your compassion is their camouflage. Your desire to help is their highway into your life.

For years after leaving prison, I felt obligated to "save" others still trapped in that lifestyle. I let former associates crash at my place, lent money I'd never see again, gave chance after chance to people who saw my compassion as weakness.

One night, after someone I was "helping" robbed me and disappeared, my mentor asked me a question that changed everything: "Are you helping them, or are you helping yourself feel better about your past?"

The truth hit like a sledgehammer. My "compassion" was actually guilt. My "help" was actually enabling. My "kindness" was actually weakness dressed up as virtue.

True compassion includes boundaries. Real kindness includes saying no. Authentic love includes letting people experience the consequences of their choices.

The Compassion Paradox

The paradox is this: The more you protect your own internal coherence, the more you can genuinely help others. The stronger your boundaries, the deeper your compassion can run. The better you guard your soul, the more light you have to share.

But this requires accepting a hard truth: Some people don't want help. They want hosts. Some people aren't looking for growth. They're looking for supply. Some people aren't seeking healing. They're seeking targets.

And your job is not to save them. Your job is to save yourself first, so you have something genuine to offer those who actually want growth.

The Seven Deadly Myths About Reading People

Myth 1: "I shouldn't judge people "Truth: Judgment and discernment are different. Judgment says "you're bad." Discernment says "you're bad FOR ME." You have every right to discern who belongs in your life.

Myth 2: "Everyone deserves a second chance "Truth: Second chances are earned, not deserved. And some people are on their hundredth chance. Patterns matter more than promises.

Myth 3: "I should see the good in everyone "Truth: Seeing the good doesn't mean ignoring the dangerous. You can acknowledge someone's light while protecting yourself from their darkness.

Myth 4: "If I'm strong enough, toxic people can't hurt me "Truth: This is like saying "If I'm healthy enough, poison can't hurt me." Toxicity is toxic regardless of your strength. Strength means avoiding poison, not surviving it.

Myth 5: "They're only toxic because they're hurting "Truth: Hurt people hurt people, but that doesn't obligate you to be their victim. Their pain explains their behavior but doesn't excuse it.

Myth 6: "I can help them change" Truth: You can't change anyone who doesn't want to change. And Dark Triad individuals don't see themselves as needing change—they see others as needing manipulation.

Myth 7: "Cutting people off is cruel" Truth: Keeping toxic people in your life is cruel—to yourself, to those who genuinely care about you, and ultimately to the toxic person who needs consequences, not enabling.

The Freedom Formula

When you master the Guardian Protocol, something miraculous happens: You stop being afraid of people.

Not because you become hard or cynical, but because you become clear. You see people's patterns, understand their stories, recognize their purposes. The mystery disappears. The manipulation becomes visible. The games become obvious.

And from this clarity comes freedom:

- Freedom from wondering "what did I do wrong?" (Nothing. They're toxic.)

- Freedom from trying to fix the unfixable (Some people don't want fixing.)

- Freedom from guilt about boundaries (Protection isn't cruelty.)

- Freedom from toxic entanglements (You can walk away.)

- Freedom to invest in aligned relationships (Your energy goes where it grows.)

But most importantly, freedom to become who you're meant to be without the constant drain of misaligned relationships.

The Story of Two Futures

Let me paint you two pictures of your life five years from now.

Future One: You continue letting everyone into your life who knocks. You pride yourself on being "open" and "non-judgmental." You give chances to people who've shown you their fragmentation. You explain away red flags. You justify toxic patterns. You maintain relationships that drain you because ending them feels "mean."

In five years, you're exhausted. Your own internal framework is fragmented from constantly adapting to toxic people. Your patterns serve others' purposes. Your stories are about survival, not growth. Your purposes have shrunk to just getting through each day. You're successful maybe, but you're not alive. You're performing life, not living it.

Future Two: You become the guardian of your soul. You develop Guardian Sight. You trust your ability to read patterns, decode stories, recognize purposes. You place people in appropriate circles of access. You maintain boundaries without guilt. You invest deeply in integrated relationships while protecting yourself from toxic ones.

In five years, you're energized. Your internal framework shows strong coherence because you've protected it from corruption. Your patterns serve your authentic purposes. Your stories are about growth and contribution. Your purposes expand because you have energy to pursue them. You're not just successful—you're fully alive.

The difference between these futures isn't luck. It's not circumstances. It's not even talent. The difference is whether you take responsibility for who you let into your life.

The Ultimate Truth

Here's what I learned from those years locked up: The signs were always there. They're always there.

Research by Gigerenzer shows that intuition is actually "fast and frugal" heuristics—your brain processing thousands of micro-signals below conscious awareness. Studies on "thin-slicing" by Ambady and Rosenthal prove that accurate judgments about someone's character can be made in under thirty seconds.

You already have Guardian Sight. You've always had it. You've just been trained to ignore it.

Trained to be "nice" instead of discerning. Trained to give chances instead of enforcing boundaries. Trained to doubt your instincts instead of trusting them. Trained to explain away red flags instead of respecting them.

This chapter is your permission slip to trust what you see. To believe what people show you. To protect what matters. To choose who gets access to your soul.

Your Guardian Assignment

For the next 30 days, practice the Guardian Protocol on everyone you meet:

Week 1: Master the Thirty-Minute Surface Read. Use the PATTERNS method on every new person. Document what you observe. Notice how often your first impression proves correct.

Week 2: Apply the Thirty-Day Deep Dive to existing relationships. Create Pattern Maps for five people in your life. Use the STORIES framework and PURPOSE compass to evaluate their demonstrated character.

Week 3: Practice the Circle Assignment. Place everyone in your life into one of the Five Circles of Access based on demonstrated patterns, story integrity, and purpose clarity. Notice who's too close, who's too far, and who needs to be moved.

Week 4: Implement Protection Protocols. Practice the mantras daily. Enforce one new boundary with someone who's been violating your space. Move one toxic person to a more appropriate circle. Celebrate your sovereignty.

The Final Recognition

As I finish this chapter, I want you to understand something profound: Learning to read others' internal framework isn't about becoming suspicious or cynical. It's about becoming sovereign.

When you can see clearly, you can love deeply—because you're loving real people, not performances. When you can recognize toxicity, you can appreciate health—because you know the difference. When you can identify predators, you can celebrate protectors—because you've learned to distinguish between them.

Those years locked up taught me to see patterns, decode stories, and recognize purposes in ways most people never develop. The predators I studied showed me exactly what to look for. The manipulators revealed their methods. The parasites demonstrated their extraction techniques. And the rare integrated people—the ones whose patterns, stories, and purposes worked in harmony even in that brutal environment—showed me what authentic character looks like under the worst possible pressure.

I don't thank the predators for what they taught me. They destroyed lives and deserved every consequence they faced. But I learned from them. I learned that toxic people exist, that they're identifiable, and that I have the power to keep them out of my life.

You have that same power. You've always had it. The only question is whether you'll use it.

The choice is yours. Choose wisely. Your soul depends on it.

The Three Evaluation Scenarios for Real Life

Let me give you three practical scenarios showing exactly how to evaluate people's framework in the contexts that matter most to your actual life.

Scenario 1: The Workplace Colleague

You have a new team member who joins your department. Friendly, competent, seems great on the surface. Here's how to read them properly.

The Thirty-Minute Surface Read:

Watch how they treat the administrative assistant on their first day. Notice whether they introduce themselves to the janitor or just walk past. Observe how they interact with the security guard. These micro-interactions with people who can't advance their career tell you who they are when there's no strategic advantage to kindness.

Listen to the first three stories they tell in the break room. Are they always the hero who saved the day? Always the victim of unfair circumstances? Do their former colleagues exist as real people with motivations, or just as obstacles they had to overcome? Is there genuine feeling when they talk about why they left their last job, or just calculated positioning?

Notice what excites them in conversation. Do their eyes light up when discussing the actual work, or only when talking about advancement opportunities? What do they ask about—the team's dynamics and how they can contribute, or the office politics and who has power?

The Thirty-Day Deep Dive:

Create your Pattern Map. How do they behave Monday morning versus Friday afternoon? When a project goes well versus when there's a crisis? In front of the boss versus alone with peers? With senior colleagues versus junior staff?

Track their stories. Does the narrative about why they left their previous company stay consistent when they tell different people? Do the details shift based on what plays better with each audience? Do they take responsibility for any mistakes, or is everything always someone else's fault?

Watch the gap between claimed and demonstrated purposes. Do they say they value teamwork but consistently take solo credit? Do they talk about wanting to learn but never ask questions? Do they claim to care about quality but cut corners when nobody's watching?

The Crisis Observation:

When the first real deadline pressure hits or a project encounters problems, watch carefully. Do they problem-solve collaboratively or become controlling? Do they stay to help the team finish or leave at five regardless? Do they share credit in success and responsibility in failure, or claim victories and distribute blame?

Red Flags That Require Immediate Circle Adjustment:

If they take credit for others' work, that's Predator patterning—move them immediately to Circle 4 (Social Access only) and document everything in writing. If they create drama around minor issues and always need rescuing, that's Parasite patterning—enforce strict boundaries around your time and emotional energy. If they triangulate team members against each other and gather information asymmetrically, that's Puppeteer patterning—share nothing personal and trust nothing they tell you about others.

Circle Assignment:

If their framework shows genuine integration after thirty days—patterns consistent, stories honest, purposes clear—consider moving them to Circle 3 (Mind Access) for professional collaboration and trust. If concerning patterns emerge, keep them firmly in Circle 4 with professional courtesy only. If they show toxic traits, move to Circle 5 and interact only when absolutely necessary for work, always with witnesses or documentation.

Scenario 2: The Potential Romantic Partner

You've met someone you're attracted to. The chemistry is strong. Now comes the crucial part—reading their framework before your heart overrides your head.

The Thirty-Minute Surface Read (First Date):

How do they treat the server? This single interaction tells you more than an hour of conversation. Are they polite and patient, or demanding and dismissive? Do they say "please" and "thank you," or just bark orders? When the server makes a small mistake, do they respond with grace or irritation? This is your future treatment once the initial charm wears off.

What role do they play in the first three stories they tell? Are they always the innocent victim of crazy exes, terrible bosses, and unfair circumstances? That's a massive red flag—you'll be the next villain in their victim narrative. Do they share stories where they're sometimes wrong, sometimes learning, sometimes helped by others? That's healthy self-awareness.

Notice their attention patterns. Do they maintain eye contact when you're talking, or are their eyes scanning the room for someone better? Do they ask follow-up questions about what you share, or are they just waiting for their turn to talk? Do they put their phone away, or check it constantly? These micro-behaviors reveal whether they see you as a person to connect with or an option to evaluate.

Watch how they handle the small disappointments of a first date. The restaurant has a wait. The movie is sold out. It starts raining. Do they adapt with humor and flexibility, or complain and blame? Do they make it an adventure, or make you feel responsible for things outside your control?

The Thirty-Day Deep Dive (First Month):

Are they consistent across contexts? Meet their friends—do they treat you the same way in public as in private? See them stressed—do they stay emotionally stable or become someone unrecognizable? Observe them around family—are they the same person, or does a different personality emerge?

Do their stories about exes remain consistent? The first time they tell you why their last relationship ended, write it down. If you hear them tell someone else a month later and the story has shifted—different villain, different lesson, different facts—you're seeing story manipulation in real time. Healthy people have consistent narratives because they're telling the truth. Toxic people rewrite history based on audience.

Watch for the gap between words and actions. They say family is important—do they call their parents, remember birthdays, show up for family events? They claim to value health—do their patterns include exercise, good sleep, nourishing food? They talk about honesty—do they keep small commitments, tell you the truth about minor things, own their mistakes?

Most importantly, how do they respond when you say "no" to something small? When you can't meet up because you're busy. When you don't want to share something personal yet. When you need space or time alone. Do they respect your boundary graciously, or do they push, guilt, pressure, or punish?

The Crisis Observation:

Wait for the first real stress—they have a bad day at work, family drama emerges, they get sick, plans fall through. Do they reach for you for genuine support, or do they dump their emotional chaos on you expecting you to fix it? Do they take responsibility for their part in problems, or blame everyone else? Do they stay kind under pressure, or become mean?

Red Flags That Should End the Relationship Immediately:

Love bombing—excessive intensity, grand gestures, and "I love you" within weeks—is Predator patterning designed to create dependency. Run. Boundary violations that escalate—showing up uninvited, going through your phone, demanding passwords—is control masquerading as love. Leave. Isolation tactics that separate you from friends and family—"they don't really get you like I do"—is preparation for abuse. Exit.

Constant crisis and chaos where you're always rescuing them is Parasite patterning. Stories where every ex is "crazy" and they're always the victim is Predator warning. Gathering excessive information about you while sharing little about themselves is Puppeteer manipulation. Temperature swings from hot to cold without explanation is intermittent reinforcement creating addiction. Guilt or shame when you enforce any boundary is toxic control.

Any of these patterns mean: Move them immediately to Circle 5. End the relationship. Block if necessary. Do not give second chances. These patterns don't improve—they escalate.

Circle Assignment Timeline:

Do not grant Circle 2 (Heart Access) before at least six months of demonstrated consistency. Do not even consider Circle 1 (Soul Access) before two years of proven integration through multiple life seasons and stresses. At the first major red flag, move immediately to Circle 4 and slow everything down. At the second red flag, move to Circle 5 and end it. Your future self will thank you.

The Dating Mantra:

"Chemistry is not character. Intensity is not intimacy. Excitement is not integration. Take time. Observe patterns. Trust what you see. My future peace depends on present discernment."

Scenario 3: The Long-Time Friend or Family Member

This is the hardest scenario because history creates obligation, shared memories generate guilt, and family ties produce pressure to maintain access regardless of toxicity. But it's also the most important evaluation you'll do.

The Current State Pattern Documentation:

Over the next thirty days, honestly document the reality of this relationship. After each interaction, do you feel energized or drained? Not occasionally—consistently. Do they show up for you when you need support, or only when they need something from you? Do they celebrate your wins genuinely, or does your success seem to threaten them? Do they respect your boundaries, or guilt you for having them? Do they take responsibility for their part in conflicts, or is everything always your fault?

Write it down. Be honest. Your journal doesn't judge—it just records truth.

The Historical Story Analysis:

Look back over the years of this relationship. Has their narrative about you stayed consistent, or does it shift based on what they need? Do they tell stories where you're a full person with your own life, or are you just a supporting character in their drama? Have they ever acknowledged their role in past conflicts, or is it always you who has to apologize? When they share vulnerability, does it create genuine connection, or do they weaponize it to manipulate you?

Think about the last five times they told others about your relationship. What story do they tell? Are you cast as the good child who always helps, setting you up for continued extraction? Are you positioned as the problem, justifying their poor treatment of you? Are you described with pride as your own person, or as an extension of them?

The Long-Term Purpose Recognition:

Ask yourself with brutal honesty: What purpose do I serve in their life? Am I genuine relationship—someone they invest in mutually? Am I supply—someone who provides resources, validation, or service? Am I status—someone who makes them look good? Am I scapegoat—someone who takes blame for their problems?

Now flip it: What purpose do they serve in mine? Is it actual relationship built on demonstrated care? Or is it obligation, guilt, habit, or hope that they'll someday become who I wish they were?

The Hardest Truth:

Just because someone has been in your life for years—just because you share DNA or history—doesn't mean they've earned the circle they're currently in. Most people have parents in Circle 1 or 2 based purely on biology, siblings in Circle 2 based purely on growing up together, old friends in Circle 2 based purely on longevity.

But access should be based on demonstrated character, not duration or biology. Integration should be earned through consistent patterns, honest stories, and clear purposes—not assumed through relationship type.

The Circle Reassignment Process:

First, acknowledge the truth to yourself. Write it in your journal: "This relationship is draining me. The pattern is toxic. The framework is fragmented. I've been keeping them close out of guilt/obligation/hope, not because they've earned this access through demonstrated character."

Second, accept the grief. It's okay to mourn what you hoped they would be. It's okay to be sad that biology or history isn't enough. It's okay to feel loss even when the relationship was toxic—you're losing the fantasy of what it could have been.

Third, make the decision based on observed reality. Given their actual patterns, story integrity, and purpose demonstration, what circle do they actually belong in? Not where you wish they could be, but where their behavior has proven they should be.

Fourth, implement the change gradually. Use the Extraction Process if moving to Circle 5. If moving from Circle 1 or 2 to Circle 3 or 4, reduce contact frequency, decrease vulnerability sharing, and increase boundary enforcement.

Fifth, hold the boundary despite guilt, history, or pressure. They will likely escalate when they feel access being reduced. They may cry, rage, guilt-trip, recruit others to pressure you, promise to change. Hold firm. Patterns predict futures better than promises.

The Family Exception That Isn't:

Many people say: "But they're family. I can't just cut them off. Blood is thicker than water."

Truth: The full quote is "The blood of the covenant is thicker than the water of the womb"—meaning chosen bonds can be stronger than biological ones. Being family doesn't grant automatic access to your soul. You can love someone from Circle 4 or even Circle 5. You can maintain family connection without granting deep access to someone whose framework is toxic.

Christmas dinner? Attend if you choose. Deep emotional vulnerability? Absolutely not. Family gatherings? Show up for the people you care about. Late-night crisis calls? Boundary that immediately. Polite surface conversation? Sure. Access to your dreams, fears, and authentic self? Never.

The Reassignment Mantra:

"I honor what we were. I accept what we are. I choose what I need. History doesn't obligate me to sacrifice my present. Love doesn't require self-destruction. I can care from a distance. I can wish them well from Circle 4 or 5. This is wisdom, not cruelty. This is sovereignty, not selfishness. This is protection, not punishment."

The Daily Protection Practices

Once you've evaluated people and assigned appropriate circles, you need daily practices to maintain your sovereignty and protect your internal coherence.

Morning Protection Ritual:

Before your day begins, set your intention for guardian consciousness: "I am the guardian of my soul. Today I choose who gets access and at what level. My patterns are precious—they're creating my future. My stories are sacred—they're shaping my reality. My purposes are protected—they're defining my destiny. I will observe clearly, decide wisely, and protect courageously."

Touch your head: "What stories will I tell myself today?" Touch your heart: "What purposes will I serve today?" Touch your hands: "What patterns will I practice today?" This thirty-second ritual creates conscious integration before the world starts pulling you in different directions.

Midday Energy Check:

At lunch or midday, pause and assess your energy levels. Who have you interacted with today? Which interactions left you feeling energized, expanded, more yourself? Which interactions left you feeling drained, diminished, less than you were? Are your circles appropriately assigned based on these energy impacts?

If someone consistently drains you, they're in the wrong circle. Move them further out. If someone consistently energizes you and they're distant, consider moving them closer. Trust your nervous system—it knows before your mind can articulate.

Evening Boundary Review:

Before bed, reflect on any boundary violations that occurred today. Were any boundaries crossed? Did you enforce them or excuse them? What access adjustment is needed tomorrow? What protection practice would serve you?

Write it down. "Today [person] violated [boundary] by [specific behavior]. Tomorrow I will [specific consequence]." Vague intentions create vague results. Specific commitments create actual change.

Weekly Circle Audit:

Every Sunday evening, review your Five Circles. Is everyone still in the right circle based on recent behavior? Who needs to move closer because they've demonstrated consistent integration? Who needs to move further away because patterns have revealed toxicity? Who needs complete extraction because they've shown you clearly they're dangerous?

Make the adjustments. Update your journal. Recommit to your sovereignty.

Monthly Deep Assessment:

Once a month, do a comprehensive evaluation of your relational ecosystem. Pull out your Pattern Maps for key relationships. Review the documented evidence. Ask yourself: Are these relationships helping me build coherence between my patterns, stories, and purposes, or are they creating fragmentation?

Celebrate the healthy relationships—write gratitude for people who add light to your life. Grieve the toxic ones—acknowledge the loss of what you hoped they could be. Make any necessary major circle adjustments. Your life is too short and your soul is too valuable to waste on people who extract rather than contribute.

The Guardian's Oath

I want you to write this in your journal right now. Date it. Sign it. Mean it.

"I am the guardian of my soul. I decide who enters my life, who stays in my life, and who leaves my life.

This is not selfishness—this is sovereignty. This is not judgment—this is discernment. This is not cruelty—this is wisdom.

I will observe patterns without judgment but with clarity. I will trust what I see without apology or explanation. I will protect my internal coherence without guilt or hesitation. I will grant access based on demonstration, not declaration. I will maintain boundaries based on need, not obligation.

My patterns are precious—they're creating who I'm becoming. My stories are sacred—they're shaping my reality. My purposes are protected—they're defining my destiny.

I guard my soul like my life depends on it. Because it does."

The Path Forward

In the next chapter, we'll explore The Art of Conscious Change—how to transform your internal framework without overwhelming yourself, how to work with resistance rather than against it, and how to create lasting change rather than temporary modification.

You've learned to see clearly—to read patterns, decode stories, and recognize purposes in yourself and others. You've learned to protect yourself—to assign appropriate circles of access and maintain sovereign boundaries. Now you'll learn to evolve consciously—to change your own patterns, rewrite your own stories, and clarify your own purposes with precision and grace.

Because here's the truth: Protecting yourself from toxic people is only half the battle. The other half is becoming someone whose internal framework is so coherent, so integrated, so aligned that toxic people naturally repel from you while healthy people naturally gravitate toward you.

When your patterns, stories, and purposes work in harmony, you become magnetic to other integrated people and repellent to fragmented ones. You won't have to work as hard at the Guardian Protocol because your own coherence will do much of the filtering for you.

But building that coherence requires understanding the art of conscious change—the physics of transformation, the leverage points of identity, and the methods that actually work versus the ones that just waste time and energy.

You'll discover why dramatic change usually fails while one-degree shifts create lasting transformation. You'll learn to work with your resistance rather than fighting it. You'll understand how to change one thing completely rather than ten things partially.

But for now, sit with this truth: You have Guardian Sight. You have sovereign power. You have sacred responsibility.

The question isn't whether you can protect yourself. The question is whether you will.

Your soul is counting on you. Your future self is depending on you. Your purposes are waiting for the protection that allows them to flourish.

Choose wisely, guardian. Choose courageously. Choose consciously.

Your life—your real life, your authentic life, your integrated life—depends on it.

"The guardian doesn't guard out of fear—they guard out of love. Love for who they're becoming. Love for what they're building. Love for the purposes they serve. The guardian knows that protecting their internal coherence isn't selfish—it's the prerequisite for serving

others from overflow rather than depletion. Guard well, guardian. Your future self will thank you." —Mark Loudermilk

CHAPTER NINE

RECOGNIZING AND NURTURING HEALTHY RELATIONSHIPS IN OTHERS

"THE QUALITY OF YOUR LIFE IS DETERMINED BY THE QUALITY OF YOUR RELATIONSHIP WITH YOURSELF AND OTHERS. AND THE QUALITY OF YOUR RELATIONSHIPS IS DETERMINED BY THE QUALITY OF THE PEOPLE YOU CHOOSE TO BUILD WITH."

The Other Half of the Equation

In the last chapter, you learned the Guardian Protocol—how to identify toxic frameworks and protect yourself from predators, parasites, puppeteers, and bullies. You learned who to keep out.

But protection is only half the equation. The other half is attraction and cultivation—learning to recognize genuinely integrated people and building deep, aligned relationships with them.

Because here's what nobody tells you: **Once you clear the toxic people out of your life, you create space. And that space either fills with more toxicity, or it fills with genuine connection. The choice is yours.**

Most people spend their whole lives defending against the wrong people but never learning to recognize and nurture the right ones. They become so good at spotting red flags that they miss green lights. They're so skilled at building walls that they forget how to build bridges.

This chapter is about the other side of relational wisdom—recognizing health, attracting integration, and cultivating relationships that multiply your growth rather than drain your energy.

The Lesson From Marcus

Let me tell you about Marcus, a client who mastered the Guardian Protocol so well he ended up alone.

Marcus came to me two years after his divorce from a narcissistic partner who had nearly destroyed him financially and emotionally. He'd done the work—therapy, boundaries, Guardian training. He could spot a toxic person within five minutes of meeting them.

The problem? He could ONLY spot toxic people.

"I went on three dates last month," Marcus told me. "First woman talked too much about her ex—red flag, Parasite pattern. Second woman asked too many questions about my income—red flag, extraction purposes. Third woman complimented me excessively—red flag, love bombing."

"Were any of them actually problematic?" I asked.

"Well... no. But they COULD have been. Better safe than sorry, right?"

Marcus had become so hypervigilant about toxicity that he was rejecting healthy people for showing normal human imperfection. His Guardian Sight had turned into paranoid suspicion.

"Marcus," I said, "you've learned to see the darkness clearly. Now you need to learn to see the light."

What Marcus discovered—and what you need to understand—is that **healthy people aren't perfect people. They're authentic people. They show their struggles, their growth edges, their humanity. And that's not a red flag. That's a green light.**

The Five Integrated Archetypes

Just as there are toxic archetypes to avoid (Predator, Parasite, Puppeteer, Bully), there are healthy archetypes to recognize and attract. These are people whose patterns, stories, and purposes work in genuine harmony.

The Builder

Pattern Recognition: The Builder creates value wherever they go. Not through grand gestures but through consistent contribution. They leave meetings more productive than they found them. They leave conversations more insightful than they started them. They leave people more capable than before they met.

Watch how they approach problems—do they complain about what's broken or immediately start thinking about solutions? Do they wait for permission to improve things or do they just start building? Do they need credit for their contributions or is the contribution itself the reward?

Story Recognition: Builders tell stories about growth, learning, and collective achievement. They use "we" more than "I." They acknowledge the people who helped them succeed. They share failures as openly as successes because both taught them something valuable.

Their narratives aren't about dominating or extracting or controlling—they're about creating, contributing, and collaborating.

Purpose Recognition: The Builder's purpose is generative—they want to leave things better than they found them. They invest in long-term value over short-term gain. They build systems that work without them, teams that thrive independently, projects that outlast their involvement.

They get excited about other people's successes. They celebrate collaborative wins more than individual achievements. They measure impact not by what they personally gained but by what they collectively created.

How to Recognize Them:

- After interactions, you feel more capable, not less

- They ask "how can we make this work?" not "why won't this work?"

- They share credit freely and take responsibility readily

- They're more interested in solving problems than assigning blame

- They invest time in developing others without expecting immediate return

How to Nurture the Relationship:

- Collaborate on projects together—Builders thrive in co-creation

- Bring them problems to solve collectively, not just to dump

- Acknowledge their contributions specifically and publicly

- Reciprocate by building value in their lives

- Give them autonomy and trust—they deliver when trusted

The Mentor

Pattern Recognition: The Mentor invests in others' growth without need for control. They guide without dominating, teach without diminishing, challenge without crushing. They ask powerful questions more than they give definitive answers.

Watch how they respond when you succeed—do they celebrate genuinely or feel threatened? When you struggle, do they judge or guide? When you make mistakes, do they shame or teach?

Story Recognition: Mentors tell stories that illuminate principles rather than showcase themselves. Their narratives include their own failures and lessons learned. They speak about their mentors with gratitude and their mentees with pride.

They don't position themselves as having all answers—they position themselves as having useful questions and hard-won wisdom they're willing to share.

Purpose Recognition: The Mentor's purpose is developmental—they want to cultivate capability in others. They measure success not by how much they know but by how much others grow. They're genuinely fulfilled when their mentees surpass them.

They get excited about potential, not just performance. They see beyond current limitations to future capabilities. They invest in people others might overlook.

How to Recognize Them:

- They ask questions that make you think rather than telling you what to think

- They celebrate your growth even when it moves you beyond their guidance

- They challenge you to exceed what you think you're capable of

- They share wisdom freely without needing to be seen as wise

- They acknowledge their own ongoing learning and growth

How to Nurture the Relationship:

- Be coachable—Mentors invest where they see genuine openness to growth

- Apply what they teach and report results—they want to see impact

- Ask thoughtful questions—they thrive on depth of inquiry

- Acknowledge how they've influenced your development

- Eventually mentor others using what they taught you—that's the ultimate honor

The Companion

Pattern Recognition: The Companion shows up consistently through all seasons—not just the celebratory ones. They're present in crisis without making it about them. They offer support without needing to save you. They hold space without needing to fix you.

Watch for reciprocity—do they share vulnerability as well as receive it? Do they celebrate your wins as genuinely as you celebrate theirs? Do they maintain connection through busy seasons or only reach out when they need something?

Story Recognition: Companions tell stories where relationships matter more than achievements. They remember details about your life that you mentioned months ago.

They reference shared experiences with warmth. They speak about friendship as something you build, not something that just happens.

Their narratives demonstrate investment in others' wellbeing beyond what those others can provide in return.

Purpose Recognition: The Companion's purpose is relational—they value connection for its own sake, not as means to an end. They invest in friendships that may never provide professional networking benefit. They show up for people who can't advance their career.

They measure richness in relationships, not just resources. They prioritize presence over productivity. They understand that being there for someone is sometimes more valuable than doing something for someone.

How to Recognize Them:

- After difficult times, they check in consistently, not just once

- They remember and follow up on things you've shared

- They offer help before being asked and without strings attached

- They're as happy to listen as to talk

- They maintain friendships through geographic distance and life changes

How to Nurture the Relationship:

- Reciprocate the consistency—show up for them too

- Share authentically, not just surface pleasantries

- Create rituals—regular coffee, annual trips, monthly calls

- Acknowledge how much their friendship means specifically

- Introduce them to other quality people in your life

The Champion

Pattern Recognition: The Champion believes in you before you believe in yourself. They see potential where you see limitations. They challenge you to grow without making you feel inadequate. They hold you accountable to your own stated purposes without judgment.

Watch how they respond to your self-doubt—do they rescue you from it or challenge you through it? When you're succeeding, do they feel competitive or celebratory? When you're struggling, do they lower expectations or raise support?

Story Recognition: Champions tell stories that highlight growth edges and possibilities. They reframe your "I can't" into "you haven't yet." They remind you of past successes when you're drowning in current failures. They see patterns of capability you've forgotten.

Their narratives about you are more generous than your narratives about yourself, but grounded in evidence you've demonstrated.

Purpose Recognition: The Champion's purpose is elevating—they want to help others reach their highest potential. They're fulfilled not by being the best but by bringing out the best in others. They measure success by the people they've helped rise.

They get genuinely excited about your goals, sometimes more than their own. They invest time helping you strategize, prepare, and execute. They become your biggest advocate without needing recognition for the support.

How to Recognize Them:

- They remember your goals better than you do

- They call you out when you're playing small

- They celebrate your wins like they're their own

- They see capabilities in you that you don't yet see in yourself

- They offer accountability without judgment

How to Nurture the Relationship:

- Take action on what they help you see—Champions invest where they see movement

- Update them on progress—they're genuinely interested in your journey

- Receive their belief in you without diminishing it with self-deprecation

- Champion their dreams with equal enthusiasm

- Acknowledge specifically how they've helped you grow

The Mirror

Pattern Recognition: The Mirror reflects truth with love. They tell you what you need to hear, not what you want to hear. But they do it with care, not cruelty. They hold up reality without judgment, helping you see yourself more clearly.

Watch for the combination of honesty and compassion—do they speak hard truths gently? Do they point out blind spots without shaming? Do they deliver difficult feedback privately and supportively?

Story Recognition: Mirrors tell stories that include complexity and nuance. They don't need you to be the hero or the villain—they see you as fully human. They acknowledge your light and your shadow with equal acceptance.

Their narratives demonstrate that they've done their own inner work—they can see clearly in others because they've learned to see clearly in themselves.

Purpose Recognition: The Mirror's purpose is clarifying—they help others see truth they've been avoiding. They value authenticity over comfort. They believe real love includes real honesty, and that enabling someone's delusions isn't kindness.

They're willing to have difficult conversations others avoid. They care more about your growth than your approval. They'll risk the relationship to tell you what you need to hear.

How to Recognize Them:

- They tell you uncomfortable truths everyone else is too polite to mention

- They do it privately, kindly, and with specific examples

- They're equally honest about your strengths as your weaknesses

- They've clearly done deep work on themselves

- They can handle receiving honest feedback as well as giving it

How to Nurture the Relationship:

- Thank them for honesty even when it stings

- Don't punish them for truth-telling by withdrawing

- Ask for their perspective when you're stuck

- Reciprocate by reflecting truth to them

- Show them how their honesty has helped you grow

The Integrated Framework: What Healthy Looks Like

Before you can recognize integrated people, you need to understand what integration actually looks like across patterns, stories, and purposes.

Pattern Integration

Healthy people show remarkable consistency across contexts. They're the same person:
- Monday morning as Friday evening

- With subordinates as with superiors

- In public as in private

- Stressed as relaxed

- Winning as losing

This doesn't mean they're robots without emotional range. It means their core way of treating people, keeping commitments, and showing up remains stable regardless of circumstance.

Story Integration

Healthy people maintain narrative integrity:

- Their stories stay consistent across time and audience

- They acknowledge their role in both successes and failures

- They can hold complexity without needing simple villains

- They speak about others with nuance and respect

- They update their narratives based on new information without rewriting history

Purpose Integration

Healthy people demonstrate clear purposes through action:

- Their time and energy investments reflect stated values

- They make sacrifices consistent with claimed priorities

- They can articulate why they do what they do

- Their short-term decisions serve long-term aims

- Their purposes transcend pure self-interest

The Integration Test

When all three elements work together, you'll notice:

- **Energy exchange is mutual** - you both leave interactions energized

- **Growth is collaborative** - you challenge each other to improve

- **Support flows both ways** - neither person is always giving or taking

- **Conflict gets resolved** - disagreements lead to understanding, not recycling

- **Trust builds over time** - consistency creates safety

- **Authenticity is default** - neither person is performing

The Attraction Principle

Here's something profound: **Once you build strong internal integration, you naturally attract other integrated people and repel toxic ones.**

It's not magic. It's magnetism.

When your own patterns, stories, and purposes work in harmony, you emit a frequency that resonates with others operating at that same level. Integrated people recognize integration in others. It's like a tuning fork—when one vibrates at a certain frequency, others nearby start vibrating at the same frequency.

Conversely, toxic people find integrated people boring, threatening, or incomprehensible. You're not providing the drama, chaos, or supply they're seeking. Your boundaries feel too firm. Your authenticity feels too exposing. Your purposes don't align with their extraction.

This is why the work you do on yourself in Chapters 4-7 (building your own integration) is inseparable from the work of building healthy relationships. You can't consistently attract what you haven't become.

The Cultivation Process

Recognizing healthy frameworks is one thing. Nurturing them into deep, lasting relationships is another. Here's how to cultivate aligned relationships intentionally.

Stage One: The Slow Reveal (Months 1-3)

Don't rush intimacy. Integrated relationships build gradually through demonstrated consistency.

What to do:

- Spend time together in various contexts (not just coffee chats)

- Observe how they handle small stresses and minor wins

- Share vulnerability incrementally, watching how they handle it

- Notice whether they reciprocate appropriate levels of openness

- Watch for pattern consistency across different situations

What to watch for:

- Do they show up when they say they will?

- Do their stories stay consistent?

- Do they respect boundaries you set?

- Do they follow through on commitments?

- Do you feel more yourself or less yourself around them?

Stage Two: The Depth Test (Months 3-6)

Once initial patterns look promising, go deeper.

What to do:

- Have conversations about values, purposes, what matters most

- Collaborate on something together (project, problem-solving, shared experience)

- Observe how they handle disagreement or disappointment

- Share something genuinely difficult or vulnerable

- See how they respond to your success and your struggle

What to watch for:

- Can they handle depth without drama?

- Do they maintain boundaries while being present?

- Can they celebrate your wins without competition?

- Can they support your struggles without trying to fix you?

- Do they bring wisdom without being preachy?

Stage Three: The Integration (Months 6-12)

If they've demonstrated consistent integration, begin building real depth.

What to do:

- Create regular rhythms (weekly calls, monthly dinners, quarterly adventures)

- Introduce them to other important people in your life

- Be someone they can count on and let them be someone you count on

- Have the difficult conversations when needed

- Build shared history through experiences and rituals

What to watch for:

- Does trust deepen naturally over time?

- Can the relationship handle conflict and emerge stronger?

- Do you both invest equally in maintaining connection?

- Does the relationship add to both your lives without drain?

- Can you be fully authentic without performance?

Stage Four: The Long Game (Year 2+)

True aligned relationships are built over years, not months.

What to do:

- Weather seasons together—joy and sorrow, success and failure

- Maintain consistency even through busy periods and geographic distance

- Continue investing in the relationship's growth and depth

- Acknowledge explicitly what the relationship means to you

- Become someone whose presence helps them build greater integration

What to watch for:

- Does the relationship deepen or plateau?

- Can it handle life changes (career shifts, relationships, moves)?

- Do you both continue growing individually and together?

- Is there genuine mutual investment?

- Does the friendship make both your lives genuinely better?

The Reciprocity Requirement

Healthy relationships require reciprocity—mutual investment, balanced exchange, shared vulnerability. But reciprocity doesn't mean identical. It means equitable.

What Reciprocity Looks Like:

In Support:

- Sometimes you're the supporter, sometimes the supported

- Both people show up in crisis without keeping score

- Asking for help is as comfortable as offering it

- Neither person always plays savior or victim

In Vulnerability:

- Both people share authentically at appropriate depths

- Risk is matched—if you share something difficult, they reciprocate

- Neither person uses vulnerability as manipulation

- Authenticity flows both directions

In Growth:

- Both people challenge each other to improve

- Both people celebrate the other's development

- Neither person needs the other to stay small

- Growth is collaborative, not competitive

In Energy:

- After most interactions, both feel energized

- Investment levels feel balanced over time

- Neither person consistently drains the other

- The relationship adds to both lives

What Reciprocity Doesn't Look Like:

The Imbalanced Supporter:

- You're always helping, they're always needing help

- Your problems get minimized while theirs get center stage

- You feel drained after interactions while they feel energized

- Taking is easy for them but giving is rare

The Conditional Friend:

- They're present when life is good but absent when it's hard

- They celebrate with you but can't sit in difficulty with you

- They reach out when they need something but disappear otherwise

- The friendship serves their purposes but not yours

The Competitive Companion:

- Your success threatens rather than celebrates them

- They need to one-up your stories

- Your growth makes them insecure

- They can support you through failure but not through triumph

When reciprocity is genuinely missing after giving the relationship adequate time to develop, it's not an aligned relationship. It's an extraction with better packaging.

The Integration Invitation

Here's something beautiful: **The best way to build aligned relationships is to become an integrated person worth building with.**

When you:

- Build clear patterns that demonstrate your values

- Tell honest stories that reflect real growth

- Serve purposes that transcend self-interest

You become someone other integrated people want to be around.

This means:

Show up consistently. Be the person others can count on. Keep your commitments. Follow through on what you say. Be present when you're present.

Share authentically. Don't perform perfection. Share your struggles and growth edges. Be real about where you're learning. Vulnerability is the currency of genuine connection.

Celebrate others genuinely. Make others' wins about them, not about you. Be the person who's genuinely happy when good things happen to people you care about.

Challenge with love. Care enough to tell truth, skilled enough to tell it kindly. Be someone who helps others see their blind spots without shaming them for having them.

Invest without scorekeeping. Give without immediately expecting return. Trust that reciprocity balances over time in healthy relationships. Be generous with time, attention, and support.

Maintain boundaries gracefully. Protection and connection aren't opposites. You can have deep relationships while maintaining healthy boundaries. In fact, boundaries make depth possible.

Keep growing. Don't stagnate. Integrated people want to be around others who are actively developing. Your growth inspires their growth and vice versa.

The Green Flags Checklist

Just as you learned red flags in Chapter 8, here are the green flags that signal someone is worth building with:

Immediate Green Flags (First Month):

- ☐ Treats service workers and strangers with respect

- ☐ Speaks about others (including exes) with nuance, not vilification

- ☐ Takes responsibility for their part in conflicts

- ☐ Can laugh at themselves without self-deprecation

- ☐ Asks thoughtful questions and actually listens to answers

- ☐ Shows genuine interest in understanding your perspective

- ☐ Maintains appropriate boundaries early on

- ☐ Follows through on small commitments

Developing Green Flags (Months 2-6):

- ☐ Stories stay consistent across contexts and time

- ☐ Can handle disagreement without drama or withdrawal

- ☐ Celebrates your wins without competition

- ☐ Supports your struggles without trying to fix you

- ☐ Shares vulnerability appropriately and reciprocally

- ☐ Demonstrates growth mindset about their own development

- ☐ Makes time for the friendship without making it feel like obligation

- ☐ Respects your other relationships and commitments

Long-Term Green Flags (6+ Months):

- ☐ Maintains consistency through various life seasons

- ☐ The relationship deepens naturally over time

- ☐ Conflict resolution leads to greater understanding

- ☐ Both people continue investing in the connection

- ☐ Trust builds through demonstrated reliability

- ☐ The friendship enriches both lives without drain

- ☐ You can be fully authentic without performance

- ☐ The relationship makes you want to be better without making you feel inadequate

The Circle Promotion System

Remember the Five Circles of Access from Chapter 8? Here's how to thoughtfully move people closer as they demonstrate integration:

From Circle 4 (Social Access) to Circle 3 (Mind Access):

- Demonstrated reliability over 3+ months

- Respectful interactions across multiple contexts

- Purposes that don't conflict with yours

- Willingness to collaborate professionally

From Circle 3 (Mind Access) to Circle 2 (Heart Access):

- Demonstrated integrity over 6+ months

- Appropriate vulnerability and reciprocity

- Celebration of your growth and wins

- Support during difficulty without agenda

From Circle 2 (Heart Access) to Circle 1 (Soul Access):

- Demonstrated consistency over 2+ years

- Multiple crisis navigations together showing their true character

- Deep mutual investment in each other's wellbeing

- Complete trust in their intentions and integrity

Never rush this progression. Circle 1 is reserved for 2-3 people maximum who have proven themselves through time, crisis, and consistency. Most people in your life should remain in Circles 3-4. That's not a limitation—it's wisdom.

Your Aligned Relationships Assignment

For the next 30 days, practice recognizing and nurturing healthy frameworks:

Week 1: The Audit

- List everyone currently in your life across all five circles

- Using the green flags checklist, identify who shows genuine integration

- Notice whether you have ANY integrated people in Circles 1-2

- Acknowledge if you've been so focused on avoiding toxic people that you haven't been cultivating healthy ones

Week 2: The Recognition

- Watch for the five integrated archetypes in your existing relationships

- Document specific examples of Builder, Mentor, Companion, Champion, or Mirror behaviors

- Notice who energizes versus drains you

- Identify one relationship that deserves deeper investment

Week 3: The Cultivation

- Reach out to one integrated person you've been underinvesting in

- Create a specific plan for deepening that relationship (regular coffee, monthly call, etc.)

- Practice reciprocity—don't just take, actively give

- Share authentically and notice how they respond

Week 4: The Invitation

- Become the kind of person integrated people want to be around

- Practice the integration invitation principles daily

- Notice what changes in your relational ecosystem

- Celebrate the healthy connections you're building

The Path Forward

In the next chapter, we'll explore The Art of Conscious Change—how to transform your own internal framework, work with resistance rather than against it, and create lasting change in your patterns, stories, and purposes.

Because here's the ultimate truth about relationships: **You attract who you are, not who you want.**

The work you do on your own integration directly determines the quality of relationships you can build. As you become more coherent internally, you'll naturally attract more coherent people. As you develop your patterns, stories, and purposes, you'll resonate with others doing the same work.

The Guardian Protocol taught you who to keep out. This chapter taught you who to let in. The next chapter will teach you how to become someone worth letting in.

Your aligned relationships are waiting. But first, you have to become someone capable of building them.

"The relationships that transform your life aren't the ones that fill your time—they're the ones that multiply your growth. Choose wisely. Invest deeply. Build slowly. And watch your life transform through the quality of the people you choose to journey with."

Chapter Ten

THE ART OF CONSCIOUS CHANGE

"Change is inevitable. Conscious change is a choice. The difference between the two is the difference between being shaped by life and shaping your life."

The Man Who Changed Everything by Changing Nothing

Thomas Riley was the kind of man who bought every self-help book published. His apartment in Boston was a monument to attempted transformation---shelves groaning with titles promising new lives in 30 days, walls covered with motivational posters, notebooks filled with goals he'd never pursued, gym memberships he'd never used.

By the time Thomas came to see me, he'd tried everything. Twice.

"I've done it all," he said, slumping into the chair across from me. "Meditation retreats, life coaches, therapy, journaling, cold showers, intermittent fasting, affirmations, vision boards. I even paid $10,000 for a weekend with a guru who made us walk on hot coals."
"And?" I asked.

"And I'm still the same fucking person I was five years ago. Maybe worse, because now I know exactly how many ways I can fail to change."

Thomas had fallen into what I call **The Change Trap**---the belief that transformation requires dramatic action, extreme measures, and superhuman willpower. He'd been trying to revolutionize his entire existence overnight, which is like trying to turn an ocean liner by jumping off the deck and pushing.

"Thomas," I said, "what if I told you that you've been doing change backward? What if the secret isn't doing more, but doing less---but doing that less with complete consciousness?"

He laughed bitterly. "Great, another approach to fail at."

"No," I said. "This time, we're going to change everything by changing almost nothing. But we're going to change that almost nothing so consciously that it transforms everything else."

The transformation that followed challenged everything I thought I knew about change.

The Physics of Personal Change

Before we dive into Thomas's story, you need to understand something that took me twenty years to learn: **Personal change follows the same laws as physical change. And in physics, the smallest forces, applied at the right points, create the largest transformations.**

Think about a massive steel door, hundreds of pounds, impossible to move by pushing against its center. But put your finger on the edge, apply gentle pressure, and it swings open. The door didn't become lighter. You just found the leverage point.

Your TOS works the same way. You have leverage points---small changes that create cascade effects throughout your entire system. Most people exhaust themselves pushing against the center of their problems. The art of conscious change is finding where to place your finger.

The Three Leverage Points of Your TOS:

The Pattern Lever: Change one keystone pattern, and dozens of other patterns reorganize around it. When you change your morning routine, you change your energy, which changes your decisions, which changes your results, which changes your identity.

The Story Lever: Update one core story, and your entire narrative framework shifts. When you change from "I'm not good enough" to "I'm learning," every experience gets reinterpreted through a new lens.

The Purpose Lever: Clarify one authentic purpose, and your entire motivational system realigns. When you find a purpose that truly matters to you, patterns that seemed impossible become automatic.

The art isn't knowing these leverage points exist---it's knowing which one to pull first.

The Surgeon's Wisdom

Let me tell you about Dr. Jennifer Martinez, a heart surgeon who taught me more about change in one conversation than most books teach in three hundred pages.

"When I operate," she said, "I don't restructure the entire chest cavity. I make the smallest possible incision, fix the specific problem, and let the body's natural healing systems do the rest. Most failed surgeries happen when surgeons try to fix too much at once."

She paused, then added something that transformed how I think about change forever:

"The body wants to heal. It's designed to heal. My job isn't to heal it---it's to remove what's blocking the healing and make one precise correction that allows natural recovery to begin."

Your psyche works the same way. You're designed to grow, evolve, and heal. The art of conscious change isn't forcing transformation---it's removing what's blocking it and making one precise adjustment that allows natural evolution to begin.

The Change Paradox That Changes Everything

Nobody tells you this about personal transformation: **The harder you try to change, the more you reinforce what you're trying to change.**

It's like quicksand. The more you struggle, the deeper you sink. The more you fight against a pattern, the more attention you give it, the more neural pathways you strengthen around it.

This is why Thomas had failed so spectacularly. Every dramatic attempt at change was actually an elaborate form of resistance. He was so focused on what he didn't want to be that he kept recreating it.

Watch what happens in your mind when you try NOT to think about a pink elephant. The very effort to not think about it requires you to think about it first to know what not to think about.

The same thing happens with patterns you're trying to break. "I won't check my phone first thing in the morning" requires you to think about checking your phone. "I won't eat junk food" requires you to think about junk food. "I won't procrastinate" focuses your attention on procrastination.

This is why willpower fails. You're using energy to resist instead of redirect. You're pushing against instead of flowing toward.

The Four Stages of Conscious Change

After studying thousands of successful transformations, I've identified four stages that everyone passes through. Most people get stuck in Stage 1 or exhaust themselves in Stage 2. The art is moving gracefully through all four.

Stage 1: Unconscious Imprisonment

"You Don't Know What You Don't Know"

This is where most people live most of their lives. Your patterns run automatically, your stories feel like truth, your purposes were chosen by others. You're not even aware there's a prison, let alone looking for escape.

The tragedy of this stage isn't the imprisonment---it's the comfort. When you don't know you're in a cage, the bars feel like home.

The Exit Door: Something has to shake you awake. Sometimes it's crisis---divorce, job loss, health scare. Sometimes it's inspiration---a book, a conversation, a moment of clarity. Sometimes it's just exhaustion from the weight of living unconsciously.

Stage 2: Conscious Incompetence

"The Painful Awakening"

This is where Thomas lived---aware of everything wrong but unable to fix it. You see your limiting patterns but can't stop them. You recognize your false stories but still believe them. You know your purposes are borrowed but can't find your own.

This is the most dangerous stage because awareness without ability creates suffering. You're awake in the prison but don't have the keys. Many people retreat back to Stage 1 because unconscious imprisonment feels better than conscious captivity.

The Exit Door: Stop trying to change everything. Choose one small thing you CAN change and change it completely. Build evidence that change is possible.

Stage 3: Conscious Competence

"The Effort Stage"

This is where real change happens, but it requires constant attention. You can choose new patterns but have to think about them. You can tell new stories but have to remind yourself they're true. You can serve new purposes but need regular reconnection to them.

Everything feels effortful because you're manually overriding years of automatic programming. It's like learning to drive---you have to think about every action.

The Exit Door: Repetition with awareness. Not mindless repetition, but conscious practice. Each repetition should include a moment of recognition: "I'm choosing this. This is who I'm becoming."

Stage 4: Unconscious Competence

"The New Normal"

This is the promised land---your new patterns run automatically, your new stories feel like truth, your new purposes pull you forward naturally. What once required massive effort now happens without thinking.

But there's a twist: This isn't the end. It's a new beginning. Because once you've integrated one change, you're ready for the next level of growth. Stage 4 in one area becomes Stage 1 in another.

The Continual Door: Regular review and renewal. What got you here won't get you there. Today's Stage 4 is tomorrow's Stage 1.

Thomas's Transformation: The Power of One

Back to Thomas, sitting in my office, defeated by five years of failed transformation attempts.

"Thomas," I said, "we're going to try something different. For the next 30 days, you're going to change exactly one thing. Not ten things, not five things, not even two things.

One thing."

"That's it?" he asked, suspicious.

"That's it. But here's the catch---you're going to change it with complete consciousness. Every single day, without exception, with total awareness."

"What's the one thing?"

"You tell me. Look at your TOS. Which single change would affect everything else? What's your highest leverage point?"

Thomas thought for a moment. "My morning routine is chaos. I hit snooze five times, scroll my phone in bed, rush through everything, and start every day already behind."

"Perfect. What's ONE change you could make to your morning?"

"I could stop hitting snooze."

"Too vague. Be specific."

"I could get up at 6 AM without hitting snooze."

"Still missing something. WHY would you get up without hitting snooze?"

This is where Thomas had his first breakthrough. He sat quietly for almost a minute, then said:

"Because every time I hit snooze, I'm telling myself my word doesn't matter. I'm starting the day by breaking a promise to myself. That's... that's actually why nothing else changes. I don't trust myself to follow through because I prove every morning that I can't."

There it was---the leverage point. Not the pattern itself, but what the pattern represented. Thomas didn't need to change his morning routine. He needed to rebuild trust with himself. The morning was just where he'd practice.

The One-Degree Method

Thomas discovered what I call **The One-Degree Method**. If you change your direction by just one degree, it seems like nothing at first. After one step, you're basically in the same place. After ten steps, barely noticeable. But after a thousand steps? You're in a completely different location.

Most people try to change direction by 180 degrees---complete reversal, total transformation, radical reinvention. This requires massive energy, creates massive resistance, and usually results in massive failure.

But one degree? One degree is sustainable. One degree is achievable. One degree doesn't trigger your system's resistance mechanisms.

Here's the formula:

1. Choose one pattern, story, or purpose to shift

2. Change it by the smallest meaningful amount

3. Practice that change with complete consciousness

4. Let the ripple effects spread naturally

5. Only add another degree when the first is automatic

Thomas chose his one degree: getting up at 6 AM without hitting snooze. That's it. He didn't add exercise, meditation, journaling, or cold showers. Just that one conscious choice, every morning, no matter what.

The Resistance Roster: Your Internal Saboteurs

As you begin conscious change, you'll meet resistance. Not external resistance---internal resistance. These are the voices, feelings, and forces that have kept you stuck. Know them by name:

The Comfort Keeper

"This feels wrong. Go back to what you know."

This voice evolved to keep you safe, but safety and growth live in different neighborhoods. The Comfort Keeper interprets all change as danger, all growth as threat.

How to work with it: Thank it for trying to protect you, then remind it that discomfort isn't danger---it's growth.

The Perfectionist

"If you can't do it perfectly, don't do it at all."

This voice pretends to have high standards but is actually terrified of judgment. It would rather you do nothing than risk doing something imperfectly.

How to work with it: Aim for "good enough" instead of perfect. Progress beats perfection every time.

The Historian

"You've tried this before. Remember how it ended?"

This voice has a photographic memory for every failure but amnesia for every success. It uses your past as evidence for your future.

How to work with it: Remind it that past attempts were practice, not prediction. You're not the same person who failed before.

The Critic

"Who do you think you are? People like you don't change."

This voice sounds like truth but is actually fear. It uses shame as a weapon to keep you small.

How to work with it: Ask it, "According to whom?" Usually, you'll find it's quoting someone from your past who had their own limitations.

The Negotiator

"Just this once won't matter. You can start again tomorrow."

This voice seems reasonable but is actually insidious. It knows that breaking your commitment once makes it easier to break it again.

How to work with it: Remind it that every choice matters because every choice is practice for the next choice.

The Compound Effect of Conscious Change

Week 1 of Thomas's experiment was hell. Every fiber of his being wanted to hit snooze. His bed felt like it had gravitational pull. His resistance voices performed a symphony of objections.

But Thomas had one advantage: he understood what was really happening. This wasn't about waking up. This was about integrity. Every morning he got up without hitting snooze, he was practicing keeping his word to himself.

Week 2 was slightly easier. Not easy---easier. The voices were still there, but quieter. Getting up at 6 AM was becoming possible, even if not pleasant.

Week 3 brought the first ripple effects. Because Thomas was up earlier, he wasn't rushed. Because he wasn't rushed, he made better breakfast choices. Because he ate better, he had more energy. Because he had more energy, he was more productive. Because he was more productive, he felt better about himself.

He hadn't tried to change any of these things. They changed naturally because he changed the one thing that mattered most---his relationship with his own word.

Week 4 brought revelation. Thomas called me, and I could hear something different in his voice. "It's not about the morning anymore," he said. "Every time I keep my word to myself about waking up, I trust myself a little more. And because I trust myself more, I'm making bolder commitments in other areas. Not because I'm trying to, but because I believe I'll follow through."

This is the compound effect of conscious change. One small change, made with complete awareness, creates a cascade of natural transformations.

The Story Update Protocol

Three months into his morning practice, Thomas hit a wall. He was getting up at 6 AM consistently, but something felt off.

"I'm doing it," he said, "but I hate it. Every morning feels like punishment."

"What story are you telling yourself about getting up early?" I asked.

"That I have to. That this is what disciplined people do. That I'm forcing myself to be someone I'm not."

"What if you told a different story?"

"Like what?"

"Like you GET to wake up early. Like this is your sacred time before the world starts demanding things from you. Like you're not forcing yourself to be someone else---you're finally becoming who you really are."

Thomas looked skeptical. "That's just positive thinking bullshit."

"No," I said. "It's choosing which true story to tell. It IS true that you have to wake up early if you want to keep your word. It's ALSO true that you get to wake up early because you're alive and capable of choice. Both stories are factually accurate. Which one serves you?"

This is the art of story updating---not replacing truth with fantasy, but choosing which truth to emphasize.

Thomas experimented with the new story. Instead of "I have to wake up," he started thinking "I get to wake up." Instead of "This is hard," he thought "This is sacred." Instead of "I'm not a morning person," he thought "I'm becoming someone who owns their mornings."

Same pattern. Different story. Revolutionary different experience.

The Purpose Clarification Process

Six months in, Thomas had transformed his mornings, updated his stories, and built tremendous self-trust. But something was still missing.

"I'm doing everything right," he said, "but I don't know why I'm doing it. I wake up early, but for what? I'm disciplined, but toward what end?"

Thomas had changed his patterns and stories but hadn't clarified his purpose. He was driving a perfectly tuned car with no destination.

"What would make all this effort worthwhile?" I asked.

"I don't know. Success, I guess?"

"Whose definition of success?"

"I... I don't know."

This is where most people get stuck. They master the mechanics of change but miss the meaning. They become efficient at going nowhere important.

"Thomas, forget what you should want. Forget what sounds good. If you could only be remembered for one thing, what would it be?"

Long silence. Then, quietly: "I want to be remembered as someone who helped kids believe in themselves. Kids who are like I was---lost, angry, convinced they don't matter."

"And are your current changes serving that purpose?"

For the first time in our work together, Thomas cried. "No. I'm just becoming a more disciplined version of someone living for himself."

"So what needs to change?"

"Everything. And nothing. I need to keep my patterns but redirect them toward something that matters."

The Integration Initiative

Thomas's next evolution was beautiful to watch. He kept waking up at 6 AM, but now he used that time to develop a mentoring program for at-risk youth. Same pattern, new purpose, transformed meaning.

He updated his stories from "I'm becoming disciplined" to "I'm becoming someone who can be trusted by kids who can't trust anyone." Same growth, new context, deeper significance.

He brought his patterns into harmony with his purpose. He started volunteering at a youth center. He began studying child psychology. He developed workshops on building self-trust---teaching kids what he'd learned about keeping promises to yourself.

This is integration---when your patterns serve your purpose, your stories support your patterns, and your purpose gives meaning to your stories.

The Seven Principles of Conscious Change

After working with thousands of people like Thomas, I've distilled conscious change into seven principles:

Principle 1: Start With Why, Not How

Most people obsess over how to change but never clarify why they want to change. Without a compelling why, no how will sustain you through resistance.

Principle 2: Change One Thing Completely

Rather than changing ten things partially, change one thing totally. Complete change in one area creates confidence for change in all areas.

Principle 3: Make the Unconscious Conscious

You can't change what you're not aware of. Bring your automatic patterns, hidden stories, and inherited purposes into conscious awareness.

Principle 4: Choose Progress Over Perfection

Perfection is paralysis disguised as standards. Progress is movement toward who you're becoming. Choose movement.

Principle 5: Work With Resistance, Not Against It

Resistance is information. It shows you what matters, what scares you, what needs attention. Listen to it, learn from it, then move through it.

Principle 6: Track the Process, Not Just the Outcome

Outcomes are often delayed and influenced by factors outside your control. Track whether you're doing the work, not just whether the work is working.

Principle 7: Celebrate Small Wins

Your brain releases dopamine when you acknowledge progress. This literally rewires your neural pathways to support continued change. Celebration isn't indulgence---it's neuroscience.

The Change Artist's Palette

Think of yourself as an artist and your life as your canvas. You have three primary colors to work with:

Pattern (Blue): The consistent actions that create the structure of your days **Story (Yellow):** The narratives that color your interpretation of experience **Purpose (Red):** The passion that provides energy and direction

When you mix:

- Pattern + Story = Habit (Blue + Yellow = Green)

- Story + Purpose = Motivation (Yellow + Red = Orange)

- Purpose + Pattern = Discipline (Red + Blue = Purple)

- All three together = Transformation (White light)

Most people try to paint their entire life with one color. They focus only on patterns (behaviorists), only on stories (cognitivists), or only on purpose (existentialists). But masterpieces require all three colors, mixed consciously.

The Breakthrough Question Sequence

When you're stuck in change, ask yourself these questions in order:

1. **What am I pretending not to know?** (This reveals unconscious awareness)

2. **What story am I telling myself about why I can't change?** (This exposes limiting narratives)

3. **What pattern would I need to change first?** (This identifies the leverage point)

4. **What purpose would make this change inevitable?** (This finds the motivational fuel)

5. **What's the smallest step I can take right now?** (This bypasses overwhelm)

6. **How will I know when I've succeeded?** (This creates clear targets)

7. **Who will I become when this change is complete?** (This connects change to identity)

The Warning I Wish Someone Had Given Me

Something nobody tells you about conscious change: **It will cost you relationships.**

Not because you become worse---because you become different. The people who knew the old you will unconsciously try to pull you back. Not from malice, but from comfort. Your change threatens their stability.

Thomas lost friends who were invested in him being the guy who talked about change but never achieved it. His transformation made them uncomfortable with their own stagnation.

He lost his girlfriend, who was attracted to his potential but threatened by his progress. She preferred the safety of his limitation to the uncertainty of his growth.

He lost his identity as someone who couldn't change. This might sound like a gain, but identities---even negative ones---provide security. Losing them feels like death because it is death---ego death.

But Thomas gained:

New friends who supported his growth. A partner who matched his evolution. An identity as someone who keeps promises to himself. And most importantly, a relationship with twelve at-risk kids who call him "Mr. T" and are learning to trust themselves because he learned to trust himself.

The cost of conscious change is everything that's kept you small. The reward is everything you're capable of becoming.

The Daily Change Practice

Here's a simple daily practice that maintains momentum in conscious change:

Morning (3 minutes)

- Touch your head: "What story will guide my change today?"

- Touch your heart: "What purpose will fuel my change today?"

- Touch your hands: "What pattern will embody my change today?"

Midday (30 seconds)

- Pause and ask: "Am I being who I'm becoming?"

- If yes, celebrate it

- If no, adjust without judgment

Evening (3 minutes)

- Review: "What did I do today that moved me toward who I'm becoming?"

- Reflect: "What did I learn about the process of change?"

- Renew: "What will I do differently tomorrow?"

This takes less than 7 minutes total but keeps you conscious of your transformation throughout the day.

The Story That Started With Failure

Let me share Maria's story---she failed at conscious change seventeen times before succeeding on the eighteenth.

Each failure taught her something:

- Failure 1-5: She learned that willpower alone wasn't enough

- Failure 6-10: She learned that changing everything at once was impossible

- Failure 11-15: She learned that doing it alone was unnecessarily hard

- Failure 16-17: She learned that perfectionism was procrastination in disguise

On attempt eighteen, Maria did something different. She chose one pattern (walking for 10 minutes daily), connected it to a meaningful purpose (being healthy for her daughter), updated her story (from "I always quit" to "I'm learning persistence"), and gave herself permission to do it imperfectly.

She walked in the rain. She walked when tired. She walked for 8 minutes when 10 felt impossible. She walked badly, slowly, reluctantly---but she walked.

After a year, Maria had walked over 1,000 miles. But more importantly, she had become someone who does what she says she'll do. That identity shift changed everything else.

"Those seventeen failures weren't failures," Maria told me. "They were research. I was learning what doesn't work so I could discover what does."

The Ultimate Change Paradox

The final paradox of conscious change: **The moment you fully accept who you are is the moment you become free to become who you're meant to be.**

Thomas discovered this in month nine. "I spent so many years hating who I was, fighting against myself, trying to become someone else. But the change only stuck when I accepted that I'm someone who struggles with mornings, and that's okay. I'm not trying to become a morning person. I'm just a night owl who chooses to wake up early because it serves my purpose."

This is the difference between change from self-hatred and change from self-love. One is violence against yourself. The other is evolution toward yourself.

Your Change Commitment

As we close this chapter, I want you to make a commitment. Not to me, not to anyone else, but to yourself.

Choose one thing---just one thing---that you'll change consciously. Not dramatically, not perfectly, but consciously. Choose your highest leverage point in your TOS:

- One pattern that would ripple through everything else

- One story that would shift your entire perspective

- One purpose that would realign your entire life

Then commit to changing it by one degree. Not 180 degrees. Not 90 degrees. One degree. But change it with complete consciousness, total awareness, absolute presence.

The Three Questions That Begin Everything

Before you move to the next chapter, answer these three questions:

1. **What is the one change that would change everything else for you?** Be specific. Be honest. Be brave.

2. **What resistance will you face, and how will you work with it?** Name your saboteurs. Plan your response. Prepare for the struggle.

3. **Who will you become when this change is complete?** See it. Feel it. Begin to embody it now.

Thomas, Transformed

Two years after that first conversation, Thomas invited me to his youth center. I watched him teach twelve kids about keeping promises to yourself. He used his own story---the five years of failed change, the morning practice, the slow building of self-trust.
One kid raised his hand: "Mr. T, what if I fail?"

Thomas smiled. "Then you fail forward. Every failure teaches you something about success. I failed for five years before I succeeded. The only real failure is not trying again."

After the session, Thomas walked me out. "You know what the craziest part is?" he said. "I changed everything by changing almost nothing. One morning routine. That's it. But that one conscious change rewired my entire life."

"No," I said. "You rewired your entire life. The morning routine was just where you practiced."

Thomas nodded, then said something I'll never forget: "I used to think change meant becoming someone else. Now I know it means becoming who I always was but was too scared to be."

"The art of conscious change isn't about force---it's about finesse. It's not about doing more---it's about doing less with more awareness. It's not about becoming someone else---it's about revealing who you've always been beneath the patterns, stories, and purposes that were never truly yours."

In the next chapter, we'll explore how to use the TOS framework for healing and recovery---how to rebuild your identity after trauma, loss, or life-altering events. You'll discover that sometimes the greatest transformations come not from adding something new, but from healing something old.

But for now, sit with this truth: You have the power to change. Not through force, not through will, but through consciousness. One degree at a time. One choice at a time. One moment at a time.

The art of conscious change isn't about becoming perfect. It's about becoming present to the process of becoming.

Your transformation starts with your next conscious choice.

What will it be?

CHAPTER ELEVEN

LOVE AND LOSS: THE PRACTICE OF IMPERMANENCE

"THE WOUND IS WHERE THE LIGHT ENTERS YOU. BUT FIRST, YOU MUST STOP PRETENDING YOU'RE NOT BLEEDING." — RUMI, ADAPTED

From Understanding to Application

You understand the framework now. You've learned the science behind how patterns, stories, and purposes shape your identity. You know that change is possible, that neuroplasticity means you're not condemned to remain who you've been.

But understanding doesn't prepare you for the moment your world ends.

Theory collapses when the person you built your life around walks away. Knowledge feels useless when you're staring at your phone at 3 AM, hoping for a text that will never come. The Trichotomy of Self sounds academic when you can't remember what it feels like to be whole.

This chapter is different. This is where we apply everything you've learned to one of life's most devastating experiences: profound heartbreak. Not the disappointment of a failed date, but the kind of loss that kills the person you were and leaves you to bury yourself in silence.

The Death That No One Acknowledges

Jack Hoyt sat in his car outside his ex-wife's house, watching his three children climb into her SUV. Fourteen years of marriage dissolved in a Tuesday morning conversation over coffee. No warning signs. No big fights. Just seven words that shattered his universe: "I don't want to be married anymore."

"The strangest part," Jack told me later, "is that everyone expected me to just... continue. Go to work. Pay bills. Function. But the person who went to work the next day wasn't me. He was a ghost wearing my clothes, speaking with my voice, living in the ruins of my life."

Jack had discovered what I call The Invisible Death—when heartbreak kills the person you were, but the world expects you to keep living as if nothing happened.

Here's what nobody tells you about profound heartbreak: it's not just the loss of a person. It's the death of an entire universe—the future you imagined, the identity you inhabited, the story that gave your life meaning. Unlike physical death, which society acknowledges with funerals and grieving periods, this death leaves you to bury yourself in silence while performing normalcy for a world that doesn't understand you're attending your own wake.

But here's the first truth Jack had to learn, the one that changes everything: **you don't control what other people do to you. You only control how you respond to it.**

His ex-wife chose to leave. That was her choice, her story, her journey. Jack couldn't control that. But he could control whether he drowned in the storm or learned to dance in the rain.

The Beauty of Impermanence

Before we dive into the deaths of heartbreak, I need to tell you something that might revolutionize how you love: everything beautiful in life is temporary. The Japanese have a term for this wisdom: *mono no aware*—the bittersweet awareness of the impermanence of all things. And far from being tragic, this awareness is what makes beauty possible.

I learned this lesson sitting with my dying father. We watched what would be one of his last sunsets together. The sky was on fire—oranges and purples I'd never seen before or since.

"You know why sunsets are beautiful?" he asked, his voice weak but clear.
"The colors?" I guessed.

He shook his head. "Because they end. If the sky was always like this, we'd stop noticing. The ending is what makes us pay attention."

He was quiet for a moment, then added: "Same with people, son. We're all sunsets. Here for a moment, blazing with color, then gone. Don't waste your sunsets wishing they were permanent. That's not what they're for."

This is The Impermanence Principle: the temporary nature of everything—roses, sunsets, moments, people—isn't a flaw in the design. It's the entire point.

Here's the distinction that matters: Conscious impermanence means being fully present while things last, then releasing with grace when they end. It means treasuring the cherry blossoms during their one week of blooming, not demanding they bloom forever. It means loving people deeply precisely because the time is limited.

Unconscious impermanence—which we'll explore later—is something else entirely. It's treating everything as disposable. It's pretending commitment while keeping one foot out the door. It's using people temporarily while promising them permanence.

The difference between these two approaches will become clear as we continue.

PRACTICE: The Impermanence Acknowledgment (2 minutes) *Right now, look at something or someone you love. Acknowledge silently: "This is temporary. That's why it matters." Notice how this awareness sharpens your attention rather than diminishing your love.*

The Three Deaths of Heartbreak

When someone leaves—whether by choice or circumstance—you experience what I have identified as the Three Deaths of Heartbreak. Each death corresponds directly to the three core elements of who you are:

The First Death: Your Story Dies

Your entire narrative about who you are and where you are going suddenly ends mid-sentence. The "we" becomes "I." The "forever" becomes "never again." Every plan, every dream, every assumption about tomorrow dies instantly.

This is the collapse of the beliefs that structured your reality. Jack went from "I am a devoted husband building a family legacy" to "I am a divorced man whose life fell apart without warning." The story that had guided every decision for fourteen years was suddenly fiction.

When your core beliefs about yourself and your future die, you're left without the meaning-making framework that helps you navigate life.

The Second Death: Your Patterns Die

All the daily routines, habits, and behaviors that structured your shared life suddenly have no context. You were "Jack, who made coffee for two every morning." Now you're "Jack, staring at two coffee cups wondering why you're still reaching for both."

This is when the behavioral architecture of your life collapses. Every morning routine included them. Every evening plan considered them. Every weekend pattern involved them. Now you have to rebuild not just your habits, but your entire way of being.

The patterns that once felt automatic—checking in throughout the day, planning for two, coming home to someone—now feel like phantom limbs. You keep reaching for routines that no longer have purpose.

The Third Death: Your Purpose Dies

When someone becomes your reason for everything—waking up, working hard, coming home—their absence creates a purpose vacuum. Every achievement feels hollow because the person you wanted to share it with is gone.

This is the collapse of your "why." Jack's purpose had been "building a beautiful family life with the woman I love." When that purpose died, he was left with the devastating question: "What was it all for?"

Most people only prepare for one of these deaths. Understanding all three reveals why complete healing requires rebuilding your entire foundation.

PRACTICE: Naming Your Deaths (5 minutes)*In your journal, write down which death feels most acute right now:*

- *What story about yourself died with this relationship?*

- *What daily pattern do you keep reaching for that no longer exists?*

- *What purpose feels hollow now that they're gone?*

Simply naming these deaths begins the healing process.

When Words and Actions Diverge: A Cautionary Tale

Let me tell you about David, because his story illustrates something crucial: how to see people clearly before you lose years of your life to beautiful lies.

David fell in love with Sarah when they were both young adults. One problem: Sarah was married. But she whispered to him in stolen moments, "You're my soulmate. One day, we'll be together."

David believed her. For sixteen years, he believed her.

I know sixteen years sounds impossible—who could be that naive? But I've counseled dozens of people who've lost similar stretches to similar illusions. Sometimes it's three years, sometimes twenty. The duration varies, but the pattern remains: we see what we desperately want to see until reality becomes undeniable.

She promised him children together—he watched her have children with the man she claimed not to love. He spent holidays alone while she played happy family. He put his life on hold, living in the margins of hers, sustained by promises that tomorrow, next month, next year, things would change.

Look at how David's entire identity became organized around Sarah:

His Daily Reality: Waiting by the phone for her calls. Keeping weekends free in case she could meet. Building his life around her schedule and availability. Never dating anyone else seriously. Living as a part-time person in a part-time relationship. Every action served the purpose of being accessible to her while putting his own life on hold.

His Core Beliefs: "I am her soulmate." "Love conquers all." "Good things come to those who wait." "She'll leave him when the time is right." Every belief justified the waiting and supported the hope.

His Life Purpose: To prove through patience and devotion that he was worthy of her love. To be ready when she finally chose him. Everything he did served this singular purpose.

David's error wasn't loving Sarah—it was building his entire identity around someone who was never fully there. He organized his days, his beliefs, and his reasons for living around a person who was always conditional, always divided, always belonging more to someone else's life than to his.

He forgot that people are guests in our lives, not permanent residents.

Finally, after sixteen years, Sarah divorced. David thought his patience had paid off. This was their moment.

Then cancer hit him. Hard. The kind that makes you reconsider everything.

And Sarah? She went cold. Not gradually—instantly. She told him she didn't love him, never really had, and never wanted to see or talk to him again. Weeks before Christmas. Via email.

Using Your Inner Compass as a Truth Detector

David's sixteen-year nightmare could have been avoided if he had understood one crucial truth: **The same framework you use to understand yourself can reveal the truth about others.**

The Trichotomy of Self isn't just for self-development—it's a powerful lens for seeing people clearly. When you learn to observe someone's patterns, stories, and purposes as an integrated whole, you gain what I call Relational Clarity—the ability to see who people truly are, not who they claim to be or who you wish them to be.

Most people evaluate relationships through a single lens—words. We listen to what people say they value, what they promise, what they claim to believe. But words are the easiest dimension to manipulate.

The Trichotomy teaches you to see in three dimensions:

Their Patterns (What They Actually Do): Observable reality. Patterns don't lie because they require consistent energy and choice. You can fake words for years. You can fake emotions for months. But you can't fake patterns—they reveal true priorities.

Their Stories (What They Actually Believe): Not the stories people tell you—the stories their patterns reveal. What someone truly believes shows up in how they behave when no one is watching, how they respond under pressure.

Their Purposes (What They Actually Serve): The deepest truth. Regardless of what someone claims their values are, their patterns reveal what they actually serve over time.

Let's apply this to Sarah—not to judge her, but to understand how seeing all three dimensions together could have saved David years of pain:

Sarah's Stated Stories (Her Words):

- "David is my soulmate"

- "I want to be with him forever"

- "I want to have children with David"

- "I love him more than my husband"

- "When the time is right, we'll be together"

Sarah's Observable Patterns (Her Actions):
- Stayed married to another man for sixteen years

- Had children with her husband, not David

- Kept David as a secret, compartmentalized relationship

- Never made concrete plans to leave her marriage

- Consistently chose convenience over commitment

- Disappeared completely during David's cancer battle

- Made promises but never aligned actions with words

What Her Patterns Revealed She Actually Served:
- Maintaining multiple sources of validation without sacrifice

- Having maximum freedom while avoiding accountability

- Using people as resources to meet immediate needs

- Serving self-interest without regard for consequences

Here's what's important: Sarah's patterns likely reflected her own unaddressed pain, her own fractured inner world, her own survival strategies from experiences we can't see. Understanding this doesn't mean David had to fix her or accept being hurt. **Her wounds were real, but they weren't his responsibility to heal.**

The point isn't that Sarah was evil or that David should have judged her more harshly. The point is that her TOS worked perfectly for her needs—but was fundamentally incompatible with David's healing and growth.

If David had used this framework:

Month 3: Sarah's patterns (staying married, no concrete plans) don't match her stories ("soulmate," "forever"). Misalignment detected.

Month 6: Her purposes (maintaining her marriage while enjoying David's attention) are clear from her patterns. They have nothing to do with leaving her husband.

Year 1: The pattern is consistent and unchanging. Her TOS is perfectly aligned—just not toward building a life with David. Decision point: accept this truth or continue living the lie.

Here's what David finally understood: **You cannot change someone else's Trichotomy of Self. You can only decide if you'll accept it in your life.**

Sarah's patterns were hers to choose. Her stories were hers to tell. Her purposes were hers to serve. David couldn't change any of it.

But David had complete control over his response.

Someone whose patterns hurt you, whose stories manipulate you, and whose purposes exclude you doesn't deserve space in your life—not because you're judging them, but because their TOS is incompatible with your health and growth.

David's final lesson was simple: **Love yourself enough to believe people's patterns more than their words. Your peace depends on it.**

The Mirror Principle

Here's the truth that changed everything for both Jack and David, the principle that became the foundation of their recovery:

"The quality of your relationships mirrors the depth of your relationship with yourself—how you love, trust, and value you sets the tone for all other relationships in your life."

When we examined their inner worlds, the patterns became clear:

Jack's Pre-Divorce Reality: Jack realized he had abandoned himself long before his wife abandoned him. He had stopped pursuing his interests, stopped maintaining friendships, stopped growing as an individual. He had dissolved into the role of husband and father, losing Jack in the process.

- Had abandoned his individual interests and friendships

- Believed "I am only valuable when I'm serving others," "My worth comes from being needed"

- Lived to make his wife happy at the expense of his own authenticity

His entire identity had become completely dependent on external validation rather than internal alignment.

David's Sixteen-Year Reality: David saw it even more clearly. For sixteen years, he had treated himself as someone worth putting on hold. He had valued himself so little that he accepted crumbs of affection as a feast.

- Treated himself as someone worth waiting, worth putting on hold

- Believed "I don't deserve love unless I prove myself," "My needs come last"

- Spent his life earning love through suffering rather than expressing love through wholeness

His relationship with Sarah perfectly mirrored his relationship with himself—neglectful, dishonest, and built on false promises.

This is The Mirror Principle: **Every relationship you have is a reflection of the relationship you have with yourself.** If you don't trust yourself, you'll attract untrustworthy people. If you don't value yourself, you'll accept being undervalued. If you abandon yourself, you'll be abandoned.

The Prerequisite Nobody Mentions

Here's what therapists rarely say directly because it sounds harsh: **You cannot build a stable relationship with anyone else until you build a stable relationship with yourself.**

This isn't motivational fluff. It's structural necessity.

Think about it through the Trichotomy:

If your patterns neglect your own needs, you'll attract people who neglect you—because that's the dynamic you're practicing and radiating.

If your stories tell you that you're not worthy of love, you'll unconsciously seek relationships that confirm this belief—because humans crave consistency, even painful consistency.

If your purposes revolve around earning someone else's approval, you'll attract people who withhold approval—because that's the game you're playing.

The solution isn't to judge yourself for this. It's to recognize that **loving yourself first isn't selfish—it's foundational.**

When you love yourself first:

- You show up as your best version, not your desperate version

- You can love others from abundance rather than need

- You can recognize incompatibility early instead of years later

- You can leave situations that harm you without feeling like you're giving up

- You can be fully present because you're not constantly seeking validation

This is why the rest of this chapter focuses on you—not on understanding them, not on closure from them, but on rebuilding your foundation from the ground up.

PRACTICE: The Mirror Question (3 minutes) *Ask yourself honestly: "If I treated my best friend the way I treat myself—how I talk to myself, what I ask of myself, what I tolerate from others—would they stay in my life?"*

If the answer is no, you've identified where your healing needs to begin.

The Impermanent Love Practice

After his divorce, Jack developed what he calls The Impermanent Love Practice—and it transformed how he experienced every relationship:

New Daily Reality: Every morning, he would look at photos of his children and remind himself: "I have them today. Not forever. Today." This meant:

- When they visited on weekends, he was fully present instead of distracted

- When they were difficult, he remembered these years would pass quickly

- When they hugged him, he held on a second longer, storing the feeling

- When they left for their mother's house, he was grateful for the time rather than bitter about the absence

New Beliefs: Instead of "My kids are mine forever" or "This divorce ruined our family," Jack embraced: "My children are temporary gifts entrusted to my care," "Every moment with them is precious because it's limited," and "Love doesn't require permanence to be real."

New Life Purpose: Rather than trying to recreate the old family structure, Jack's purpose became: "To be fully present for my children during the time we have together,"

"To model how to love without clinging," and "To show them that endings can be transformations."

"Treating my kids as temporary gifts rather than permanent possessions changed everything," Jack explained. "I stopped taking them for granted. I stopped wishing for more time and started maximizing the time I had. Ironically, accepting that they're temporary made our relationship deeper and more permanent in the ways that actually matter."

In Japan, they celebrate cherry blossoms not despite their brief blooming, but because of it. For one week, the entire country stops to appreciate these temporary flowers. People gather under the trees, fully present, fully aware that by next week, the petals will have fallen.

Jack learned to apply this to relationships. "Every relationship is a cherry blossom season," he told me. "Some last a week, some last years, but they all end. The ending doesn't diminish the beauty. If anything, it intensifies it."

The Storm Response Strategy

When Jack's ex-wife left, she didn't just leave—she immediately started dating someone else. The storm of emotion that hit Jack was Category 5: rage, betrayal, humiliation, despair.

"I wanted to destroy everything," Jack admitted. "Myself, her, him, the whole world."

But then Jack remembered something his grandmother used to say: "When the storm comes, you can decide whether to dance in the rain or drown in it."

Jack made a choice that saved his life: He decided to dance. This required completely rebuilding who he was:

Storm Response Through Daily Changes:

- Instead of rage-scrolling through her social media (old habit), Jack started journaling for ten minutes each morning (new habit)

- Instead of calling friends to vent about her betrayal (old habit), he began calling friends to plan activities and adventures (new habit)

- Instead of drinking to numb the pain (old habit), he started running to transform the energy (new habit)

Storm Response Through New Beliefs:

- From "She destroyed my life" to "She revealed what needed to change"

- From "I'm a victim of her betrayal" to "I'm the author of my response"

- From "Love is dangerous" to "Love is temporary and therefore precious"

Storm Response Through Purpose Transformation:

- From trying to win her back or punish her to focusing on his own healing

- From proving he was wronged to proving he could grow from being wronged

- From making her the center of his story to making his transformation the center

This is The Storm Response Strategy: **Use the energy of crisis to completely realign your entire being.** Every tear washed away a false story. Every moment of rage burned away an old pattern. Every wave of grief carved space for new purposes.

PRACTICE: Redirect the Storm (10 minutes daily)*For one week, every time you feel the urge to check their social media, text them, or ruminate about them:*

1. *Name the feeling: "I'm feeling [abandoned/angry/desperate]"*

2. *Redirect the energy: Do 20 push-ups, write 3 gratitude's, or call someone who builds you up*

3. *Track it: Keep a simple tally of successful redirects*

This isn't about suppressing emotion—it's about channeling it into reconstruction rather than destruction.

Another Voice: When She Left Herself Behind

Maria's story was different from Jack's and David's, but the pattern was the same. She had spent eight years in a relationship where she had become smaller and smaller, quieter and quieter, until she barely recognized herself.

"I didn't lose him," she told me six months after the breakup. "I lost me. And the worst part? I did it voluntarily. Every time I swallowed my opinion to keep the peace, every time I canceled plans with friends because he preferred I stay home, every time I dressed how he liked instead of how I felt—I was practicing abandoning myself."

When he finally left her for someone else, Maria's first response wasn't anger at him—it was rage at herself.

"I kept asking, 'How could I let this happen?' Then I realized: the same patterns I used to disappear for him were the same patterns I'd been using my whole life. With my parents, with previous boyfriends, even with my boss. I had been perfecting the art of self-abandonment since childhood."

Maria's healing didn't come from understanding why he left. It came from understanding why she stayed—and what she needed to rebuild in herself to never abandon herself that way again.

She's the one who taught me that heartbreak isn't just about losing someone. It's often about finding the person you lost while trying to keep them.

The Absence Gift Principle

David kept trying to talk to Sarah after she'd rejected him. Not to reconcile, but to understand, to get closure, to make sense of sixteen years. Each conversation left David more shattered than before.

Finally, I asked David: "When someone no longer values your presence, what's the most valuable thing you can give them?"

"Nothing?" David guessed.

"Close," I said. "Your absence."

When someone shows you through their patterns that they don't value your presence, gift them your absence. When they show you through their actions that your words don't matter, stop talking to them.

But this isn't punishment—it's protection. Protection for your inner world:

Protecting Your Daily Patterns: David blocked Sarah's number and removed all ways she could disrupt his healing routines. No more checking if she called. No more hoping for texts. No more organizing his day around potential contact.

Protecting Your Beliefs: Every conversation with her reinforced the old, destructive beliefs: "Maybe she'll change her mind," "If I just explain better," "I need closure from her." Cutting contact allowed new beliefs to emerge: "Her silence is my answer," "I create my own closure."

Protecting Your Life Purpose: As long as Sarah could reach him, David's purposes remained entangled with her approval. Only in her absence could he discover purposes that were truly his own: healing, growing, creating a life of authentic self-love.

David blocked Sarah's number that day. No dramatic goodbye. No final explanation. Just the gift of absence—both for her and, more importantly, for himself.

His absence wasn't cruelty—it was self-respect. It wasn't punishment—it was protection.

Here's the truth David learned: **Stop chasing explanations from those who never valued your questions. Their silence and absence is the closure you seek.**

When someone can abandon you during your darkest hour—when they can know you're facing cancer and still disappear—their patterns have given you the only answer you need. Seeking verbal explanation from someone whose actions already spoke volumes is like asking for directions from someone who just pushed you off a cliff.

The closure you seek isn't in their words. It's in accepting their patterns as the truth and choosing yourself anyway.

The Path Back to Yourself

Here's what both Jack, David, and Maria had to learn: **You must focus on yourself and love yourself first, so you may show up as your best version and love others properly.**

This isn't selfishness—it's wisdom. You can't pour from an empty cup. You can't give what you don't have. You can't love others well if your own foundation is cracked.

Phase 1: Accept the Temporary (Weeks 1-4)

Accept that everything and everyone is temporary, and let this truth transform your entire approach to life:

Daily Practice:

- Write this truth daily: "Everything is temporary, including this pain"

- Spend 10 minutes fully engaged with whatever is in front of you

- Create a morning ritual that honors impermanence—gratitude for what you have today

Belief Shifts:

- From "They were supposed to be permanent" to "They were a temporary teacher"

- From "I lost everything" to "I'm between chapters"

- From "Forever was a lie" to "Forever was the depth of presence in each moment"

Purpose Adjustments:

- From "building forever with them" to "being fully alive today"

- From "making them happy" to "creating moments of authentic presence"

Phase 2: Rebuild Your Foundation (Weeks 5-12)

Create patterns, stories, and purposes that prove you love yourself:

Start treating yourself like someone you're responsible for taking care of—because you are:

- Feed yourself well (you deserve nourishment)

- Move your body (you deserve strength)

- Rest properly (you deserve restoration)

- Pursue interests (you deserve joy)

- Create before consuming each day

New Empowering Beliefs:

- From "I'm broken because they left" to "I'm healing because I choose to"

- From "I need them to be complete" to "I am complete and can share from wholeness"

- From "Love failed me" to "I'm learning to love more consciously"

Independent Purposes:

- Focus on service, creation, growth, and presence

- Make your primary purpose your own authentic development

- Identify purposes that exist independent of any relationship

Phase 3: Rewrite Your Story (Weeks 13-20)

Rewrite your narratives with impermanence as wisdom, not loss:
- "They left me" becomes "They were a temporary teacher"

- "I lost everything" becomes "I'm between chapters"

- "I'll never love again" becomes "I'll love differently next time"

- "Forever is a lie" becomes "Forever is this moment, fully lived"

Phase 4: Discover What Transcends (Weeks 21+)

Find purposes that honor impermanence and transcend any individual relationship:

- Be fully present with whoever is in front of you

- Love without requiring permanence

- Give without expecting returns

- Create beauty that will outlast you

- Serve something larger than your personal happiness

The Phoenix Protocol: Seven Stages of Identity Resurrection

Stage 1: The Death Acceptance: "The person I was is gone. They died with the relationship. That's okay. Death makes room for rebirth."

Stage 2: The Grief Honor: "I will mourn fully. No timeline. No shame. No performance. I will grieve the patterns I'll miss, the stories I believed, the purposes that felt so meaningful. My grief is sacred but temporary."

Stage 3: The Pattern Clearing: "I will identify which daily habits served my authentic self versus the relationship. Which routines expressed who I really am? Which were just performance? I keep only what makes me more myself."

Stage 4: The Story Liberation: "I will write new stories where impermanence is wisdom, not loss. Where endings are transformations, not failures. Where I am complete with or without anyone else."

Stage 5: The Purpose Discovery: "I will find purposes that transcend any relationship. Purposes that honor both permanence and impermanence. Purposes that make me come alive regardless of who stays or goes."

Stage 6: The Integration Practice: "I will align my new patterns, stories, and purposes daily, knowing they too will evolve. I will treat my inner world as a living system that grows with me."

Stage 7: The Wisdom Offering: "I will teach others that loving impermanence is not about loving less, but about loving more consciously. My healed self becomes a gift to others."

The Ultimate Heartbreak Truth

About a year after his divorce, Jack sent me a text that perfectly captured the power of complete reconstruction:

"The best thing she ever did was leave. Not because I'm better without her—but because her leaving forced me to rebuild myself from the ground up. I learned that everyone is temporary. Once I accepted that, I started loving more deeply, not less. I treasure my kids more knowing they'll grow up and leave. I appreciate friends more knowing we'll drift apart. I even appreciate myself more, knowing I won't be here forever. Her leaving didn't teach me not to love. It taught me how to love properly—with full presence, complete awareness, and total acceptance of impermanence."

David, recovered from cancer and thriving, shared his own revelation:

"Cancer and heartbreak taught me the same lesson: Everything ends. But that's not the tragedy—that's the gift. My new foundation is built on this truth. My daily routines honor the temporary. My beliefs embrace impermanence. My purposes transcend individual relationships. I focus on loving myself first, so whatever time I have with others comes from wholeness, not neediness. My entire approach to life is finally aligned with reality instead of fantasy."

Maria put it most simply: "I spent eight years losing myself for someone. Now I spend every day finding myself for me. Turns out, that's the only love story that was ever going to last."

The Love That Remains

Here's what I want you to understand about healing from heartbreak: You don't heal by forgetting how to love. You heal by learning to love differently—with a foundation that's aligned with the truth of impermanence.

How to Love Consciously:

- Be fully present with whoever is in front of you
- Express love today, not tomorrow
- Create moments of beauty and connection
- Practice gratitude for temporary gifts

What to Believe About Love:

- Everyone is temporary, which makes them precious

- Love doesn't require permanence to be real

- Endings don't diminish the beauty of what was

- You are complete and can love from wholeness

What to Serve Through Love:

- Love yourself first so you can love others well

- Create beauty that transcends individual relationships

- Serve something larger than personal happiness

- Leave people better for having known you

Your Heartbreak Assignment: Complete Reconstruction

Before we move to the next chapter, I need you to do something that might feel impossible but is absolutely necessary—consciously reconstruct your entire foundation:

1. Pattern Inventory: List every way you tried to make temporary permanent in your relationship. What daily routines were organized around them? Which habits died with the relationship? Which habits were authentically yours?

2. Story Audit: Write down what believing in "forever" cost you in presence. What beliefs about yourself and love need to die? What empowering beliefs about impermanence could you embrace?

3. Purpose Excavation: What purposes did your relationship serve that were authentic vs. imposed? What purposes could transcend any individual relationship?

4. Present Moment Practice: Identify three people in your life you've been taking for granted because you assume they're permanent. Tell them today—not tomorrow—what they mean to you.

5. Foundation Declaration: Write and sign this declaration:

"I accept that everything and everyone is temporary, including me. This awareness doesn't make me love less—it makes me love more consciously. I will rebuild my foundation on this truth:

My DAILY REALITY will treasure what I have while I have it. I will be present for the sunsets, the roses, the moments, and the people.

My BELIEFS will embrace impermanence as wisdom, not loss. When people leave, I will be grateful for the time we had rather than bitter about the time we won't.

My PURPOSES will transcend any individual relationship while honoring each temporary connection. I will love myself first so I can love others from wholeness.

I am temporary. They are temporary. This pain is temporary. But the growth, the wisdom, the capacity to love—these transcend temporary and become eternal through my conscious choices."

The Chapter That Ends to Begin

Jack's youngest daughter asked him, two years after the divorce, "Dad, are you sad that Mom left?"

Jack pulled her close, knowing that she too was temporary—that one day she'd grow up, move away, start her own life. The awareness made him hold her tighter, not from fear but from presence.

"I'm sad that our family changed," he said. "But I'm not sad about what I learned. Your mom taught me something precious by leaving—that people are like seasons. Some are spring, bringing new growth. Some are summer, warm and full. Some are autumn, beautiful in their change. And some are winter, clearing space for what's next. Your mom was my season, and now that season has passed. But you know what's beautiful? Every season teaches us something. And the season I'm in now—being your dad, being present for these moments—this is the season I'm meant to be in."

His daughter looked up at him. "Am I temporary too, Dad?"

Jack's eyes filled with tears. "Yes, sweetheart. Someday you'll grow up and leave. But that's what makes right now so precious. That's why I pay attention when you talk. That's why I'm here for every soccer game. That's why I hold you extra long when you hug me. Because I know this won't last forever, and that makes it infinitely valuable."

"I love you, Dad."

"I love you too, baby. Today. Tomorrow. And every temporary moment we have together."

"Heartbreak teaches us the ultimate truth: Everything is temporary. This isn't tragedy—it's wisdom. When we align our foundation with this reality, we stop taking people for granted and start treasuring them. We stop postponing love and start expressing it. We stop waiting for perfect and start appreciating present. Love yourself first, so you can love others from wholeness. Treasure the temporary, for it's all we have and all we need. The rose petals will fall, the sunset will end, people will leave. But the beauty of having experienced them? That transcends temporary and becomes part of who you are forever."

In the next chapter, we'll explore how to use your healed and integrated foundation for peak performance and leadership—how to channel your newfound strength not just into survival, but into extraordinary contribution. You'll discover that sometimes our greatest impact comes not despite our wounds, but because of them.

But for now, sit with this truth: Your heartbreak hasn't diminished your capacity to love—it's refined it. You now know the secret that transforms ordinary love into sacred love, and ordinary living into conscious alignment:

Everything ends. That's what makes it beautiful.☐
Everyone leaves. That's what makes them precious.☐
You are temporary. That's what makes you free.☐
Your foundation can be reconstructed. That's what makes you unstoppable.

Chapter Twelve

LEADERSHIP AND INFLUENCE

"YOU CANNOT LEAD ANYONE TO A PLACE YOU HAVE NEVER BEEN. LEADERSHIP BEGINS WITH THE COURAGE TO LEAD YOURSELF THROUGH YOUR OWN TRANSFORMATION."

The CEO Who Couldn't Lead Himself

At 6:47 AM on a Tuesday morning, Jonathan Mitchell, CEO of a $200 million software company, was hiding in his car in the parking garage of his own building. He'd been sitting there for twenty-three minutes, paralyzed by what waited for him upstairs: a board meeting where he'd have to explain why his "visionary leadership" had led the company to the edge of bankruptcy.

The irony wasn't lost on him. Jonathan had built his career on leadership. MBA from Wharton. Featured on magazine covers. Keynote speaker at conferences where he taught others how to "lead with passion and purpose." He had a corner office filled with leadership books, walls covered with awards for executive excellence, and a reputation as someone who could "turn any organization around."

But sitting in that parking garage, Jonathan faced a truth that shattered everything he thought he knew about leadership: **You cannot lead others if you cannot lead yourself. And he hadn't been leading himself---he'd been performing leadership while his own life fell apart behind the scenes.**

His marriage was failing because he worked 80-hour weeks but called it "dedication." His health was crumbling because he lived on caffeine and ambition but called it "high performance." His children barely knew him because he was always "building their future" instead of being present for their childhood. His company was dying because he made decisions based on ego rather than wisdom, but called it "bold leadership."

Jonathan had mastered the language of leadership, the strategies of leadership, the appearance of leadership. But he had never learned the foundation of all authentic leadership: leading himself.

"I was a fraud," Jonathan told me six months later, after everything collapsed and then rebuilt stronger. "I was teaching people to follow me to places I'd never actually been. I talked about work-life balance while destroying mine. I preached about authentic leadership while performing a role. I promised to lead others to success while I was leading myself toward destruction."

The Leadership Lie That Destroys Everything

The lie that most leadership training perpetuates: **Leadership is about getting others to do what you want them to do.**

This lie creates what I call **Performance Leaders**---people who master the external mechanics of leadership while remaining internally chaotic. They learn to give inspiring speeches while their own motivation runs on empty. They develop systems for others while their own lives lack structure. They teach vision while they can't see clearly past their own limitations.

Performance Leaders can be effective in the short term. They can inspire teams, hit quarterly numbers, and build impressive resumes. But eventually, the internal chaos catches up. Eventually, the gap between who they appear to be and who they actually are becomes impossible to maintain. Eventually, the foundation crumbles because it was built on performance, not presence.

The truth that changes everything: Leadership is not about getting others to follow you somewhere. Leadership is about becoming someone worth following---and you can only become that by first learning to lead yourself.

The Three Foundations of Leading Yourself

Real leadership---the kind that transforms organizations, communities, and lives---begins with what I call **Self-Leadership**: the ability to consciously direct your own daily actions, inner stories, and deeper purposes toward outcomes that serve not just yourself, but something larger than yourself.

Self-Leadership rests on three foundations:

Foundation 1: Mastering Your Daily Actions You have developed the daily habits that create the results you want and eliminated the ones that undermine what you're trying to build.

Foundation 2: Choosing Your Inner Stories You are aware of the stories you tell yourself, you choose which ones to believe, and you update them when they no longer serve your growth or your mission.

Foundation 3: Clarifying Your Deeper Purpose You know why you do what you do, and that why extends beyond your personal benefit to include the welfare of others.

When these three foundations support each other, you develop what I call **Natural Authority**---not authority granted by a title or position, but authority earned through the harmony between your words, actions, and character.

Foundation One: Mastering Your Daily Actions

Let me tell you about Maria Santos, a middle school principal in East Los Angeles who transformed one of the worst-performing schools in the district into one of the best. She didn't do it through new programs, additional funding, or administrative mandates. She did it by mastering her own daily actions first.

"When I arrived at Jefferson Middle School," Maria told me, "the place was chaos. Students roaming the halls, teachers burned out, parents distrustful. Everyone was looking for someone to blame, someone to fix it. I realized I could spend my energy trying to change eight hundred people, or I could spend it changing one person completely---myself."

Maria's transformation began with a simple recognition: **You cannot give what you do not have. You cannot create order around you if there is chaos within you. You cannot inspire discipline in others if you lack discipline yourself.**

The Morning Revolution

Maria started with her morning routine---not because it seemed important to others, but because it would determine the energy she brought to every interaction throughout the day.

"I was waking up frantic, checking emails in bed, rushing through everything, and arriving at school already stressed," she explained. "Then I expected teachers to be calm and students to be focused. I was trying to lead from anxiety."

Maria redesigned her morning with the understanding that her daily actions would ripple through the entire school:

- 5:00 AM: Meditation and intention-setting (15 minutes)

- 5:15 AM: Physical exercise (30 minutes)

- 6:00 AM: Breakfast eaten mindfully, no devices

- 6:30 AM: Review of priorities and preparation for the day

- 7:15 AM: Arrival at school with presence, not panic

"It sounds simple," Maria said, "but those two hours of daily discipline changed everything. I stopped being a reactive leader and became a responsive one. Students could feel the difference. Teachers could see it. My energy became the energy that set the tone for the building."

The Credibility Principle

Maria discovered: **Your credibility as a leader is directly connected to your credibility with yourself. If you can't trust yourself to keep commitments to yourself, why should others trust you to keep commitments to them?**

This is why so many leaders struggle with influence. They ask others to be disciplined while lacking discipline themselves. They demand accountability from their teams while avoiding accountability in their personal lives. They speak about excellence while accepting mediocrity in their own standards.

But when you master your own daily actions---when you become someone who does what you say you'll do, when you say you'll do it, because you said you'd do it---something profound happens: Others naturally want to follow your example.

The Three Levels of Daily Leadership

Level 1: Personal Daily Mastery You have developed habits that create the results you want in your own life. You wake up when you say you will, exercise when you plan to, eat in a way that serves your values, manage your time and energy consciously. People see your consistency and think: "I want that discipline in my life."

Level 2: Professional Daily Mastery You apply the same discipline to your work that you apply to yourself. You prepare thoroughly, communicate clearly, follow through completely, and continuously improve your capabilities. People see your work habits and think: "I want to work at that level."

Level 3: Influential Daily Mastery Your daily actions become a model that others naturally want to copy. Not because you're preaching or teaching, but because the results speak for themselves. People see your integrated life and think: "I want to become someone who lives like that."

Foundation Two: Choosing Your Inner Stories

Six months into Maria's transformation, Jefferson Middle School was showing improvement, but she hit an unexpected obstacle: her own success story was limiting her leadership.

"I'd always told myself I was a 'turn-around specialist,'" Maria explained. "Someone who came in, fixed broken systems, and moved on to the next challenge. That story had served me well in my career, but it was sabotaging my long-term leadership at Jefferson."

Maria's "fix-it-and-leave" story was unconsciously creating habits of short-term thinking and preventing her from building the deep relationships necessary for sustained transformation. **Her story about herself was determining her behavior as a leader, which was limiting her impact on the organization.**

The Leadership Story Examination

This is when Maria learned a crucial lesson: **The stories you tell about yourself determine the kind of leader you become. And most people are unconsciously**

living out stories that were written by others or formed in response to wounds rather than wisdom.

Maria examined what I call her **Leadership Stories**---the narratives that were driving her leadership approach:

Story 1: "I'm here to fix what's broken" **Impact:** This made her focus on problems rather than possibilities, deficits rather than strengths.

Story 2: "Good leaders don't need help" **Impact:** This prevented her from building the collaborative relationships that could multiply her impact.

Story 3: "My job is to have all the answers" **Impact:** This created pressure to perform omniscience rather than model continuous learning.

Story 4: "Leaders must sacrifice personal needs for the organization" **Impact:** This was leading her toward burnout and modeling unsustainable practices.

The Story Rewrite Process

Maria rewrote each limiting story into what I call a **Growth Story**---a narrative that creates expansion rather than limitation:

New Story 1: "I'm here to unlock what's already great" **New Impact:** This shifted her focus to strengths, possibilities, and empowerment.

New Story 2: "Great leaders build great teams" **New Impact:** This opened her to collaboration and made seeking help a sign of wisdom, not weakness.

New Story 3: "My job is to ask better questions" **New Impact:** This positioned her as a facilitator of discovery rather than a repository of answers.

New Story 4: "Leaders who sustain themselves sustain their impact" **New Impact:** This made self-care a leadership responsibility, not a personal indulgence.

The Mirror Effect of Leadership Stories

Maria discovered: **The stories you tell about yourself as a leader become the stories others tell about what leadership looks like.**

When Maria operated from "I must have all the answers," her teachers stopped bringing creative ideas because they assumed she'd already figured everything out. When she shifted to "My job is to ask better questions," teachers began proposing innovative solutions because they felt invited into the thinking process.

When she lived the story "Leaders sacrifice everything," her staff felt guilty about their own work-life balance. When she embraced "Sustainable leaders create sustainable impact," her teachers started taking better care of themselves, which improved their effectiveness with students.

This is the Mirror Effect: Your internal stories about leadership become your team's external understanding of what leadership requires.

Foundation Three: Clarifying Your Deeper Purpose

Two years into Maria's leadership at Jefferson, the school had transformed dramatically. Test scores were up, discipline problems were down, teacher retention had improved, and parent engagement was at an all-time high. But Maria was about to learn the deepest lesson about leadership: **Techniques and strategies can create improvement, but only purpose creates transformation.**

The lesson came during a conversation with Miguel, a seventh-grader who'd been one of the school's biggest behavioral challenges when Maria arrived.

"Mrs. Santos," Miguel said after a student leadership meeting, "why do you really care about us? You could work at any school. You could probably make more money somewhere else. Why are you here?"

Miguel's question forced Maria to examine something she'd never put into words clearly: her deepest purpose as a leader.

"I realized I could give him tactical answers about education reform and closing achievement gaps," Maria told me. "But what I really needed to give him was truth. Why did I actually care? What was driving me at the deepest level?"

The Purpose Discovery Process

That night, Maria went through what I call **Purpose Discovery**---digging beneath the surface reasons for her work to discover the bedrock purpose that was actually driving her leadership.

Surface Purpose: "To improve test scores and school performance" **Deeper Purpose:** "To create an environment where learning can happen" **Deepest Purpose:** "To prove to kids like I was that someone believes they matter"

Maria had grown up in a neighborhood similar to the one where Jefferson was located. She'd been a bright kid in a struggling school system, and one principal had changed her trajectory by seeing her potential and refusing to give up on her.

"My deepest purpose wasn't about education metrics," Maria realized. "It was about being for these kids what Mrs. Patterson had been for me---someone who saw their light when they couldn't see it themselves."

Purpose-Driven vs. Goal-Driven Leadership

This discovery transformed Maria's approach to leadership in ways she hadn't expected:

Before Purpose Clarity (Goal-Driven Leadership):

- Focused on quarterly improvements and annual targets

- Motivated by external validation and career advancement

- Energy fluctuated based on wins and losses

- Decisions filtered through "What will this do for the numbers?"

After Purpose Clarity (Purpose-Driven Leadership):

- Focused on long-term transformation and sustainable change

- Motivated by internal meaning and meaningful impact

- Energy remained steady because it was connected to something beyond circumstances

- Decisions filtered through "What will this do for the kids?"

The Ripple Effect of Authentic Purpose

When Maria began leading from authentic purpose rather than borrowed goals, something remarkable happened: her purpose became contagious.

Teachers started asking themselves why they really became educators. Students began connecting their own learning to larger purposes. Parents got involved not because they were required to, but because they caught the vision of what their children could become.

"Purpose is the only thing that's truly viral," Maria observed. "You can mandate goals, but you can't mandate purpose. Purpose has to be caught, not taught. And people can only catch it from someone who authentically has it."

The Three Levels of Leadership Purpose

Through working with hundreds of leaders across different contexts, I've identified three levels of purpose that determine both the sustainability and impact of leadership:

Level 1: Personal Benefit Purpose "What can I gain from this leadership role?"

- Limited sustainability---burns out when personal needs are met or obstacles become too great

- Creates transactional relationships where people follow for personal benefit

- Works for short-term results but fails during crises

Level 2: Organizational Purpose "What can I achieve for this organization?"

- Moderate sustainability---lasts as long as the organization thrives

- Creates conditional loyalty tied to organizational success

- Effective for institutional growth but limited by institutional boundaries

Level 3: Transcendent Purpose "What can I contribute to something larger than myself or my organization?"

- Maximum sustainability---endures through changing circumstances

- Creates deep loyalty based on shared values and vision

- Generates extraordinary results because it connects individual effort to universal meaning

Bringing It All Together: The Self-Leadership Model

Now everything comes together: **True leadership is when your daily actions, inner stories, and deeper purpose work together in service of others' growth.**

This creates what I call **Natural Authority**---the kind of influence that doesn't need titles, positions, or external validation because it emerges from the harmony between who you are, what you believe, and why you serve.

Robert Chen: From Performance to Presence

Let me show you how this works through the story of Robert Chen, a sales manager who transformed not just his team's performance, but their entire relationship with work.

When Robert first became a manager, he led through what I call **Action Copying**---mimicking the behaviors of successful leaders without understanding the internal harmony that made those behaviors effective.

He implemented morning team meetings (action) because successful leaders have team meetings. He talked about vision and values (story) because that's what leaders are supposed to do. He set aggressive targets (purpose) because that's how you drive performance.

The results were mediocre. His team performed adequately but without engagement. Turnover was high. Energy was low. Robert was working harder than ever but creating less impact than he'd hoped.

The Breakthrough

Everything changed when Robert stopped copying external behaviors and started developing internal harmony:

Action Harmony: Instead of mimicking other leaders' meeting styles, Robert developed morning practices that connected his own habits with his team's needs. His meetings became opportunities to connect daily actions with larger purposes rather than just reporting on numbers.

Story Harmony: Instead of repeating generic vision statements, Robert identified and shared the authentic stories that drove his commitment to the team's success. He talked about his own struggles with sales, his growth through mentorship, and his desire to create for others what had been created for him.

Purpose Harmony: Instead of pursuing targets for their own sake, Robert connected every goal to the larger purpose of helping his team members develop capabilities that would serve them throughout their careers, not just during their time with the company.

The Results of Harmony

Within six months, Robert's team transformation was remarkable:

- Sales performance increased 340%

- Employee satisfaction scores reached company-wide highs

- Team turnover dropped to near zero

- Three team members were promoted to leadership roles in other departments

- The waiting list to join Robert's team grew to over 30 people

But the real measure of Robert's leadership development wasn't in the numbers---it was in the transformation of the people he led.

"Robert didn't just manage us," one team member told me. "He modeled what it looked like to take responsibility for your own growth. We started holding ourselves to higher standards because we saw him holding himself to higher standards. We started taking care of our own development because we watched him continuously developing himself."

The Leadership Multiplication Effect

This is the ultimate test of authentic leadership: **Do the people you lead become better leaders themselves?**

Performance Leaders create dependency. People become reliant on the leader's energy, vision, and decision-making. When the leader leaves, performance drops because the team was following the person, not embodying the principles.

Authentic Leaders create multiplication. People develop their own daily mastery, story consciousness, and purpose clarity. When the leader leaves, performance often improves because team members have become leaders themselves.

Maria's transformation at Jefferson illustrates this perfectly. When she took a district-level position after four years, Jefferson didn't decline---it continued improving. Why? Because Maria hadn't just led the school; she had developed leaders throughout the school. Teachers who had learned daily discipline from watching her became disciplined themselves. Staff who had witnessed her story consciousness began examining and updating their own limiting narratives. Administrators who had caught her purpose clarity found their own authentic reasons for serving students.

The Leadership Paradox

The paradox that every authentic leader must embrace: **The goal of leadership is to make yourself unnecessary.**

This seems counterintuitive to leaders who derive their sense of importance from being needed. But it's the natural result of leading from internal harmony rather than ego needs.

When you lead from daily mastery, you teach others to master their own habits rather than depending on your discipline.

When you lead from story consciousness, you help others examine and rewrite their own stories rather than accepting your stories as truth.

When you lead from purpose clarity, you help others discover their own authentic purposes rather than requiring them to serve yours.

The result isn't that you become less important---it's that you become important in a different way. Instead of being the person who has all the answers, you become the person who helps others find their own answers. Instead of being the person who drives all results, you become the person who develops others' capacity to create results. Instead of being irreplaceable, you become the kind of leader who creates other irreplaceable leaders.

The Daily Practice of Self-Leadership

Authentic leadership isn't a destination you reach; it's a practice you maintain. The daily framework that both Maria and Robert use to keep their leadership grounded in self-leadership:

Morning Check-In (10 minutes):

- Action Check: "What habits will I practice today that serve my team's growth?"

- Story Check: "What mindset will I live today that models what I want to see?"

- Purpose Check: "How will I serve something larger than myself today?"

Midday Reset (2 minutes):

1. "Am I leading from my authentic self or from performance?"

2. "Are my actions matching my stated values?"

3. "What does my team need from me right now?"

Evening Reflection (5 minutes):

1. "How did my self-leadership impact others today?"

2. "What internal work do I need to do to serve better tomorrow?"

3. "Where did I model harmony, and where did I default to performance?"

The Leadership Ripple Effect

The most profound truth about authentic leadership is that it doesn't stop with your immediate team or organization. When you lead from internal harmony, you create ripples that extend far beyond your official sphere of influence.

The Parent Leadership Revolution

Consider Rachel Thompson, a single mother of three who discovered that self-leadership at home was the foundation for every other leadership role in her life.

"I was trying to teach my kids responsibility while I was irresponsible with my own commitments," Rachel realized. "I was demanding they do their homework while I avoided my own learning and growth. I was asking them to be honest while I was lying to myself about my habits, my stories, and what I really wanted from life."

Rachel's self-leadership transformation started with the recognition that **parenting is leadership, and you cannot lead your children to places you haven't been willing to go yourself.**

Daily Leadership at Home: Rachel developed morning and evening routines that demonstrated the behaviors she wanted her children to develop. Instead of lecturing about discipline, she modeled it. Instead of demanding they clean their rooms, she maintained her own space with care and attention.

Story Leadership at Home: Rachel examined the stories she was passing to her children through her words and actions. She stopped saying things like "We can't afford that" and started saying "That's not where we choose to spend our money right now." She stopped telling them "I'm so busy" and started saying "I'm choosing to prioritize other things right now."

Purpose Leadership at Home: Rachel connected family rules and expectations to larger purposes rather than arbitrary parental authority. "We clean up after ourselves because we respect our home and each other," not "because I said so." "We help each other because that's what families do," not "because you have to."

The Exponential Impact

The results of Rachel's self-leadership extended far beyond her family:

Her children began demonstrating leadership qualities at school because they were learning leadership at home. Her oldest daughter started a peer tutoring program. Her middle son began mediating conflicts on the playground. Her youngest started taking initiative with chores without being asked.

But the ripples went further. Rachel's self-leadership transformation inspired changes in her workplace, where colleagues began asking about her increased energy and effectiveness. Her modeling of work-life harmony influenced company policies. Her approach to team projects elevated the performance of everyone around her.

Community Leadership Through Self-Leadership

Rachel's influence extended into her community as well. Her neighborhood noticed the change in her family dynamic and began asking for advice. She started informal parenting groups that focused on self-leadership as the foundation for family leadership. These groups grew into community leadership development initiatives.

"I never intended to become a 'leader' in the traditional sense," Rachel told me. "I just wanted to be a better parent. But when you start leading yourself well, people notice. They want to learn how to create what you've created. Before you know it, you're influencing dozens, then hundreds, then thousands of people---all because you decided to take responsibility for your own habits, stories, and purposes."

Breaking the Generational Pattern

One of the most profound applications of self-leadership is breaking negative generational patterns that have been passed down through families, organizations, and communities.

Michael's Generational Leadership Revolution

Michael Rodriguez came from three generations of men who led through intimidation, criticism, and emotional distance. His grandfather had been a harsh disciplinarian. His father had been demanding and never satisfied. Michael found himself repeating these patterns with his own children and his team at work.

"I was perpetuating a leadership style that had damaged me, and I was damaging others with it," Michael realized. "The pattern was going to continue through my kids and their kids unless I stopped it."

Michael's transformation required developing daily mastery that contradicted generational programming, story consciousness that challenged inherited narratives, and purpose clarity that transcended family dysfunction.

New Daily Development:

- Instead of leading through criticism, Michael developed habits of encouragement

- Instead of demanding immediate compliance, he created habits of collaborative problem-solving

- Instead of emotional distance, he practiced emotional presence and vulnerability

Story Reconstruction:

- From "Strong leaders don't show weakness" to "Authentic leaders show their humanity"

- From "Children need to fear authority" to "Children need to respect authentic authority"

- From "Emotions are a sign of weakness" to "Emotional intelligence is a leadership strength"

Purpose Transformation:

- From "My job is to control outcomes" to "My job is to develop people's capability to create good outcomes"

- From "Leadership means being feared" to "Leadership means being worthy of respect"

- From "I must be right" to "I must help others discover what's right"

The Generational Transformation

The impact on Michael's children was immediate and profound. His teenage son, who had been rebellious and distant, began coming to Michael for advice. His daughter started including him in her plans instead of hiding them. Both children began demonstrating leadership qualities in their own contexts.

But perhaps most significantly, Michael's elderly father noticed the change. "You're different with your kids than I was with you," he observed. "Maybe I was wrong about some things."

At age 67, Michael's father began his own journey of self-leadership, examining habits that had shaped three generations of their family. **Michael's decision to lead himself differently had not only transformed his children's future but had also healed his father's past.**

Your Leadership Moment

Jonathan Mitchell, the CEO we met at the beginning of this chapter, rebuilt his company and his life through self-leadership. Two years after hiding in that parking garage, he was featured in Harvard Business Review---not for his turnaround strategies, but for his approach to leadership development.

"I learned that leadership isn't something you do to others," Jonathan said in the interview. "It's something you become for others. And you can only become it by first becoming it for yourself."

Jonathan's company not only recovered but thrived, becoming known for developing leaders at every level. The business success was remarkable, but Jonathan measured his real leadership impact differently:

"The question isn't whether people follow you," he told me. "The question is: do the people who follow you become better leaders themselves? Are you creating dependency or developing capability? Are you building a culture that requires your presence or one that embodies your principles?"

Before you close this chapter and move to the next, I want you to consider this truth: **You are already leading someone. Even if it's just yourself, you are already influencing others through your example, your energy, and your choices.**

The question isn't whether you're a leader. The question is: **What kind of leader are you becoming through the habits you practice, the stories you believe, and the purposes you serve?**

Three Final Questions:

- If everyone in your sphere of influence developed the same daily habits you practice, what kind of culture would that create?

- If everyone around you believed the same stories about themselves and the world that you believe, how would that shape their possibilities?

- If everyone you influence served the same purposes that drive you, what kind of impact would that create in the world?

The Choice That Changes Everything

Maria Santos is now superintendent of schools for her district, overseeing 47 schools and 35,000 students. But she still begins each day the same way she did when she was learning to lead herself: with the recognition that **leadership is an inside-out proposition that begins with the person in the mirror.**

"Every morning, I ask myself three questions," Maria shared. "Am I leading my habits or are they leading me? Am I choosing my stories or are they choosing me? Am I serving my purposes or am I being driven by them? The answers determine not just what kind of day I'll have, but what kind of influence I'll be."

This is the choice that changes everything: the choice to lead yourself first, so that your leadership of others emerges from authenticity rather than authority, from presence rather than position, from who you are rather than what you do.

The revolution begins with you. The transformation spreads through you. The legacy flows from you.

"Leadership is not about having people follow you to where you've never been. It's about becoming someone worth following because of where you've led yourself. Master your daily actions, choose your stories, clarify your purposes, and you'll discover that influence isn't something you have to manufacture---it's something that naturally emerges from the harmony of who you are."

In the next chapter, we'll explore how to use your transformed self for the long game---building not just a successful life, but a meaningful legacy that outlasts your time on earth. You'll discover that the greatest leadership isn't measured by what you accomplish, but by what continues to grow long after you're gone.

But for now, look in the mirror and see not just who you are, but who you're becoming through your daily choices. See not just your current influence, but the ripple effects your self-leadership could create across generations.

The world doesn't need more people with leadership titles. It needs more people with leadership character.

Which one will you become?

Chapter Thirteen

Wealth and Prosperity

"The difference between those who have and those who have not isn't opportunity, education, or luck. It's understanding that wealth flows to those who become worthy of it through how they think, what they do daily, and what they choose to serve."

The Library and the Lamborghini

Two brothers. Same parents. Same neighborhood. Same opportunities.

Today, one drives a Lamborghini to his office overlooking Central Park. The other drives a ten-year-old Honda to his job at the same company where he's worked for fifteen years.

Want to know the difference?

It happened in a library when they were both nineteen.

Marcus was drowning in his economics textbook, memorizing formulas he'd forget by next semester. His brother David sat across from him, but he wasn't reading textbooks. He was devouring Andrew Carnegie's autobiography, studying how Ray Kroc built McDonald's, learning how problems become profits when you understand the pattern.

Marcus looked up, exhausted. "Why are you wasting time on that? It's not going to be on the test."

David's response changed everything—he told me this story himself, years later, in that office overlooking Central Park: "You're studying to pass their test. I'm studying to pass life's test. You're learning what they want you to know. I'm learning what I need to know."

That moment. Right there. That's when two brothers' destinies diverged.

Marcus graduated with honors, got a good job, did everything right. David dropped out sophomore year, started three failed businesses, lived on his friend's couch for a year, and nearly gave up five times.

But here's what Marcus never saw during those years: David wasn't failing. He was being forged.

The Million-Dollar Mind Shift

Let me tell you something that will either upset you or set you free: formal education teaches you to work in someone else's system. Self-education teaches you to build your own.

Think about what David discovered in those biographies that Marcus missed in his textbooks. Every single self-made millionaire understood something profound: **Problems equal profits.** The bigger the problem you solve, the bigger the check you receive.

But schools don't teach you to hunt for problems. They teach you to avoid them.

David learned something else in that library, something that took me twenty years to understand: Wealth isn't about what you know. It's about who you become while learning what others won't learn, trying what others won't try, and continuing when others won't continue.

"The poor see problems as punishments. The middle class see problems as annoyances. The wealthy see problems as paychecks waiting to be collected."

The Emotional Price of Staying Poor

Before I tell you about transformation, let me tell you about the alternative. Let me tell you what poverty really costs.

It's not the ten-year-old Honda. It's the dreams that die in the driver's seat.

It's not the small apartment. It's feeling small inside it.

It's not the empty bank account. It's the empty feeling when you realize another year passed and nothing changed.

I know because I lived it. For fifteen years, I lived it. Every morning, I'd wake up with that weight on my chest—not depression, but something worse: resignation. The quiet acceptance that this is all there is.

You know that feeling? When your kid asks for something—nothing fancy, maybe just the name-brand cereal instead of generic—and you have to say no. Not because you're teaching them values. But because you can't afford the extra dollar-fifty.

That moment breaks something inside you. Or it breaks something open.

There's a particular sound poverty makes. It's not dramatic. It's the quiet sigh when you check your bank balance. It's the pause before you swipe your card, hoping. It's the calculations you do in the grocery store, putting items back one by one.

But the worst sound? The silence when your spouse stops mentioning dreams because they know you can't afford them. The quiet when your kids stop asking because they already know the answer.

"Poverty isn't just about money. It's about becoming smaller to fit inside your circumstances instead of expanding your circumstances to fit your becoming."

The Journey Is the Destination

Here's what nobody tells you about building wealth: The money is the least important part.

When David was living on that couch, eating ramen, watching his third business fail, he wasn't failing—he was forming. Every setback was stripping away who he thought he was and revealing who he could become.

The journey to wealth is a journey to yourself. The person who can create millions is not the person who wants millions. They're completely different humans. The journey transforms you from one to the other.

Think about it: If you gave a million dollars to someone with a poverty mindset, what happens? They'd be broke within two years. Statistics prove it. Lottery winners, athletes, inheritance recipients—90% return to their starting point or worse.

Why? Because they got the money without taking the journey. They received the reward without the reformation.

"Wealth is not what you have. It's what you've become that allows you to have it and keep it and grow it."

Jennifer's Revolution: The Awakening Moment

Let me tell you about Jennifer Park, because her story isn't about meal prep. It's about the moment a human being decides to stop accepting the unacceptable.

Jennifer was thirty-four, single mom, working reception at a dental office. Thirty-two thousand a year. Every month was a negotiation with reality: Which bill can wait? Which necessity isn't really necessary?

But Jennifer had developed something most people never develop: She had learned to hear differently.

Every day at lunch, her coworkers complained:

- "I can never find healthy food that's quick"

- "Meal prep takes all Sunday"

- "I waste so much money on takeout"

Most people hear complaints and join the chorus. Jennifer heard a symphony of opportunity.

That night, she sat in her kitchen after putting her daughter to bed. She had seventeen dollars in her checking account. But she also had YouTube. And she had something more valuable than money: She had reached the point where the pain of staying the same exceeded the pain of change.

Here's what Jennifer told me later, and I want you to feel the weight of this: "I realized I had been living my mother's life. And her mother's life. The same struggles, the same limitations, the same story of 'people like us.' That night, I decided my daughter would watch me rise, not just survive."

"The moment you decide to be the one who breaks the generational pattern is the moment your wealth story begins."

The Inner Revolution: Rewiring How You Think

Jennifer didn't just start a meal prep business. She rewired her entire way of thinking about herself and what was possible.

For six months, she lived two lives. By day, she answered phones and smiled at patients. By night, she studied everything: nutrition, bulk sourcing, food safety, packaging, systems, marketing. Not in a classroom. In her kitchen, with YouTube University and library books.

But the real transformation wasn't in her skills. It was in her skull.

The Old Jennifer thought: "I can't because... I don't have... People like me don't... If only I had... It must be nice to... That's for other people..."

The New Jennifer thought: "How can I... What if I tried... People like me are exactly who... Because I don't have, I must... It will be nice when... I'm becoming those other people..."

She stopped saying, "I'm just a single mom trying to get by." She started saying, "I'm building an empire, one meal at a time."

She stopped thinking, "People like me don't build businesses." She started thinking, "People like me build businesses that matter because we know what problems feel like."

She stopped believing, "I need credentials to succeed." She started believing, "My life is my credential. My struggle is my qualification. My hunger is my degree."

"Your credentials aren't what hang on your wall. They're what you've crawled through to get to where you're standing."

The 4 AM Revelation

4 AM became Jennifer's power hour. But not for the reason you think.

It wasn't about productivity. It was about identity.

When you wake at 4 AM to build your dreams, you're making a declaration to the universe and to yourself: "I matter. My vision matters. My future matters more than my comfort."

Every morning she rose in darkness, she was choosing her becoming over her being.

Here's the profound truth about those early morning hours: You're not just building a business. You're building evidence. Evidence that you're not who you were. Evidence that you can do hard things. Evidence that you're becoming someone who deserves wealth because you're becoming someone who creates value.

Five meals for one coworker. Then ten. Then fifty.

Within two years, her company hit two million in revenue.

But here's what the revenue doesn't tell you: The moment Jennifer's daughter watched her mom buy their first house. The moment Jennifer hired another single mom and said, "I see you. I was you. Let me show you what's possible." The moment she realized she hadn't checked her bank balance in fear for six months.

That's not business success. That's human revolution.

"Success is when your bank account changes. Wealth is when you change."

The Daily Habits of Wealthy Thinking

Wealthy people don't have better habits. They have different mornings, different thoughts, different responses to the same struggles that everyone faces.

Marcus woke up at 7:30, rushed through coffee, commuted in traffic thinking about his boss, worked till 6, came home exhausted, watched Netflix, went to bed. Repeat for fifteen years.

David woke up at 5:00. Not because he had to. Because that's when opportunity wakes up.

But here's the deeper truth: Those early morning hours aren't about time management. They're about becoming management.

The Poverty Morning Mindset: "I have to get up" → "I have to go to work" → "I have to pay bills" → "I have to survive"

The Wealth Morning Mindset: "I get to wake up" → "I get to build" → "I get to create value" → "I get to become"

In those quiet hours, transformation happens:

You don't just read success stories. You feel your own story changing. You don't just study business models. You model a new version of yourself. You don't just hunt for opportunities. You become someone opportunities hunt for.

"Poverty sleeps until it has to wake up. Wealth wakes up before it has to. That's not discipline. That's desire."

The Sacred Morning Ritual

Here's exactly what happens in a wealth-building morning:

5:00-5:15 AM - The Awakening Ritual You don't check your phone. You check in with your becoming. You ask: "Who am I becoming today that I wasn't yesterday?" You declare: "Today, I build. Today, I create. Today, I become."

This isn't positive thinking. This is identity architecture.

5:15-6:00 AM - The Education Investment You read, but not for entertainment. You read for transformation. You study someone who's done what you want to do. You learn one thing that makes you more valuable.

"Poor people read to escape reality. Rich people read to create a new one."

6:00-6:30 AM - The Problem Hunt You scan the world for problems. Not to complain. To capitalize. Every complaint you hear is a check waiting to be written. Every frustration is a fortune in disguise.

6:30-7:00 AM - The Value Creation You work on your thing. Your project. Your business. Your becoming. Not for hours. Just for progress. Thirty minutes of creation beats eight hours of consumption.

"You don't need more hours in your day. You need more intention in your hours."

Rewriting Your Money Story

The stories you tell yourself about money aren't just thoughts. They're prophecies.

But here's what's profound: These stories were written before you could write. You inherited them. Absorbed them. Accepted them as truth before you knew you had a choice.

What did you learn about money at your dinner table? "Money doesn't grow on trees" = Money is scarce "We can't afford that" = We are not enough "Rich people are different" = Wealth is not for us "Must be nice" = We're victims, not victors

These aren't your truths. They're hand-me-down limitations, worn-out stories that fit your parents but strangle your potential.

"You're not poor. You're living someone else's poverty story. Time to write your own."

The Story Archaeology Process

Week One: Excavation Write down every money memory from childhood. Every phrase. Every feeling. Every moment that shaped your money story. Then write next to each: "This was their truth, not mine."

Week Two: Examination Listen to yourself talk about money for one week. Catch every poverty phrase:

- "I can't afford..."

- "Must be nice to..."

- "People like me don't..."

- "I'm not good with..."

These are your poverty mantras. You're literally praying for scarcity.

Week Three: Reformation Replace every poverty story with a wealth story:

"I can't afford that" becomes "How can I make that happen?" One is a coffin. The other is a key.

"That's too expensive" becomes "That's not my priority right now" One is powerlessness. The other is power.

"I'm broke" becomes "I'm between breakthroughs. I'm in transition. I'm building." One is permanent. The other is passing.

"Money is hard" becomes "Money flows to value, and I'm becoming valuable" One is a wall. The other is a way.

"Your vocabulary creates your reality. Speak poverty, live poverty. Speak wealth, live wealth. Your tongue is your treasure map."

Tommy's Transformation: The Janitor Who Built an Empire

Tommy was forty-seven, high school dropout, janitor, eleven dollars an hour. Most people would say his story was already written.

Tommy disagreed.

While cleaning offices at night, he studied them. Not just emptying trash—understanding. Why did some businesses thrive while others just survived? What problems did they all share?

Then he noticed: These offices were always running out of supplies. The office managers hated dealing with it. Ordering was a hassle. Delivery was unpredictable. Nobody wanted to manage it.

Tommy saw what others missed: a problem so annoying that people would pay to make it disappear.

But here's where Tommy's story becomes legendary. He didn't quit his janitor job to start his business. He transformed his janitor job into his business education. Every office he cleaned became his classroom. Every complaint he overheard became curriculum.

"Your current job isn't your prison. It's your paid education if you're paying attention."

For three months, he studied supply chain management on YouTube during his dinner break. For two months, he learned subscription business models at the library before his shift. He mastered QuickBooks using their free trial.

Cost of his MBA: Zero. Value of his education: Priceless.

But here's what matters: While Tommy was learning, he was becoming. Each video he watched, he wasn't just gaining knowledge. He was shedding the story of "I'm just a janitor" and writing the story of "I'm a businessman in training."

The Psychology of the First Sale

Tommy's first pitch. Picture this: A forty-seven-year-old janitor walking into the office manager's room, the same room he'd emptied trash from for three years.

His hands shook. His voice cracked. The old story screamed: "You're just the janitor! Who do you think you are?"

But the new story whispered: "You're the solution to their problem. You deserve to be here."

He made his offer: "I'll handle all your supplies for a flat monthly fee. You'll never run out. You'll never think about it. You'll never deal with it again."

The manager looked at him. Really looked at him for the first time in three years.

"How much?"

Tommy named his price. Three times what he calculated he needed, because Jennifer's story taught him something: "Never negotiate against yourself. Your poverty mindset will always undercharge.

"Deal."

That "deal" was worth more than the contract. It was the moment Tommy's new story became real. He wasn't a janitor who had an idea. He was a business owner who happened to still clean.

"The first sale doesn't change your bank account. It changes your being. You're no longer someone who wants to be. You're someone who is."

The Compound Effect of Becoming

Here's what happened next—and notice how success really builds:

One office said yes. Tommy delivered obsessively. On time. Every time. That office told another office. Second office was easier—he had proof now. By the tenth office, he hired another janitor to handle deliveries. By the twentieth office, he quit his janitor job. By the fiftieth, he had a system. By the hundredth, he had a business. By the two hundredth, he had freedom.

Today: Three million in annual revenue. Twelve employees. Twenty hours a week of actual work.

But Tommy told me something that stopped me cold: "The hardest part wasn't building the business. It was believing I was allowed to."

"We don't build businesses. We build ourselves, and then we build businesses. The business is just evidence of who we've become."

The Four Levels of Money Consciousness

There are four levels of wealth consciousness, and you must climb them in order:

Level 1: Survival Consciousness ($0-30K) "I need to make enough to survive" You trade time for money. You think in days and weeks. Your focus: Don't drown.

Level 2: Stability Consciousness ($30K-100K) "I need to make enough to be secure" You trade skills for money. You think in months and years. Your focus: Stay safe.

Level 3: Success Consciousness ($100K-1M) "I want to create systems that create wealth" You trade value for money. You think in years and decades. Your focus: Build and grow.

Level 4: Significance Consciousness ($1M+) "I want to solve problems that matter" You trade solutions for money. You think in decades and generations. Your focus: Impact and legacy.

You can't skip levels. Each level requires a different you.

"Poor people ask 'How can I survive?' Rich people ask 'How can I thrive?' Wealthy people ask 'How can others thrive through me?'"

Finding Your Why Beyond Survival

Poor people have survival purposes: Pay rent. Feed kids. Get through the month. There's no shame in survival. But there's tragedy in stopping there.

Because here's what happens when your only purpose is survival: You survive. That's it. You get exactly what you aimed for—not dying.

Rich people have success purposes: Build wealth. Achieve status. Prove themselves. Better. But still incomplete.

Wealthy people—truly wealthy people—have significance purposes: Solve real problems. Create lasting value. Lift others as they rise.

Jennifer didn't just build a meal prep company. She created jobs for other single mothers. She became proof that single moms can build empires.

Tommy didn't just build a supply company. He created systems that gave other janitors a pathway out. He became a bridge others could cross.

David didn't just build wealth. He came back for Marcus.

"Survival asks 'How can I get?' Success asks 'How can I grow?' Significance asks 'How can I give?'"

The Moment Everything Changes

Marcus was forty when he finally understood. Sitting in his cubicle, tenth year at the same company, he realized his brother's success wasn't luck. It was choice, compounded daily for twenty years.

That night, Marcus called David. "Teach me," he said. Just that. Teach me.

David's response reveals everything about wealth consciousness: "I'll show you everything I know. But first, you have to decide—do you want to get rich, or do you want to become rich?"

There's a universe of difference.

Getting rich is about having. Becoming rich is about being.

Getting rich can be lost. Becoming rich is forever.

Marcus chose becoming.

The Sacred Hours Strategy

Marcus kept his job but claimed his mornings. 5 AM became his sanctuary.

While his family slept, he studied. While his coworkers commuted, he created. While others watched Netflix, he built.

But here's what Marcus understood that most don't: He wasn't adding activities to his day. He was subtracting himself from his old story and adding himself to a new one.

Every morning he woke at 5 AM, the old Marcus died a little. Every book he read, the new Marcus was born a little more. Every problem he solved, his identity shifted.

"You don't change your life. You change yourself, and your life changes as evidence of who you've become."

He read fifty-two books in fifty-two weeks. Not for entertainment. For transformation. Each book was someone's lifetime of lessons for the price of lunch.

He identified a problem: Small businesses couldn't afford good marketing. He built a solution: Automated marketing systems they could afford. He launched at forty-one. He went profitable at forty-two. He quit his job at forty-three.

Today, Marcus makes more in a month than his old annual salary.

But here's what matters more: Marcus's children watch their father build instead of blame. They see possibility instead of limitation. They're inheriting wealth consciousness, not poverty consciousness.

"The greatest wealth you can give your children isn't money. It's showing them what's possible when someone decides to become."

The Unspoken Truth About Wealth

Here's what David told Marcus that changed everything:

"For twenty years, I felt guilty about my success. Why me? Why not you? Then I realized: My success without your success is incomplete. True wealth is when everyone in your circle rises."

This is the final evolution of wealth consciousness: Understanding that your wealth is not separate from others' wealth. It's connected. Your rising lifts others. Your success gives permission. Your breakthrough becomes their possibility.

"Poverty consciousness believes wealth is limited—if I have more, you have less. Wealth consciousness knows wealth is created—if I have more, I can create more for others."

The Price of Transformation

Let me tell you something about the journey that nobody talks about:

You will lose friends. The ones who need you to stay small so they can feel big.

You will face ridicule. The ones who tried and quit need you to quit too, to validate their quitting.

You will doubt yourself. At 3 AM, building while others sleep, you'll wonder if you're crazy.

You will want to quit. Multiple times. The old you will scream to go back to comfort. But here's what else happens:

You will find your tribe. People who celebrate your rising because they're rising too.

You will discover strength. The kind that only comes from doing what you thought you couldn't.

You will experience freedom. Not just financial. The freedom of becoming who you really are.

You will feel purpose. The deep satisfaction of solving real problems for real people.

"The price of wealth is paid in the currency of becoming. It costs who you were to become who you're meant to be."

Your Wealth Meditation

Every night before sleep, Marcus does this. Tommy does this. Jennifer does this. Now you do this:

Close your eyes. See yourself one year from today.

What problems have you solved? Who have you become in the solving? What skills have you built? What value have you created? Who have you lifted with your rising?

Now see yourself five years from today.

You're not the same person. You can't be. The person who creates millions cannot be the person who dreams of thousands. You've transformed.

What does that person know that you don't know yet? What does that person do that you don't do yet? Who is that person that you aren't yet?

Now here's the key: That person isn't in the future. They're in you now, waiting to be revealed. Every choice you make either feeds that person or starves them.

"You're not building a business. You're building the person who can build the business. You're not creating wealth. You're creating the person who can create wealth."

The Three Pillars of Wealth Psychology

Pillar 1: Pattern Recognition Poor people see isolated events. Rich people see patterns. Wealthy people create patterns.

Every problem that gets solved repeatedly for money is a pattern. Every complaint you hear repeatedly is a pattern. Every frustration people face repeatedly is a pattern.

"Poverty is random. Wealth is pattern. Master the pattern, master the money."

Pillar 2: Value Creation Consciousness Poor people think: "How can I get paid?" Rich people think: "How can I get paid more?" Wealthy people think: "How can I create more value?"

The shift is subtle but profound. When you focus on value, payment is a byproduct. When you focus on payment, value is an afterthought.

"Chase money and it runs. Create value and money chases you."

Pillar 3: Systems Thinking Poor people work in the system. Rich people work the system. Wealthy people create systems.

Jennifer didn't cook meals. She created a meal system. Tommy didn't deliver supplies. He created a supply system. Marcus didn't do marketing. He created a marketing system.

"Your income is limited by your hours until you build systems that work beyond your hours."

The Moment of Choice

Right now, reading this, you're at your own library moment. Your crossroads. Your choice.

You can close this chapter and continue exactly as you are. There's no shame in that. Survival is not a sin.

Or you can decide that starting tomorrow—no, starting tonight—you begin the revolution. Not just in your bank account. In your being.

You can decide that your current circumstances are not your ceiling—they're your classroom.

You can decide that every problem you see is profit in disguise.

You can decide that you'll wake before comfort wakes.

You can decide that you'll build while others blame.

You can decide that you'll become while others wish.

"The moment you decide to become wealthy is not when you make the money. It's when you decide you're worthy of making it."

Your Declaration of Becoming

If you're ready, stand up. Actually stand. Because this moment deserves your full presence.

Say this with the conviction of someone who just realized their life is not a dress rehearsal:

"I am done accepting ordinary results from ordinary thinking. Starting now, I am rebuilding myself for wealth—not just in my wallet, but in my worth.

I will wake before comfort wakes. I will learn while others are entertained. I will build while others consume. I will invest while others spend. I will solve problems while others create them. I will become valuable while others demand value.

This is not hope—this is decision. This is not someday—this is today. This is not temporary—this is my new permanent.

I am not trying to get rich. I am becoming rich. The person I'm becoming creates wealth naturally, automatically, inevitably.

I release my inherited poverty stories. I reject my learned limitations. I refuse my assumed ceilings.

I am the one who breaks the pattern. I am the one who changes the story. I am the one who rises and lifts others with my rising.

My becoming makes wealth inevitable."

The Final Truth About Wealth

The library is open. YouTube is free. Problems are everywhere. Your transformation is waiting.

David and Marcus both learned the same truth, just twenty years apart: Poverty is not a lack of money—it's accepting that lack as permanent. Wealth is not an abundance of money—it's the abundance that comes from knowing you can create value anywhere, anytime, for anyone.

But here's the deepest truth, the one that changes everything:

You're not poor. You're just not finished becoming.

Every morning you wake up, you're writing your story. Every problem you solve, you're building your proof. Every habit you change, you're changing your destiny. Every skill you build, you're building your worth. Every system you create, you're creating your freedom.

The world is waiting for what you'll build when you finally believe you're allowed to build it.

Your janitor's closet might be your office. Your kitchen table might be your boardroom. Your morning hours might be your MBA. Your current struggle might be your future testimony.

But your decision—your decision to rise—that's your revolution.

"Wealth is not a destination. It's a becoming. You don't arrive at wealth. You arrive at yourself, and wealth is the evidence."

Start tonight. Wake up tomorrow different.

Not because you have to.

Because you finally understand that you can.

Because you finally understand that the person you're becoming deserves wealth.

Because you finally understand that your rising gives others permission to rise.

Because you finally understand that wealth was never about the money.

It was always about who you become on the way to the money.

The journey is the destination.

The becoming is the wealth.

Who will you become in the becoming?

Chapter Fourteen

THE DAILY PRACTICE

"THE DIFFERENCE BETWEEN THOSE WHO TRANSFORM AND THOSE WHO MERELY DREAM OF TRANSFORMATION IS FOUND IN THE MUNDANE MAGNIFICENCE OF THEIR DAILY PRACTICE. DESTINY IS NOT SHAPED IN THE DRAMATIC MOMENTS—IT'S FORGED IN THE FORGETTABLE MORNINGS WHEN NOBODY'S WATCHING."

The Man Who Wrote Himself Into Existence

At 4:47 AM, in a cramped studio apartment above a Chinese restaurant in Queens, Anthony Ramirez sits at a wobbly kitchen table with a $1.99 notebook from the dollar store. The apartment reeks of yesterday's General Tso's chicken. His neighbors are arguing through paper-thin walls. Outside, sirens wail their urban lullaby.

Anthony doesn't notice any of it. He's too busy having the most important conversation of his day—the one with himself.

Three years ago, Anthony was invisible. Not literally, but functionally. A thirty-eight-year-old warehouse worker who moved through life like a ghost—present but not noticed, alive but not living. He was sleepwalking through existence, letting his days happen to him rather than creating them.

But here's what you need to understand about Anthony three years ago, because it's probably where you are right now: He wasn't unhappy. That's the insidious truth about a life without daily practice. You're not miserable—you're numb. You're not failing—you're floating. You're not dying—you're just not living.

Anthony had what I call Comfortable Cage Syndrome. His life was tolerable enough to endure but not meaningful enough to matter. He made enough money to survive but not enough to thrive. He had enough energy to get through the day but not enough to build dreams. He had enough friends to not feel alone but not enough depth to feel connected.

"The opposite of depression isn't happiness—it's meaning. And meaning is cultivated in daily choices; without it, life decays into empty existence."

Then Anthony discovered something that sounds too simple to be revolutionary: When you write something down, it transforms from imagination to material. It moves from the realm of maybe to the territory of tangible. The pen doesn't just record reality—it creates it.

But let me tell you what Anthony really discovered, the thing that changed everything: Daily practice isn't about doing. It's about becoming. Every morning you show up, you're voting for who you're becoming. Every day you skip, you're voting for who you've been.

The Adaptation Principle: Your Body's Secret Wisdom

"Your body is constantly adapting to the life you're living. The question is: Are you designing that adaptation or defaulting into decay?"

After three decades as a nurse and respiratory therapist, I've learned something that burned itself into my consciousness: Your body is always adapting. Every single day, it's restructuring itself to match the demands you place on it—or the lack thereof.

But here's what most people don't understand: Your mind is adapting too. Your identity is adapting. Your very sense of what's possible is adapting.

I've watched the entire circle of life from the emergency room. I've delivered babies, treated young adults with sports injuries, watched middle-aged people develop diseases of disuse, and held the hands of sixty-year-olds shuffling with walkers through nursing homes, their bodies betraying them decades too early.

But I've also seen seventy-year-olds running marathons, eighty-year-olds teaching yoga, ninety-year-olds who could out-walk people a third their age.

The difference isn't genetics. It isn't luck. It isn't even motivation. The difference is daily practice.

Not dramatic interventions. Not expensive treatments. Not heroic efforts. Daily. Consistent. Unconscious-becoming-conscious. Practice.

The Tale of Two Destinies: A Mirror of Your Future

Let me tell you about two men I treated on the same day, both exactly seventy years old. Their stories contain everything you need to know about the power of daily practice—and the cost of avoiding it.

William's Gradual Descent

William came in with a hip fracture from falling in his bathroom. But the hip fracture was just the latest milestone in a decades-long journey of decline.

Twenty years ago, William was fifty. Active. Capable. Full of plans. Then life got busy. The morning walks became occasional. The occasional became rare. The rare became never. His body adapted to his new normal: sitting.

"When did you stop exercising?" I asked him.

"I never stopped," he said. "I just... paused. And the pause became permanent."

That's how it happens. Not dramatically. Gradually. You skip one day, then two, then a week, then you can't remember the last time you moved intentionally.

William's body had adapted perfectly to his lifestyle. His muscles had atrophied to the exact level needed to move from bed to chair to car. His cardiovascular system had downsized to meet his minimal demands. His bones had thinned from lack of stress. His flexibility had decreased to the range needed for reaching the remote.

But here's the part that broke my heart: William's mind had atrophied too.

"What was the last new thing you learned?" I asked.

He couldn't answer. Not because he forgot—because it had been so long that the question didn't compute.

When I asked William about exercise now, he said, "I'm too old for that now."

When I asked about learning something new, he said, "You can't teach an old dog new tricks."

When I asked what he looked forward to, he said, "Just getting through the day."

William wasn't dying. He had died. Years ago. His body just hadn't gotten the memo yet.

Robert's Daily Revolution

Robert came in for a minor cut from trail running. This man had been moving his body daily for fifty years. But here's the crucial detail: Robert wasn't always a runner. He wasn't naturally athletic. He wasn't blessed with good genes.

"I was forty when I started," Robert told me while I cleaned his wound. "Overweight. Pre-diabetic. Couldn't climb stairs without gasping. Just like my father at that age." "What changed?" I asked.

"I watched my father die at sixty-five. Not dramatically—gradually. Each year smaller than the last. Each month less capable. Each day more resigned. One morning, I looked in the mirror and saw his trajectory in my reflection. That's when I decided: I would not inherit his decline."

Robert started with five minutes of walking. Just five. "I couldn't do more," he admitted. "But I could do five. So every morning, before my mind could argue, I walked for five minutes."

Month one: Five minutes became ten. Year one: Walking became jogging. Year five: Jogging became running. Year thirty: Running became trail running.

"But the movement was just the visible part," Robert explained. "The real practice was mental. Every morning, I had to choose who I was becoming over who I'd been. Every single morning for thirty years."

Robert's secret weapon wasn't just physical movement. "I read something new every morning," he told me. "Fifteen minutes. Biography, science, philosophy—doesn't matter as long as it's something I didn't know yesterday. My rule is simple: Never go to bed the same person who woke up."

When I asked Robert why he still exercised daily at seventy, he said, "I'm too old NOT to. Every day I skip is a day closer to William's trajectory."

When I asked about the daily learning, he said, "The day I stop growing is the day I start dying. And I'm not ready to die."

Same age. Same starting point. Completely different vessels they were navigating life in. Completely different minds piloting those vessels.

The difference? Twenty minutes of movement and fifteen minutes of learning. Daily. For decades.

"We don't rise to the level of our dreams. We fall to the level of our daily practice."

Anthony's Four Pillars: The Architecture of Becoming

After six months of experimentation and failure, Anthony discovered that transformation requires four non-negotiable daily practices. Miss any one, and the whole structure becomes unstable.

Pillar 1: Move Your Vessel - The Physical Prophecy

"I realized my body was a prophecy," Anthony told me. "Every day I didn't move, I was prophesying a future where I couldn't move."

Anthony started with one push-up. One. "I couldn't do two," he admitted. "My arms shook. My chest burned. I wanted to die of embarrassment even though nobody was watching. Thirty-eight years old and I couldn't do two push-ups."

But here's what Anthony understood that most don't: The number doesn't matter. The consistency does.

"That one push-up wasn't about fitness," he explained. "It was about identity. I was becoming someone who does push-ups. Not someone who does fifty push-ups—that came later. Just someone who does push-ups. Period."

Week one: One push-up every morning. "The hardest part wasn't the push-up. It was the getting on the floor. Once I was down there, the push-up was easy."

Week two: Two push-ups. "I could have done two in week one, but I didn't. I was building consistency, not strength."

Month two: Twenty push-ups. "My body adapted faster than my mind. My muscles were ready for twenty. My identity was still catching up."

Year one: Fifty push-ups, twenty minutes of movement. "Now I don't think about it. I don't decide. I don't motivate myself. It's just who I am. I'm a person who moves every morning. It would feel weird not to."

But Anthony's physical practice evolved into something more sophisticated—what he calls "The Awakening Advantage Protocol."

The Cortisol Revolution: Leveraging Your Biology

"I discovered that my body gives me a gift every morning," Anthony explains. "The cortisol awakening response—this 50-75% surge in cortisol that happens within 30-45 minutes of waking. It's not stress—it's rocket fuel for transformation. But I was wasting it scrolling my phone."

Anthony developed a five-element morning sequence that works with his biology, not against it:

Element 1: Hydro-Mineral Reset (3 minutes) "I keep a glass of room temperature water with a pinch of Himalayan salt and lemon juice beside my bed. The body loses 1-2 pounds of water overnight, and dehydration impairs cognitive function by up to 12%. I drink this slowly while doing a body scan—flexing every muscle group for two seconds each, noticing where I'm tight and where I'm strong."

Element 2: Light Therapy Activation (10 minutes) "I step outside or stand by my brightest window. Light exposure within an hour of waking is the primary signal for circadian rhythm regulation. I combine this with movement—what I call the Dynamic Awakening Sequence."

Anthony's movement practice includes spinal wave flow (creating wave-like movements from tailbone through entire spine), breath-synchronized movement (combining flowing motions with specific breathing patterns), and strength activation (bodyweight exercises focused on consistency over intensity).

Element 3: The 4-7-8 Coherence Protocol (5 minutes) "This breathing technique creates coherence between heart, mind, and nervous system. Four counts inhale, seven counts hold, eight counts exhale. During the hold phase, I visualize breath moving between heart and brain, creating harmony between emotional and rational centers."

Element 4: Thermal Activation (Optional) "I end my shower with 60-90 seconds of cold water. Cold exposure triggers a 530% increase in noradrenaline, activates brown fat, and builds resilience through controlled stress. I focus on maintaining calm breathing rather than fighting the sensation."

"Your body isn't just transportation for your brain. It's the physical manifestation of your mental state. A body in motion creates a mind in motion."

But here's the deeper truth Anthony discovered: Movement isn't just about physical health. It's about mental possibility.

"When I proved I could transform my body from one push-up to fifty, I started believing I could transform other things too. My body was proof that change was possible. Every push-up was evidence that I wasn't stuck."

Pillar 2: Document Your Journey - The Written Witness

"Most people think journaling is recording what happened," Anthony said, showing me his stack of dollar-store notebooks—forty-three of them now. "That's a diary. Journaling is creating what's happening."

Every morning, after his movement, Anthony writes. Not essays—conversations. With himself. With his resistance. With his future.

His first entry, three years ago, was eight words: "I don't know what to write. This is stupid."

His second entry: "Still stupid. But I'm here. That's something."

His third entry: "Maybe stupid is okay. Maybe stupid is starting."

"I discovered I'd never actually met myself," he said, flipping through those early pages. "Thirty-eight years old and I'd never had an honest conversation with Anthony. The journal introduced us."

His early entries were painful to read:

- "I'm nobody special."

- "People like me don't change."

- "It's too late to matter."

- "I'm embarrassed to want more."

- "Who am I kidding?"

But daily writing revealed something: These weren't truths. They were stories. Old stories. Inherited stories. Stories that had never been questioned because they'd never been written down where he could see them.

"Writing forces honesty," Anthony explained. "You can lie to others. You can even lie to yourself in your head. But when you write it down, lies look like lies. 'I don't have time' looks ridiculous when you write it after scrolling Instagram for an hour."

"The pen is mightier than the sword because the pen can rewrite the story the sword is fighting for."

After six months, Anthony's entries evolved:

- "I'm nobody special YET."

- "People like me don't change UNLESS THEY DO."

- "It's too late to matter TO WHO?"

- "I'm embarrassed to want more BUT I WANT IT ANYWAY."

- "Who am I kidding? NOBODY. THIS IS REAL."

"The journal became my laboratory," Anthony said. "Every morning, I experimented with new thoughts. New stories. New possibilities. Some worked. Some didn't. But they were all mine, not inherited, not imposed, not assumed. Mine."

Pillar 3: Feed Your Evolution - The Learning Imperative

"I realized I hadn't learned anything new in five years," Anthony told me. "Not really learned. I'd consumed entertainment. I'd absorbed information. But I hadn't learned—meaning I hadn't changed based on new knowledge."

Here's what Anthony discovered: Your mind has a metabolic rate. Feed it the same thoughts, and it maintains the same temperature. Feed it new thoughts, and it heats up, speeds up, lights up.

"I was mentally malnourished," Anthony said. "Feeding my mind the equivalent of junk food—social media, news outrage, TV reruns. Empty calories that left me mentally bloated but intellectually starving."

Anthony developed what he calls his Daily Mental Meal—fifteen minutes of deliberate learning distributed throughout the day:

Morning Input (5 minutes): After journaling, one article, video, or book passage that challenges an assumption. "Not entertainment—evolution. I look for ideas that make me uncomfortable. Comfort is the enemy of growth."

Commute Processing: "I don't listen to music or news during my commute. I process what I learned in the morning. I ask: 'How does this challenge my current thinking? What would change if this were true?'"

Evening Integration (5 minutes): Before bed, Anthony writes one sentence: "Today I learned that..." "This forces me to process, not just consume."

But here's the crucial distinction: Anthony doesn't learn for knowledge. He learns for transformation.

"Every day, I look for one idea that threatens my current identity. One concept that makes me uncomfortable. One truth that challenges my stories. If I'm not slightly disturbed by what I'm learning, I'm not learning—I'm just confirming."

After one year:

- 365 new ideas encountered

- 365 assumptions challenged

- 365 sentences of digestion

- 91 hours of conscious evolution

"I'm not the same person I was a year ago," Anthony says. "Not because I tried to change, but because I fed my mind different food. You can't have the same thoughts when you're exposed to different ideas. You can't tell the same stories when you know different endings are possible."

"Your mind is like your body—feed it junk and it becomes junk. Feed it wisdom and it becomes wise. Starve it and it doesn't maintain—it deteriorates."

Pillar 4: Converse with Your Future - The Time Travel Practice

Six months in, Anthony added something that transformed everything: He started having conversations with his future self. Not imagination—actual written dialogues.

"I realized I was living reactively," Anthony explained. "Just responding to whatever each day brought. I had no relationship with where I was going. I was driving without a destination."

Every Sunday, Anthony writes to himself one year from now:

"Dear Future Anthony, Today I'm struggling with [specific challenge]. I'm afraid that [specific fear]. I'm hoping you've figured out [specific goal]. What do you need me to do today to become you? What should I keep doing? What should I stop? What matters most looking back?"

Every Monday, he writes back as that future self:

"Dear Present Anthony, I'm here. I made it. You're on the right path. That challenge you're facing? It's building strength you'll need. That fear? It's pointing to your growth edge. Focus on this today: [specific action]. Release this story: [specific limitation]. Remember: Every day you practice, you're building me. I'm not a hope. I'm an inevitability if you keep practicing."

"It sounds crazy," Anthony admits, "but these conversations make my future real. Not wished for—inevitable. When you're in dialogue with your future self, you stop wondering if you'll make it and start asking how to make it faster."

But here's what's really happening: Anthony is building what psychologists call "future self-continuity"—a felt connection to who he's becoming. Most people see their future self as a stranger. Anthony sees his as a friend, a mentor, a destiny.

"Most people hope their future will be different. Conscious practitioners have conversations with their future selves to ensure it."

The Daily Navigation: Conscious Response Protocols

"Transformation doesn't happen only in the morning," Anthony discovered. "It happens in how you respond to everything the day throws at you."

Anthony learned that daily practice isn't just about morning routines—it's about developing what he calls "Conscious Response Protocols" throughout the day.

The Midday Trinity Check-In

Every day at noon, Anthony pauses for what he calls the Trinity Assessment:

- Biology: "How is my energy, focus, and physical state right now?"

- Identity: "Who am I being today, and who am I becoming through my choices?"

- Purpose: "What meaningful contribution will I make today?"

"This five-minute check-in keeps me conscious instead of just reacting to whatever's happening," Anthony explains.

The Stoic Response Arsenal

Anthony developed specific protocols for common daily challenges, based on ancient Stoic principles but backed by modern neuroscience:

When Someone Cuts You Off in Traffic: "The old Anthony would rage. Road rage was my specialty," he admits. "Now I have a protocol. The moment I feel that spike of anger,

I say out loud: 'That person has their own struggles I know nothing about. I control only my response.' This cuts off the emotional reactionary centers in my brain, bypassing rage and anger."

The neuroscience: When you consciously engage your prefrontal cortex by stating a rational response, you interrupt the amygdala's automatic fight-or-flight reaction. This verbal self-instruction literally rewires your response pattern in real time.

When Facing Difficult People: "I use what I call 'Stoic Preparation,'" Anthony explains. "Before entering any challenging situation, I spend thirty seconds imagining how a difficult person might behave. Not to expect the worst, but to prepare virtuous responses. 'If they're rude, I'll respond with patience. If they're aggressive, I'll remain calm. If they're unreasonable, I'll be reasonable.'"

When Encountering Unexpected Problems: "Marcus Aurelius taught me this: 'The impediment to action advances action. What stands in the way becomes the way.' When problems arise, I ask: 'How is this obstacle actually an opportunity? What virtue can this situation develop in me?'"

The Sacred Mantras: Rewiring Through Repetition

Anthony weaves ancient wisdom phrases throughout his daily routine, using them as circuit breakers for negative thought patterns.

Stoic Virtue Mantras:

- Before difficult conversations: "Wisdom in perception"

- During conflicts: "Justice in action"

- Facing fears: "Courage in difficulty"

- When tempted: "Temperance in pleasure"

Buddhist Loving-Kindness During Waiting: "Instead of getting frustrated in lines or traffic, I practice loving-kindness. I start with myself: 'May I be happy, may I be peaceful, may I be free from suffering.' Then I extend it to others around me, even difficult people. This transforms frustration into compassion."

The Stress Inoculation Protocol: Every time Anthony encounters stress, he uses what he calls the "Pause-Breathe-Choose" method:

- Pause: "I stop whatever I'm doing for three seconds"

- Breathe: "One deep breath, focusing on the exhale"

- Choose: "I ask 'What would the person I'm becoming do right now?'"

"This three-second protocol has saved my relationships, my job, and my sanity more times than I can count," Anthony reflects.

The Evening Integration: Conscious Completion

Anthony discovered that evening routines must facilitate the transition from action to rest while consolidating the day's experiences into wisdom.

The 3-2-1 Optimization Formula

- 3 Hours Before Sleep: Final meal ends (allows proper digestion without disrupting sleep architecture)

- 2 Hours Before Sleep: All work-related activities cease (allows cortisol to naturally decline)

- 1 Hour Before Sleep: Complete blue light elimination (allows natural melatonin rise)

The Evening Trinity Questions

Before bed, Anthony answers three questions in writing that create closure while reinforcing identity development:

Question 1: Did I expand today? "This examines whether I grew beyond my comfort zone, learned something new, challenged a limiting belief, or developed a capability. Growth requires expansion, and this question ensures daily movement beyond my current self."

Question 2: Did I contribute today? "This assesses my impact on others' lives, whether through work, relationships, community involvement, or simple kindness. Contribution creates meaning and connects individual actions to larger purposes."

Question 3: Did I honor today? "This evaluates whether I lived according to my values, treated myself and others with respect, and approached life with reverence rather than just consumption. Honor creates dignity and self-respect."

The Compound Interest of Consistency

Here's the math that should either inspire or terrify you:

1% better each day = 37.78 times better after one year ($1.01^{365} = 37.78$) 1% worse each day = 0.03 of your original capacity after one year ($0.99^{365} = 0.03$)

But here's what the math doesn't tell you: The 1% isn't in your performance. It's in your identity.

Every day you practice, you become 1% more of who you're becoming. Every day you skip, you become 1% more of who you've been.

Anthony tracked his compound growth:

- Physical: Started with one push-up, now does fifty

- Mental: Started reading one page, now finishes a book weekly

- Written: Started with eight words, now writes three pages

- Learning: Started with one YouTube video, now takes online courses

- Identity: Started as "warehouse worker," now teaches literacy

"The magic isn't in the dramatic moments," Anthony says. "It's in the boring Tuesday mornings when you do it anyway. It's in showing up when inspiration is absent. It's in the compound interest of keeping promises to yourself."

"Consistency isn't about perfection. It's about persistence. Miss a day? Fine. Miss two days? You're building a new pattern—the pattern of not practicing."

The Resistance Prophecy: The Fourteen-Day War

I need to prepare you for what's coming, because when it arrives, you'll think something's wrong. Around day 10-14 of daily practice, your mind will stage a rebellion. Anthony calls it The Fourteen-Day War.

Here's exactly what will happen:

Day 1-3: The Honeymoon You're excited. Motivated. This time is different. You're finally doing it.

Day 4-7: The Reality Check It's harder than you thought. You're sore. You're tired. But you're still committed.

Day 8-10: The Doubt Creep Is this working? Shouldn't you feel transformed by now? Maybe you need a better system.

Day 11-14: The Rebellion Your old identity fights for survival. You'll "forget." You'll get "sick." You'll have "emergencies." You'll become convinced this doesn't work for "people like you."

Day 15+: The New Normal (IF you survive the war) It becomes easier. Not easy—easier. The practice starts practicing you.

This isn't failure—it's biology. Your brain has efficiency as its prime directive. It doesn't want to build new neural pathways when the old ones work fine for survival. Your old identity is fighting for its life.

Anthony calls it The Bargaining Phase: "Your old self starts negotiating. 'How about every other day?' 'Weekends off?' 'I've proven I can do it, so I can stop.' That's not your wisdom talking—that's your resistance."

When resistance peaks, Anthony implements what he calls "Minimum Viable Practice":

1. One push-up (not a workout, just one)

2. One sentence in your journal (not a page, just one)

3. One new fact learned (not a chapter, just one fact)

4. One breath of awareness (not meditation, just one breath)

"Keep the practice alive, even if barely," Anthony says. "A tiny flame is easier to rebuild than a dead fire is to restart."

"Resistance is not your enemy. It's your compass. It always points toward your growth. The more resistance you feel, the more important the practice is."

Anthony's Three-Year Revelation: The Complete Transformation

Three years into his daily practice, Anthony showed me something that stopped me cold. He'd mapped his transformation through his journals, and the progression was profound:▢
Year 1: "I discovered I existed"

- "I found out I had been living someone else's life"

- "I realized I had choices I'd never made"

- "I learned I had a voice I'd never used"

- "I discovered I had dreams I'd buried"

Year 2: "I learned I could change"

- "I proved my body could transform"

- "I proved my mind could expand"

- "I proved my stories were rewritable"

- "I proved my limitations were lies"

Year 3: "I became who I was meant to be"

- "I no longer practice; I am practice"

- "I no longer hope; I create"

- "I no longer dream of teaching; I teach"

- "I no longer seek purpose; I am purpose"

"Look," Anthony said, pointing to an entry from three years ago: 'Future Anthony, I hope you're teaching kids to read. I hope you matter. I hope you're proud of who you've become.'

Then he showed me his calendar for next week: Five literacy workshops at local schools. Forty-three kids he's teaching to read. Three other former warehouse workers he's mentoring through their own transformations.

"I didn't hope my way here," Anthony said. "I practiced my way here. Every single day. Moving my body so I'd have energy to serve. Writing my thoughts so I'd know what I actually thought. Learning constantly so I'd have something worth teaching. Talking to my future self so I'd know where I was going."

Then he said something I'll never forget:

"The practice isn't what I do. The practice is who I am. I don't have a morning routine—I have a morning ritual of becoming. I don't have habits—I have identity. I don't have discipline—I have inevitability. Every morning, I'm not deciding whether to practice. I'm practicing being Anthony. The Anthony I chose to be. The Anthony those forty-three kids need me to be."

"You don't build habits. You build identity. The habits are just evidence. The practice is just the process. The person you become—that's the point."

Your Two Futures: The Choice That Changes Everything

After three decades watching bodies and minds respond to use and disuse, let me paint you two futures with complete clarity:

Future A: Daily Practice

At 70, you're Robert. Trail running. Learning. Growing. Your body serves you because you've served it daily. Your mind expands because you've fed it daily. Your purpose deepens because you've questioned it daily. Your stories empower because you've rewritten them daily.

You look back at who you were when you started practicing and barely recognize that person. Not with shame—with compassion. That person had the courage to begin. That person did the hardest thing: they chose to change.

You look forward and see more becoming. Not because you have to, but because growth is who you are now. Practice isn't something you do—it's something you are.

Future B: No Daily Practice

At 70, you're William. Every year smaller than the last. Every month less capable. Every day more resigned. Your body has adapted to sitting. Your mind has adapted to reruns. Your stories have become cages. Your purposes have shrunk to survival.

You look back and see the same person, just older. Smaller. More fragile. More afraid. The same patterns, just more entrenched. The same stories, just more believed. The same limitations, just more accepted.

You look forward and see... less. Less mobility. Less possibility. Less time. Not because that's natural aging—because that's what happens when you don't practice. You don't get to maintain. You either grow or you decay. You chose decay by choosing not to choose. The choice is being made right now, in this moment, with what you do tomorrow morning.

"At seventy, you'll either be grateful for every morning you practiced or you'll be haunted by every morning you didn't. The choice isn't made then. It's made now."

Your Beginning

Tomorrow morning, when your alarm goes off—or better yet, when you naturally wake five minutes before your alarm because your body has learned to trust you—you have a choice.

You can hit snooze and choose who you've been.

Or you can rise and choose who you're becoming.

You can scroll your phone and consume other people's lives.

Or you can write in your journal and create your own.

You can protect your comfort and accept your decline.

Or you can challenge your capacity and ensure your growth.

You can treat tomorrow like another day to survive.

Or you can treat tomorrow like another opportunity to become.

The choice isn't actually tomorrow morning.

The choice is right now.

Set your alarm. Put your journal next to your bed. Choose what you'll learn tomorrow. Write a quick note to your future self.

Start imperfectly. Start scared. Start small.

But start.

Because Anthony started. Because Robert started. Because everyone who ever transformed started.

And because your future self—the one you'll meet in one year, five years, thirty years—is counting on you to start.

Not hoping. Counting.

The practice is waiting.

Your becoming is waiting.

Tomorrow morning at 4:47 AM—or whenever you choose to begin your revolution—your transformation begins.

Or your decline continues.

The choice, as always, has already been made.

You're living it right now.

Choose differently.

Choose daily practice.

Choose becoming.

Choose you.

CHAPTER FIFTEEN

YOUR LEGACY AND FUTURE SELF

"THE TRAGEDY OF LIFE IS NOT DEATH, BUT WHAT WITHERS INSIDE US FROM NEGLECT—THE UNEXPRESSED CREATIVITY, THE UNLIVED COURAGE, THE PERSON WE ALMOST BECAME. YOUR LEGACY ISN'T WHAT REMAINS WHEN YOU'RE GONE—IT'S WHAT YOU DID WITH THE DAYS YOU WERE GIVEN."

The Man Who Attended His Own Funeral

In the fall of 1888, Alfred Nobel opened the morning newspaper over breakfast in his Paris home and read something that should have been impossible: his own obituary. "The Merchant of Death is Dead," the headline proclaimed.

The newspaper had made a mistake—it was Alfred's brother Ludwig who had died, not Alfred. But as Alfred read about his life's accomplishments, his blood turned cold. The obituary painted him as a man who had amassed a fortune by developing more efficient ways to kill people. Dynamite. Weapons. Destruction. This was his legacy?

Alfred Nobel—brilliant chemist, successful industrialist, wealthy beyond measure—suddenly saw his life through the eyes of history. And history saw him as a dealer of death.

That morning, Nobel experienced what most of us never will: He saw exactly what his patterns had created, what story he'd been telling, what purpose he'd been serving. And he was horrified.

That mistaken obituary changed everything. Nobel spent the remaining eight years of his life frantically rewriting his story. Not through words, but through actions. He rewrote his will, leaving his entire fortune—worth billions in today's money—to establish prizes for those who contribute to peace, literature, science. To life, not death.

Alfred Nobel discovered what most people never learn: **You don't have to wait until the end to change your legacy. You can transform who you're becoming at any moment you choose.**

But here's what makes Nobel's story even more profound: He didn't just change what he did with his money. He changed his entire relationship with time itself.

Before that morning, Nobel lived like most successful people—accumulating, achieving, building empires. After that morning, he lived backward from his death. Every decision filtered through one question: "When they write my real obituary, what do I want it to say?"

The ancient Romans had a phrase for this: *memento mori*—remember you must die. Not to live in fear, but to live with urgency. Not to dwell on endings, but to treasure beginnings. When you truly understand that your days are numbered, you stop wasting them on things that don't matter.

The Awakening That Changes Everything

"The mass of men lead lives of quiet desperation." - Henry David Thoreau

Thoreau wrote those words in 1854, but walk through any office building, any subway car, any suburban mall today, and you'll see he was prophetic. Look into people's eyes—really look—and you'll see it: the vacant stare of someone who stopped truly living years ago but whose body keeps showing up.

They're not thriving. They're surviving. They're not creating. They're consuming. They're not living intentionally. They're existing accidentally.

I see them every morning on my commute. Same train. Same seat. Same glazed expression. They clutch their coffee like it's life support, scroll through their phones to avoid eye contact with their own emptiness, count the hours until Friday like prisoners marking days until release.

Ask them how they are, and they'll tell you: "Same shit, different day."
Four words that perfectly capture a soul that's given up.

But here's what I've learned after almost 3 decades working emergency rooms: The difference between those who are truly alive and those who are merely existing isn't circumstances—it's consciousness.

The Cost of Unconscious Living

Let me tell you what sleepwalking through life really costs.
It's not the ten-year-old Honda. It's the dreams that fade in the driver's seat.

It's not the job you hate. It's the resignation that creeps in slowly—first you compromise on the small things, then the bigger things, until one day you can't remember what you refused to compromise on.

It's not being single or married. It's the envy that burns when you see someone loving their life and you can't remember what that feels like.

It's not being busy. It's the numbness that requires increasingly stronger stimulation—more alcohol, more Netflix, more scrolling—just to feel anything.

It's not the occasional bad day. It's the anger that erupts at tiny inconveniences because you're actually frustrated with your entire existence.

It's knowing you're wasting your life but feeling too tired, too trapped, too far gone to change.

"Life doesn't punish you for sleeping through it. It simply passes you by while you dream of waking up."

The Woman Who Rewrote Her Ending

Let me tell you about Margaret Chen, because her story reveals something profound about the relationship between legacy and daily practice.

Margaret was 68 years old when her husband of 45 years died suddenly. At his funeral, listening to the eulogies, she heard story after story about the lives he'd touched, the kindness he'd shown, the difference he'd made. People traveled from across the country to honor him.

Sitting in that church pew, Margaret felt something crack open inside her. Not grief—though there was that too—but a more terrifying realization: **If she died tomorrow, who would come to her funeral? What would they say?**

She'd spent 45 years as "James's wife." A good wife, a dutiful wife, a wife who made his career possible by sacrificing her own ambitions. She'd been a competent mother, a reliable friend, a pleasant neighbor. But when she tried to imagine her own eulogy, all she could hear was: "She was nice. She did her duty. She didn't cause trouble."

The realization hit her like a physical blow: **She had been a supporting character in her own life story.**

That night, unable to sleep, Margaret did something that would change everything. She wrote two obituaries.

The first one was honest and devastating:

"Margaret Chen, 68, died having lived a life of quiet accommodation. She raised three children who barely knew her, supported a husband who rarely asked what she wanted, and pursued no dreams of her own because she was too busy enabling everyone else's dreams. She was kind, but not particularly memorable. She was present, but not particularly engaged. She existed, but never quite lived. She will be remembered for being reliably pleasant and conveniently invisible."

Margaret told me later that writing those words felt like drowning. But she kept going. She wrote the second obituary—the one she wanted:

"Margaret Chen, 85, died after living two distinct lives. For her first 68 years, she existed in the shadows of others' expectations. For her final 17 years, she stepped into the light of her own possibilities. She became a master gardener whose community garden fed 200 families. She mentored teenage girls in the foster system, teaching them they didn't have to settle for the hand they were dealt. She took up painting at 70 and held her first gallery show at 75. She traveled to 23 countries, learned conversational Spanish, and wrote a cookbook that became a community treasure. But more than her accomplishments, people will remember her laughter, her courage to start over, and her fierce insistence that it's never too late to become who you were meant to be."

When Margaret finished writing, the sun was coming up. She looked at both versions of her life and made a decision that most people never make: **She chose to live the second obituary starting that day.**

Not someday. Not after things settled down. Not when she felt ready.

That day.

The Philosophy of Two Deaths

The Stoics understood something most modern people have forgotten: **You die twice in this life.**

The first death is spiritual—it's the moment you stop becoming and start merely existing. Marcus Aurelius called it *"the living death of resignation."* Seneca warned that most people don't live—they merely prepare to live, always putting off authentic existence until conditions are perfect.

This first death is insidious because it doesn't arrive dramatically. There's no moment where you consciously decide to give up. Instead, it happens through a thousand small surrenders:

The first time you say "I'm too old to try that" even though you're 35.

The day you stop reading books that challenge you and only consume entertainment.

The morning you realize you can't remember the last time you felt genuinely excited about anything.

The moment you catch yourself saying "This is just how life is" about circumstances you have the power to change.

The first death happens when you accept limitation as permanent, when you mistake comfort for contentment, when you trade possibility for predictability.

But here's the liberating truth the Stoics discovered: **The first death is reversible.**

You can resurrect. You can awaken. You can choose to become alive again at any moment between your first death and your second.

Margaret Chen experienced her first death slowly over 45 years. Then, at 68, she chose resurrection. She had 17 years of authentic living after decades of unconscious existing.

But here's what's remarkable: **Those 17 years mattered more than the previous 45.**

Not because she achieved more—though she did. Not because she accumulated more—she actually gave most of her money away. But because she finally started *practicing being herself* instead of practicing being who everyone else needed her to be.

The Dual Obituary Protocol: Your Awakening Exercise

What Alfred Nobel experienced by accident and Margaret Chen created intentionally, you can do right now.

I want you to write your own obituary. Twice.

Not someday. Not when you have time. Right now. Today. Because what you discover in the gap between these two documents will tell you everything you need to know about the work ahead of you.

Obituary One: The Autopsy of Who You Are

Open your journal. Date the top of a fresh page. Now write your obituary as if you died today. Not the polished version your family would publish to be nice. The truth. What would an objective observer write about the person you've actually been?

The Patterns: What did you do daily? How did you spend your mornings, your evenings, your weekends? If someone followed you with a camera for a month, what patterns would emerge? What did your calendar reveal about your true priorities? What did your credit card statements say about what you valued? What did the apps on your phone suggest about how you spent your consciousness?

Don't write what you intended to do. Write what you actually did. The person you've been is defined by your patterns, not your plans.

The Stories: What did you believe about yourself and the world? What narratives actually guided your decisions, not the ones you wish guided them? What did you tell yourself about why you couldn't, shouldn't, or wouldn't change?

Be specific: Did you believe you were too old, too young, too inexperienced, too far behind, too damaged, too ordinary? Did you believe success was for other people? Did you believe your past determined your future? Did you believe you had to choose between your dreams and your responsibilities?

The Purposes: What did you actually serve with your time, energy, and resources? Not what you wished you served. Not what you told people you valued. What did your actual life reveal about your real priorities?

If an alien anthropologist studied your life, what would they conclude mattered most to you? Comfort? Safety? Approval? Consumption? Distraction? Or something transcendent?

The Impact: Who did you actually influence and how? Not who you hoped to influence. Not your intentions. Your actual, measurable impact.

What changed in the world because you were in it? What would be different if you had never existed? What would people remember you for a year after your death? Five years? Twenty?

The Regrets: What opportunities did you see and avoid? What dreams did you have before life taught you to be "realistic"? What person did you almost become before you chose safety over possibility?

What would your 18-year-old self think of who you became? What would disappoint them most?

Now read what you've written. Sit with it. Feel it.

This is not judgment—it's data. It's the measurement of the gap between who you say you are and who you've been becoming through your daily patterns.

Margaret Chen told me that writing her first obituary was the most painful thing she'd ever done. More painful than her husband's death, because this death was preventable and she had caused it through ten thousand small compromises.

But she also said it was the most necessary thing she'd ever done. Because you can't change what you won't acknowledge. You can't transform who you won't see clearly.

Obituary Two: The Blueprint of Who You Could Be

Now turn the page. Fresh paper. This time, write the obituary you want. The one that would be read if you lived into your highest potential. If you aligned your patterns, stories, and purposes. If you became who you're capable of becoming.

This isn't fantasy—it's architecture. You're building the blueprint for your transformation.

The Patterns: Describe the daily practices of this person. How did they start each day? What did they prioritize even when it was inconvenient? What habits distinguished them from who they used to be?

Be specific: Did they move their body daily? Did they create something every day? Did they serve others consistently? Did they read books that stretched their mind? Did they practice presence with the people they loved?

The Stories: What did this person believe about themselves and possibility? What narratives guided their boldest decisions? How did they interpret failure—as evidence of inadequacy or as feedback for growth? How did they view setbacks—as endpoints or as plot twists in a larger story?

What did they believe about time? About age? About starting over? About learning new things? About second chances?

The Purposes: What transcendent cause energized this person's daily life? What contribution gave their existence meaning beyond mere survival and comfort? How did they serve something larger than their own needs?

Did they teach? Create? Build? Heal? Protect? Connect? Preserve? Innovate? What specific thing became better because they dedicated their life to it?

The Impact: Whose life is different because this person existed? Be specific with names if you can. What specific changes occurred in the world due to their presence? What will they be remembered for by the people whose lives they touched?

The Character: What virtues defined them? What made people trust them? Respect them? Admire them? Turn to them in crisis? What did they refuse to compromise on even when it cost them?

Now read both obituaries side by side.

The distance between them is your life's work.

Every gap you see—between the patterns you have and the patterns you need, between the stories you tell and the stories you should believe, between the purposes you serve and the purposes worth serving—that's not failure. That's your curriculum.

The Gap: Where Transformation Lives

Here's what Margaret discovered when she compared her two obituaries: The gap between them wasn't as wide as she feared.

She didn't need to become a different person. She needed to become more of who she already was beneath all the accommodation and people-pleasing.

She'd always loved plants—she just needed to transform casual gardening into serious practice.

She'd always felt drawn to helping young women—she just needed to stop waiting for permission and start showing up.

She'd always appreciated beauty—she just needed to stop consuming other people's art and start creating her own.

The gap between your two obituaries isn't about becoming someone new. It's about becoming more fully yourself.

The ancient Greeks had a concept called *eudaimonia*—often translated as "flourishing" or "the good life." But the literal translation is more powerful: *eu* (good) + *daimon* (spirit or self). Eudaimonia means living in accordance with your true spirit, your authentic self.

Your second obituary is your *daimon* speaking. It's who you are beneath all the programming, all the compromises, all the shoulds and supposed-tos. It's not fantasy—it's truth you've been suppressing.

The philosopher Søren Kierkegaard wrote: *"The greatest danger is not that we aim too high and miss, but that we aim too low and hit."*

Most people's first obituary is a perfect shot at a target too low. They succeeded at becoming mediocre, average, forgettable. They hit exactly what they aimed for—a life of comfortable unconsciousness.

Your second obituary is you aiming higher. The question isn't whether you can hit that target. The question is whether you're willing to aim for it at all.

The Architecture of Your Future Self

Here's a truth that changes everything: **Your future self is under construction right now.**

Every pattern you practice today is a brick in their foundation. Every story you believe is shaping their worldview. Every purpose you serve is determining their character.

But most people build their future self accidentally, unconsciously, without any intentional design. They're like contractors who show up to a job site and start laying bricks randomly, without blueprints, without vision, without intention.

Then they act surprised when the building collapses or doesn't serve their needs.

The antidote to accidental becoming is architectural intention.

Think about how you'd build an actual house. You wouldn't just start hammering boards together and hope for the best. You'd:

1. Envision what you need the house to do

2. Design blueprints for that vision

3. Break the blueprint into phases

4. Build one phase at a time

5. Adjust as you learn what works

Building your future self requires the same intentionality.

Margaret's second obituary was her vision. But vision alone builds nothing. She needed to reverse-engineer that obituary into daily patterns she could practice.

She looked at "master gardener" and asked: What does a master gardener do daily? They're in their garden. They study plants. They experiment. They teach others.

So Margaret created a pattern: One hour in the garden every morning. No exceptions. Rain, snow, or sunshine—one hour. That pattern, practiced daily for 17 years, created mastery.

She looked at "mentored teenage girls in foster system" and asked: What does a mentor do? They show up consistently. They listen without judging. They model possibility.

So Margaret created another pattern: Tuesday evenings at the youth center. Every Tuesday for 15 years. That pattern, practiced weekly, changed 47 lives directly and countless more indirectly.

Your second obituary tells you what to build. Daily patterns are how you build it.

The Roman emperor Marcus Aurelius understood this perfectly. Every morning, he would write in his journal—not about what happened, but about who he was practicing being. His *Meditations* weren't a diary. They were architectural blueprints.

He would write things like: "Today I will practice patience with difficult people. I will remember that anger doesn't serve my purpose. I will act with dignity regardless of how others act."

He was practicing being emperor before the day required it. He was building his future self through conscious pattern repetition.

You can do the same thing. Look at your second obituary. What does that person do daily that you're not doing? Start doing one of those things today. Not perfectly. Not even well at first. Just start.

The Legacy Paradox: Forgetting Yourself to Find Yourself

Here's something the self-help industry doesn't want you to know: **The best legacies are created by people who aren't trying to create legacies.**

They're too busy serving something larger than themselves to worry about how they'll be remembered. Too engaged in meaningful work to calculate their historical impact. Too focused on daily practice to obsess about long-term outcomes.

Consider three lives:

Viktor Frankl didn't set out to create a legendary book. He was trying to survive Auschwitz by finding meaning in suffering. He was trying to help other prisoners maintain their humanity. He was trying to preserve the insights he was gaining about human psychology under extreme conditions. *Man's Search for Meaning* emerged from his attempt to serve others, not his attempt to be remembered.

After liberation, Frankl could have hidden from his trauma. Instead, he dedicated his life to helping other survivors heal through logotherapy—his method of finding meaning even in suffering. His legacy wasn't planned. It was the natural byproduct of a life dedicated to alleviating human suffering.

Katherine Johnson didn't calculate orbital trajectories to become famous. When she showed up at NASA in 1953, she was solving problems that fascinated her, using her mathematical gifts to contribute to something larger than herself—humanity's expansion into space.

She worked in a segregated building, denied credit for her calculations, invisible in official histories. But she kept calculating because the work mattered, not because she would be remembered. Her legacy as a pioneering mathematician was a byproduct of her dedication to the work itself.

Fred Rogers didn't create *Mister Rogers' Neighborhood* to build a legacy. He created it because he believed children deserved better television. He believed every child needed to hear that they were special just for being themselves. He believed in treating children with the same dignity and respect adults deserved.

For 33 years, he showed up every day to do work that looked simple but was revolutionary. He wasn't building a brand. He was serving children. His enduring influence came from his commitment to that purpose, not from strategic legacy-building.

The paradox: The people who create the most lasting legacies are the ones least concerned with being remembered. They're too absorbed in being useful.

Margaret Chen understood this intuitively. When she started her community garden, she wasn't thinking: "This will be my legacy." She was thinking: "My neighbors need fresh food and don't have money or space to grow it."

When she started mentoring girls in foster care, she wasn't calculating her impact. She was showing up for Tuesday night sessions because those girls needed someone to believe in them.

The legacy came later, as a natural consequence of patterns practiced in service of purposes larger than herself.

This is the ancient wisdom that modern culture has forgotten: **Your legacy is not something you create. It's something you leave behind naturally when you stop performing and start serving.**

The question isn't "What legacy do I want to create?" The question is "What am I in service to, and am I serving it with my actual daily life?"

The Practice of Becoming

So here's where we arrive, at the end of this book, at the end of this chapter, at the beginning of your actual work:

You have two obituaries. You know the gap between them. You understand that gap is your curriculum.

Now what?

Now you practice.

Not someday. Not when you feel ready. Not when conditions are perfect.

Now.

Because here's the final truth I need you to understand: **Transformation doesn't happen when you feel ready. It happens when you start practicing who you want to become before you feel ready.**

Margaret didn't feel ready to mentor teenage girls. She had no training, no credentials, no confidence. She showed up anyway because those girls needed someone, and waiting until she felt qualified meant they would keep waiting too.

She didn't feel like a real artist when she first picked up a paintbrush at 70. She felt foolish, amateur, presumptuous. She painted anyway because creating beauty mattered more than avoiding judgment.

You become who you practice being.

Not who you wish you were. Not who you plan to become someday. Who you practice being today, tomorrow, and the day after.

Your second obituary is your architectural blueprint. Now you build it, one pattern at a time.

Look at that obituary. Choose one thing. Just one. One pattern that person has that you don't. One story that person believes that you don't. One purpose that person serves that you don't.

Choose one.

Then practice it tomorrow.

Not perfectly. Not even well. Just practice.

Then practice again the next day.

And the next.

And the next.

This is how transformation actually works. Not through inspiration, but through patient, persistent practice of who you're becoming.

The Final Question

My mother asked me a question 30 years ago that started my own resurrection: "Son, are you happy?"

I couldn't answer. That inability to respond to such a simple question launched a decades-long investigation into authentic living that led to everything in this book.

Now I'm asking you the same question:

Are you happy?

Not "are you comfortable." Not "are you successful." Not "are you doing what you're supposed to do."

Are you happy? Is your life aligned with who you actually are beneath all the programming? Are you practicing being yourself, or practicing being who everyone else needs you to be?

And if the answer is no, or even if the answer is "I don't know," then the next question is simpler:

What are you going to do about it, starting today?

You've written two obituaries. You know who you've been. You know who you could become. The gap between them is your remaining work.

Every morning from this day forward, you wake up with a simple choice: Practice who you've been, or practice who you're becoming.

There is no third option. Inaction is just unconscious action—the continued practice of old patterns.

Alfred Nobel got eight years between his awakening and his death. Margaret Chen got seventeen. You don't know how many years you have left between this moment and your second death.

But you do know this: **You have today.**▯

And today is enough to begin.

The person in your second obituary isn't waiting to be discovered. They're waiting to be practiced into existence. One pattern. One story. One purpose. One day at a time.

Your Work Begins Now

You know what you need to do.

You've known the whole time you were reading this.

The question was never "What should I do?" The question was always "Will I do it?"

Will you write your obituaries? Will you face the gap honestly? Will you choose one pattern to practice? Will you start today?

Or will you close this book, feel temporarily inspired, and return to exactly who you've been?

Most people choose comfort over transformation. They choose familiar patterns over aligned ones. They choose unconscious existence over intentional becoming.

But you're not most people.

If you were, you wouldn't have read this far. You wouldn't have stayed with ideas that challenged you. You wouldn't be feeling that subtle vibration of recognition that comes when truth meets readiness.

You're ready.

Not to be perfect. Not to transform overnight. Not to become enlightened by Tuesday.

You're ready to start practicing. You're ready to take one step. You're ready to choose one pattern that serves your second obituary instead of your first.

That's all transformation ever requires: The willingness to practice being who you're becoming before you feel like that person.

Margaret Chen started at 68. You can start today, regardless of your age, your circumstances, your past, your resources, or your readiness.

You can start today.▯

So start.

Write your obituaries. Find the gap. Choose one pattern. Practice tomorrow.

Then practice again.

And again.

And again.

Until one day, years from now, when someone writes your actual obituary, it sounds a lot like the second one you wrote today.

That's your life's work.☐

That's everyone's life's work.☐

That's the only work that matters.

"Every man has two lives. The second begins when he realizes he only has one. You've just begun your second life. The question is: What will you do with it?"

Journal Prompts: Your Legacy and Future Self

Take your journal. Find a quiet space where you won't be disturbed for at least an hour. These aren't questions to answer quickly. They're questions to live with.

1. The Brutal Truth Write your first obituary. All of it. Don't skip this. Don't summarize. Write the actual obituary that would be accurate if you died today. Include your patterns, your stories, your purposes, your impact, your regrets. Be as honest as you've ever been about anything.

2. The Possible Self Write your second obituary. The one you want. The one that represents who you're capable of becoming if you align your patterns, stories, and purposes. Make it specific. Use names. Include details. Make it real enough that you can reverse-engineer it into daily practice.

3. The Gap Analysis Compare both obituaries side by side. Write down every gap you see. Where is the distance between who you are and who you could be most painful? Most urgent? Most achievable? What does this gap tell you about where your work needs to begin?

4. The One Pattern From all the gaps you identified, choose ONE pattern to install. Just one. What will you practice starting tomorrow? Be specific: What time? What will you actually do? How will you track it?

5. The Story Shift What story from your first obituary needs to change for your second obituary to become possible? Write the old story, then write the new story you need to practice believing.

6. The Purpose Question Your second obituary reveals what you want to serve. But are you serving it now? What would need to change about how you spend your time for your daily life to align with your stated purpose?

7. The Final Commitment Write one promise to your future self. Make it specific, measurable, and time-bound: "I, [your name], promise to [specific action] for [specific duration] because [your deepest why]."

Sign it. Date it. Keep it where you'll see it tomorrow morning.

Because tomorrow morning, your second life begins—if you choose to start living it.

AFTERWORD

"THE PERSON YOU ARE TODAY IS NOT THE PERSON YOU HAVE TO BE TOMORROW. BUT TOMORROW'S PERSON IS BEING CREATED BY TODAY'S CHOICES."

The 30-Day Challenge: Your New Start Protocol

If you've read this far, you've done what most people never do—you've examined your life. You've looked at your patterns, questioned your stories, and considered your purposes. You've accepted that you have more control over who you become than you've been told.

But reading about transformation is entertainment. Creating transformation is work.

The 30-Day Challenge isn't about perfection—it's about proof. Proof that you can keep promises to yourself. Proof that small changes create large results. Proof that you're not condemned to repeat the same patterns indefinitely.

Before you begin, understand this: These thirty days will be among the most difficult and most rewarding of your life. Your old identity will fight for survival. Your comfortable patterns will beg to be restored. Your familiar stories will whisper that change is impossible for "people like you."

This resistance isn't failure—it's your metamorphosis beginning. Stay in the cocoon. Trust the process. Become the butterfly.

Week 1: Foundation Building (Days 1-7)

Theme: "I am becoming someone who keeps promises to myself"

Daily Pattern: The Trinity Morning (15 minutes total)

1. **Hydrate and Activate** (3 minutes): One glass of water with pinch of salt. Stand by your brightest window or step outside. Take ten deep breaths while doing gentle stretches.

2. **Move Your Vessel** (5 minutes): Choose ONE movement and do it daily:

    ○ 1 push-up (advanced: 5 push-ups)

    ○ 30-second plank (advanced: 1-minute plank)

    ○ 20 jumping jacks (advanced: 50 jumping jacks)

    ○ Walk to the end of your driveway and back (advanced: walk around the block)

3. **Document Your Journey** (7 minutes): Write exactly three things in your journal:

    ○ One thing you're grateful for today

    ○ One pattern you practiced yesterday that served you

    ○ One micro-goal for today that moves you toward who you're becoming

Evening Ritual: The Day's Verdict (5 minutes): Before bed, write one sentence answering: "Did I keep my promises to myself today?" Yes or no. No explanations, no excuses, no stories—just honest accounting.

Week 1 Goal: Seven days of showing up. Not perfectly, but consistently. You're proving to yourself that you can be trusted with your own transformation.

Week 2: Identity Integration (Days 8-14)

Theme: "I am becoming someone who chooses consciousness over comfort"
Continue Week 1 practices and add:

Story Archaeology (10 minutes daily): Each day, identify one limiting story you tell yourself and write it down. Then write three alternative stories that could be equally true:

Day 8: "I'm not a morning person" becomes "I haven't practiced being a morning person yet" *Day 9*: "I'm bad with money" becomes "I'm learning to make better financial decisions" *Day 10*: "I always quit" becomes "I'm someone who's practicing persistence" *Day 11*: "People like me don't change" becomes "People like me are exactly who change" *Day 12*: "It's too late to start over" becomes "Every moment is a chance to begin again" *Day 13*: "I don't have willpower" becomes "I'm building my willpower muscle daily" *Day 14*: "This won't work for me" becomes "This is working differently than I expected"

Midday Check-in: Set an alarm for noon. When it rings, ask: "Am I being who I'm becoming, or who I've been?" Adjust accordingly.

Week 2 Goal: Catch your unconscious thoughts becoming conscious. Notice the stories running your life. Begin rewriting them.

Week 3: Purpose Clarification (Days 15-21)

Theme: "I am becoming someone whose actions align with my values"
Continue Weeks 1 & 2 practices and add:

The Future Self Dialogue (10 minutes daily): Write a brief conversation with yourself one year from now:

Present You: "Future Me, what should I focus on today?" *Future You*: "Present Me, today focus on [specific action] because it builds [specific capability] that you'll need for [specific goal]."

Value-Based Decision Making: Before making any significant decision today (what to eat, how to spend free time, how to respond to conflict), ask: "What would someone with my values do here?"

Service Practice: Each day, do one small thing to contribute positively to someone else's life:

- Send an encouraging text

- Hold a door open with full presence

- Listen without trying to fix or solve

- Compliment someone genuinely

- Help without being asked

- Share knowledge that serves others

- Practice patience in a frustrating situation

Week 3 Goal: Connect your daily actions to larger purposes. Experience how serving others serves your own transformation.

Week 4: Integration and Evolution (Days 22-30)

Theme: "I am becoming someone who transforms consistently"
Continue all previous practices and add:

The Compound Assessment: Every three days, write:

1. What pattern is becoming easier/more natural?

2. What story am I believing less?

3. What purpose is becoming clearer?

4. Where do I see evidence of change in my life?

5. What does my Future Self need me to focus on next?

Resistance Protocol: When resistance hits (and it will), use the "Minimum Viable Practice":

- Can't do 5 push-ups? Do 1.

- Can't write 3 paragraphs? Write 1 sentence.

- Can't meditate for 10 minutes? Take 3 deep breaths.

- Can't do the full morning routine? Just hydrate and move.

The Critical Question: Each morning of Week 4, ask: "If I lived every day like I'm planning to live today, where would I be in five years?" Let the answer guide your choices.

The Legacy Question: Each evening of Week 4, ask: "What did I do today that my Future Self will thank me for?" Write it down. Celebrate it.

The Challenge Rules

Rule 1: Progress Over Perfection Missing one day doesn't erase twenty-nine days of progress. Get back on track immediately. Don't use imperfection as permission for abandonment.

Rule 2: No Negotiating With Resistance When your mind offers alternatives ("How about I start tomorrow?" "Every other day would be fine"), respond with: "I'm practicing keeping commitments to myself. Today is practice."

Rule 3: Track Process, Not Outcome Don't measure weight lost, money saved, or dramatic revelations. Measure: "Did I do what I said I'd do today?" This builds the most important muscle—self-trust.

Rule 4: No Lone Wolf Transformation Tell someone about your 30-day commitment. Share your daily victories and struggles. Transformation happens faster in community.

Rule 5: Prepare for Day 14 Around day 14, you'll want to quit. This isn't failure—it's biology. Your old patterns are fighting for survival. Push through Day 14, and Days 15-30 become much easier.

After 30 Days: The Graduation Question

On Day 31, sit quietly and ask yourself: "Who am I becoming?"

Not who you were. Not who you hope to be someday. Who you are **becoming** through your daily choices.

Write your answer. Then ask: "Do I want to keep becoming this person?"

If yes, design your next 30 days. If no, adjust and try again.

Remember: This isn't a 30-day cure. It's a 30-day proof of concept. You're proving to yourself that you can change, that patterns create identity, that small daily choices compound into extraordinary transformations.

The person you are on Day 31 will barely recognize the person you were on Day 1. Not because you'll be completely transformed, but because you'll have become someone who transforms consciously rather than changes accidentally.

"The 30-Day Challenge isn't about the thirty days. It's about proving to yourself that you're not condemned to remain who you've been. You're capable of becoming who you choose to be, one day at a time."

RESOURCES

"THE DAY YOU STOP LEARNING IS THE DAY YOU START DYING. FEED YOUR EVOLUTION DAILY."

Resources for Continued Growth

Essential Reading: Books That Transform Lives

Philosophy & Wisdom

- *Meditations* by Marcus Aurelius - Daily wisdom from the most powerful man in the ancient world who understood that true power comes from self-mastery

- *Letters to a Stoic* by Seneca - Practical philosophy for practical people facing practical problems

- *Discourses* by Epictetus - How a former slave became freer than his masters by mastering his mind

- *Man's Search for Meaning* by Viktor Frankl - Why those who have a "why" can endure almost any "how"

- *Notes from Underground* by Fyodor Dostoevsky - The psychology of the underground man and the complexity of human consciousness

- *Crime and Punishment* by Fyodor Dostoevsky - How conscience and moral awakening transform identity

- *Thus Spoke Zarathustra* by Friedrich Nietzsche - The call to create your own values and become who you are

- *Beyond Good and Evil* by Friedrich Nietzsche - Questioning inherited moral frameworks to discover authentic values

- *Fear and Trembling* by Søren Kierkegaard - The leap of faith required for authentic living

- *The Sickness Unto Death* by Søren Kierkegaard - Understanding despair as the pathway to authentic selfhood

- *Being and Nothingness* by Jean-Paul Sartre - Why you are "condemned to be free" and responsible for who you become

- *Existentialism is a Humanism* by Jean-Paul Sartre - How radical freedom and responsibility create authentic existence

Psychology & Behavior

- *Atomic Habits* by James Clear - The most practical book ever written about habit formation

- *The Power of Now* by Eckhart Tolle - Why the present moment is the only place transformation can happen

- *Mindset* by Carol Dweck - How believing "I can learn this" changes everything

- *Thinking, Fast and Slow* by Daniel Kahneman - Understanding the two systems that drive your decisions

Purpose & Meaning

- *A New Earth* by Eckhart Tolle - Moving beyond ego into authentic purpose

- *The Gifts of Imperfection* by Brené Brown - Why vulnerability is the birthplace of courage and creativity

- *Flow* by Mihaly Csikszentmihalyi - The psychology of optimal experience

Practical Transformation

- *The 7 Habits of Highly Effective People* by Stephen Covey - Principles that transcend trends

- *The Four Agreements* by Don Miguel Ruiz - Ancient Toltec wisdom for modern freedom

- *Can't Hurt Me* by David Goggins - What happens when someone refuses to accept limitations

Digital Resources: Tools for Daily Practice

Meditation & Mindfulness

- Headspace: Guided meditations for beginners and advanced practitioners

- Calm: Sleep stories, nature sounds, and daily mindfulness exercises

- Insight Timer: Free meditations from teachers worldwide

- Waking Up: Sam Harris's approach to consciousness and meditation

Habit Tracking

- Way of Life: Simple color coding for daily habits

- Strides: Comprehensive habit and goal tracking

- Productive: Minimalist habit tracker focused on streaks

- Physical Journal: Sometimes the lowest tech is the most reliable

Learning Platforms

- Coursera: University-level courses on psychology, philosophy, and personal development

- MasterClass: Learn from the world's best at their craft

- Blinkist: Key insights from non-fiction books in 15-minute summaries

- Audible: Transform your commute into a mobile university

Community & Accountability

- Local philosophy groups (Meetup.com)

- Stoicism Facebook groups and forums

- Reddit communities: r/getmotivated, r/decidingtobebetter, r/Stoicism

- Find a transformation partner in your area

Professional Support: When to Seek Help

Therapy & Counseling Sometimes transformation requires professional guidance. Consider therapy when:

- Past trauma interferes with your ability to change patterns

- Depression or anxiety makes daily practice impossible

- Relationship patterns repeatedly sabotage your progress

- You need specialized help with addiction, eating disorders, or other clinical issues

Coaching & Mentorship

- Life coaches for accountability and goal achievement

- Business coaches if entrepreneurship is part of your transformation

- Fitness coaches if physical transformation is your focus

- Spiritual directors if you're exploring transcendent purposes

Medical Support

- Sleep studies if poor sleep undermines your energy for change

- Hormone testing if motivation and energy are consistently low

- Nutritional counseling if diet patterns need professional guidance

- Mental health medication when appropriate (never a replacement for but sometimes a support for personal work)

Creating Your Personal Learning System

The 15-Minute Daily Learning Protocol

1. **Morning Input** (5 minutes): One article, video, or book passage that challenges an assumption

2. **Commute Processing**: Think about what you learned, how it applies to your life

3. **Evening Integration** (5 minutes): Write one sentence: "Today I learned..."

4. **Weekly Review**: What patterns are you noticing in your learning? What themes keep appearing?

5. **Monthly Application**: Choose one thing you've learned and implement it for

30 days

The Three-Book Rule Always have three books in rotation:

1. **One Challenging Book**: Something that stretches your mind and makes you uncomfortable

2. **One Practical Book**: Something with immediate applications to your current challenges

3. **One Inspirational Book**: Something that reconnects you to your deeper purposes

Building Your Philosophy

- Keep a "Principles" notebook where you write down insights that guide your decisions

- Regularly review and update these principles as you grow

- Test your principles against your daily choices—do you actually live what you claim to believe?

The Lifelong Practice

Remember: Resources are tools, not destinations. The goal isn't to consume more content—it's to transform more consistently.

Use this test: After engaging with any resource, ask:

1. What is one specific thing I can apply today?

2. How does this challenge my current patterns, stories, or purposes?

3. What would change in my life if I fully embodied this wisdom?

If you can't answer these questions, you're consuming entertainment, not education.

The Ultimate Resource The most important resource for your continued growth isn't a book, app, or course. It's your own daily practice of conscious living. Everything else is just support for the real work—the work of becoming who you were meant to be, one choice at a time.

"Read to transform, not to accumulate. Learn to apply, not to impress. Grow to contribute, not to compete. The library of wisdom is vast, but the practice of wisdom is personal."

ACKNOWLEDGEMENTS

To **my mother**, who asked the simple question that shattered everything: "Son, are you happy?" Your courage to speak truth when silence would have been easier changed the trajectory of my life. You taught me that love sometimes looks like uncomfortable questions.

To **the philosophers I've never met but who saved my life**: Marcus Aurelius, whose *Meditations* taught me that the quality of my thoughts determines the quality of my life. Epictetus, who showed me that freedom lives in the gap between stimulus and response. Seneca, who proved that wisdom without action is merely intellectual entertainment. Viktor Frankl, who survived the unthinkable and taught us that meaning can be found in any circumstance. These men wrote their words across centuries to reach me in my darkest moments.

To **the gang members, murderers, and lost souls** I grew up with in 1980s Los Angeles—you were my first teachers. You taught me what happens when patterns serve destruction, when stories justify violence, when purposes shrink to survival. Most of you are gone now, but your lessons live on as warnings whispered to everyone who will listen.

To **Maria Santos**, the janitor who became my first example of how ordinary work becomes sacred calling when aligned with authentic purpose. You showed me that circumstance doesn't determine consciousness—consciousness determines how we experience circumstance.

To **Anthony Ramirez** and all the invisible people grinding in warehouses, wiping tables, stocking shelves—you are the real heroes of transformation. You prove daily that change doesn't require perfect conditions or unlimited resources. It requires only the courage to begin and the discipline to continue.

To **Marcus Chen**, **Jennifer Park**, **David Kim**, **Rachel Martinez**, and **Thomas Chen**—though your names have been changed, your stories are real. Thank you for trusting me with your transformations. Your willingness to excavate your patterns, examine your stories, and elevate your purposes gave this framework flesh and blood.

To **Dr. Sarah Kim**, **Robert the runner**, **William in his hospital bed**—every person I've encountered in thirty years of emergency medicine taught me something about the architecture of human resilience. You showed me that the body adapts to whatever life we demand of it, and the mind follows the body's lead.

To **my patients** who died too young from diseases of lifestyle and choices compounded over decades, and to those who lived vibrantly into their nineties because they understood that daily patterns create destiny—you both taught me that time is the ultimate teacher, and consistency is the ultimate test.

To **Phoenix and Sage Publishing** for believing that this message needed to reach beyond my own transformation. Publishing is an act of faith—thank you for having faith in uncomfortable truths packaged as practical wisdom.

To **every reader** who has ever journaled their way from confusion to clarity, who has ever changed a single pattern and watched their entire life reorganize around that change, who has ever discovered that their limiting stories were just inherited fictions waiting to be rewritten—this book is your book. You are the evidence that transformation is possible.

To **the teachers I've learned from** without knowing their names: the mother at the grocery store who spoke gently to her crying child, showing me what patience looks like. The construction worker who picked up trash that wasn't his, showing me what responsibility looks like. The teenager who helped an elderly man cross the street, showing me what service looks like. You taught me that the most profound lessons happen in the most ordinary moments.

And finally, to **everyone still attending their own funeral**, still living the same day repeatedly, still believing that this is all there is: This book is my attempt to build you a ladder out of the grave you've been living in. The ladder only works if you're willing to climb. But if you're reading these words, some part of you is already reaching up.

"We rise by lifting others, and we transform by helping others transform. This book is my attempt to pass forward what was passed to me—the scandalous possibility that you are not condemned to remain who you've been, but are invited to become who you were meant to be."

Mark Loudermilk New York, 2025

ABOUT THE AUTHOR

"I'M NOT GIFTED OR LUCKY. I'M JUST SOMEONE WHO DISCOVERED THAT CHANGE IS POSSIBLE FROM ANY STARTING POINT—IF YOU'RE WILLING TO STOP ACCEPTING THE UNACCEPTABLE AND START PRACTICING THE POSSIBLE. MY TRANSFORMATION ISN'T EXTRAORDINARY. IT'S SIMPLY WHAT HAPPENS WHEN YOU ALIGN WHO YOU ARE WITH WHO YOU WERE MEANT TO BE."

Mark Loudermilk shouldn't be alive.

By every measure that matters in criminology textbooks, he should be dead or imprisoned. Grew up with gangs in 1980s, 1990s Los Angeles—the murder capital of America at that time—he spent his teenage years incarcerated, surrounded by people who are now serving life sentences or buried.

Then he made one decision that changed his life: he left California and never looked back.

What followed was an obsessive pursuit of reinvention. Mark became a respiratory therapist, then a registered nurse, then studied computer science—collecting degrees like a man building evidence for his own defense. But credentials didn't change him. Thirty years working emergency medicine did.

In the ER, Mark witnessed the full spectrum of human existence compressed into twelve-hour shifts. He watched babies born taking their first breath and watched many take their last breath. He treated teenagers with gunshot wounds identical to his own scars, and watched marathon runners in their seventies while fifty-year-olds needed walkers to cross the room. The human body, he learned, becomes whatever life demands of it. So does the human spirit.

The question that changed everything came from his mother over coffee: *"Son, are you happy?"*

Mark realized he couldn't answer. That silence launched a decades-long investigation into what actually creates transformation—not the kind you claim in job interviews, but the kind that rewrites your DNA. He studied philosophy, psychology, neuroscience, neuroplasticity, ancient wisdom traditions, anything that could explain how human beings fundamentally change.

What emerged was the **Trichotomy of Self**—the understanding that identity is created by three forces working in concert: the patterns you repeat daily, the stories that guide your choices, and the purposes you ultimately serve.

This framework transformed Mark from someone running from his past into someone helping others design their future. But more importantly, it revealed a truth that threatens every excuse we make for staying stuck: **you are not condemned to remain who you've been.**

Mark doesn't consider himself special. He's simply proof that radical transformation is possible at any age, from any starting point, with any history—if you're willing to align your daily actions, deepest beliefs, and ultimate purposes with who you actually want to become.

He wrote this book for three types of people:

Those ready to break the pattern — sensing there's more to life than the daily routine they've settled into

Those seeking alignment — successful by external measures but hungry for deeper purpose and meaning

Those who know change is possible — ready to move from wanting transformation to actively creating it

Today, Mark lives in New York, where he continues his work in emergency medicine while teaching the principles that saved his life. His message is simple but revolutionary: **You become what you repeatedly do, believe, and serve.** Choose all three consciously, and you choose your destiny. Choose unconsciously, and your destiny chooses you.

The most profound transformations, he's learned, don't happen in dramatic moments. They happen in quiet morning hours when no one's watching—when you choose who you're becoming over who you've been.

Connect with Mark:

Website: treydoravr.com ▢
Website: phoenixsagepublishing.com▢
Speaking inquiries: mark@treydora.com

www.ingramcontent.com/pod-product-compliance
Lightning Source LLC
Chambersburg PA
CBHW051608120626
46551CB00014B/1717